Of God

Miracles of Religion and Politics Today

by

Stan Warner

DORRANCE
PUBLISHING CO
EST. 1920
PITTSBURGH, PENNSYLVANIA 15238

The contents of this work, including, but not limited to, the accuracy of events, people, and places depicted; opinions expressed; permission to use previously published materials included; and any advice given or actions advocated are solely the responsibility of the author, who assumes all liability for said work and indemnifies the publisher against any claims stemming from publication of the work.

Dorrance Publishing Co
585 Alpha Drive
Pittsburgh, PA 15238
Visit our website at *www.dorrancebookstore.com*

ISBN: 979-8-8852-7267-4
eISBN: 979-8-8852-7709-9

Introduction

God reveals His will to a kindergarten boy. His direction saves two young lives.

An ordinary fourth grader in deep despair offers a prayer. To his fright and wonder, a heavenly man appears. Weeks later, while playing a game at school, God calls the young one by name and tells him how to deal with peer pressure and more. Weeks later, the boy is savagely attacked and then lied to by an evil unseen man. God instructs the boy how to defend himself from the attack. Still weeks later, in such a remarkable way, God teaches the youth about prayer. This and more happened in an eventful couple months.

Of God follows over sixty-five years of an ordinary life brightened with wonder-filled miracles from God. You will share in the discovery of these wonder-filled experiences.

These experiences were given to me, but not just for me. They are being given to you. This is your opportunity to experience these circumstances, secondhand, for sure, but they are going to be your experiences too. Most of you, for this I hope and pray, will come to find they are from God. This will happen as the Holy Ghost warms your heart and mind confirming these words carry truth. As this happens, each experience will belong to you too.

This work is not associated with any church or organization. My agenda is for you to vicariously live some of my life through all these experiences so wonderfully orchestrated from *God.* Sharing is part of my way of being thankful for the love and instruction given to me.

There are three most remarkable visions shared –

A vision of the time long past, as our Heavenly Father taught us before we were born into this mortality.

A vision of an Exalted Man on His throne. We witness one of His processes of accomplishing miracles in our time.

A vision of the next life after death and the conditions of the disobedient and unrepentant from this life.

In September 2019, Stan is given a warning that a China man-made plague or something worse will be released very soon, and he is given the way to prevent it. He sends that information in letters to all the major nations.

Using the scriptures, an outline is added of the time remaining until the "Second Coming."

Acts 2:17 "And it shall come to pass in the last days, saith God, I will pour out of my Spirit upon all flesh: and your sons and your daughters shall prophesy, and your old men shall dream dreams…"

Many years ago, it was so wisely stated – Faith comes by hearing the word of God through the testimony of the servants of God. That testimony is always attended by the Spirit of prophesy and revelation.

Comments by Readers

"I felt the Spirit all the way through the book."

"I love the unpretentious simplicity of descriptions and the relatable situations you find yourself in. The reader can definitely say – this could be me!"

"This is a very good book. People need to find meaning in life and your book is a testimony to one man's journey."

"I love it."

Two different religious leaders said nearly the exact same thing, commenting – "It is extremely rare that one person received so many spiritual experiences."

CONTENTS

Chapter 1 .... **1**
Awaking to God and Satan
First Memory 1
Running 1
Beach 2
Right and Wrong 3
Different Churches 4
Bad Dream 4
School 4
Fishing 5
Prayer 5
TV 7
Old Movie 8
Foursquare 8
Evil 11
Hope 14
Two Missions 14
Who to Tell 15
Sunday Mornings 16
Churches 16
Hawk 17
Bad Dream Ends 20

Thanksgiving 20
Missions 20
Prepare 21

Chapter 2 ....**23**
Teen Years and Military Service
Card Game 23
Plato 24
Transcendental Meditation 25
White Hair and Memories 25
Ted 26
A Short Word 26
Good By 27
Back to the USA 27
Engaged 28
Vietnam 28
Zen 28
Wrong Place 28
Book of Mormon 29
Camp Evans 30
Off to China Beach 34
Raul 34
Baptism 36
Hymn 36
Fasting 38
The Spirit at a Meeting 39
Sick 40
Back to the USA, again 40
Fort Lewis, Washington 40

Chapter 3 ....**43**
Back to Civilian Life
Back to Bev 43
A Bishop 43

Bev and I Marry 44
Another Ward 44
Set Apart 45
Twins 45
Fireside 45
Melchizedek Priesthood 47
A Name and a Blessing 48
First Blessing on the Sick 50
Second Blessing on the Sick 52
The Fly 52
Apostle 54
Temple of the Lord 56
Great Compliment 56
Church Conference 57
General Conferences 58
The Traffic 59
To Salt or Not to Salt 59
Who Done It 61
Elders Quorum 62
Falling Away 63
Dan 63
President Kimball 64
New Song 64
Neighbor 67
Politician 68
Warning 69
The Young Woman 69
Lost Law and Justice 70
Constitutional Law Class 71

Chapter 4 73
After Law School a Deeper Study of the Gospel of Jesus
Dark Trial 73
Scam 73

There Has Always Been a Fire 77
Another Blessing 77
Campaign for Congress 79
Washington State 80
Argentina for Two 80
Knife 80
Two Towers 82
Second Campaign for Congress 83
The Song "I Believe in Christ" 84
Gospel Doctrine Class 85
Face Down 86
Look 86
Teaching Moments 88
Harshness 91
Accused 92
Old Lady of Sorrow 93
Sermon by the Prophet Joseph Smith 95
Sister 97
PS 99
More Understanding of the Bad Dream 101
Discern 102
A Three-Year-Old 102
Wanted, A New Song 103
To Share or Not 103
Friends 104
Joshua the Prophet 104
I Took Joshua to the Place 105
A Gateway 106
When we pray…the future changes 106
Old Testament 107
Childhood Friend 109
Prayer by Joshua 111
Sacrament Meeting Prayer 112
Family History 113

Before this Volume is Closed 114
Prayer 115

Chapter 5 ....**117**
The Holy Ghost Just Keeps Teaching
On Occasion 117
Holy Spirit 118
Most Grateful 121
Some Family and Friends 122
Driving Past the Temple 122
A Brother in a Priesthood Class 125
When I Finished 127
Trials for Joshua in His Youth 128
Disappointing Experiences 130
Some evenings later 130
A man named Joseph F. Smith 131
The Dark Place in the Next Life 131
Praise to Our Glorious God! 134
Raul 135
Future Cities in Future Kingdoms 136
Dreams 138
Publishing this Book 140
K 141
The Joy of the Next Life 142
Evil Spirits 143
More on Healing 144
This Healing 149
My Testimony 151
One More Dream 152
Following Answers to Prayers 153
Are You Tired? 156
Typesof Priesthood Blessings 157

Chapter 6 .... **161**
Politics and Religion
How sad 161
A Congressional hearing 161
Rock Solid Politics 163
Why is Stan Warner a 2016 Republican Candidate
for the President of the United States 170
Warning 180
China WWIII Alternative 183

Chapter 7 .... **189**
The Wonderous Second Coming, So Close
The City of Enoch 199
History is Family History 202
My Chains are Gone 204
Forest and Trees 205

Chapter 1

Awakening to God and Satan

I will start with a prayer.

Oh God our Heavenly and Eternal Father, we are thankful for Thy love for us. Please send an angel to each that read this book to bless them and help them to feel a closeness to Thee. I ask this in the name of our Savior, Jesus. Amen.

First Memory. This is a very clear memory. At two years and three months old, I was on the left side of the backseat of my grandpa's (maternal grandfather) car. Grandpa Linke was in the driver's seat. My mom, dad, and grandmother were also in the car, but I do not remember who was sitting where. We were parked next to a large, long building (Oakland Kaiser Hospital). A woman dressed in a light color was walking along a walkway. She was on the right side of our car walking toward us. The woman walked to the passenger side of the car. The lady handed her bundle, my baby brother, David, wrapped in light blankets to my mother. I was happy to have a baby brother. That is where this memory ends.

We lived in an apartment in a modest part of Oakland, California.

Running. I was at a park with my dad and mom. Dad took me by my hand and he started running on the grass. Slowly, at first, to let me get in stride, then faster and faster we went. Soon my feet were only touching the ground half as often as they should, and we were really going fast. He was lifting me with his hand. With his help, I was moving much faster than I would have thought possible. Soon the rush was over and he was tired. He lay down on the blanket and would not run with me again, despite my pleading. All the happy times were greatly appreciated. Later in my life, dad's moving me seemed a little like God's helping in my life.

Beach. I am four or an early five-year-old. We are at the ocean beach in San Francisco, at the west end of Golden Gate Park with David, Mom, and Dad. David is walking next to me; we are wading in the very shallow surf. Dad and Mom are on a blanket not too far away.

As we walked, I was given into my mind the clear feeling of eminent danger! The impression was given in a calm manner. My acceptance of the impression was one of great alarm. Something awfully bad was going to happen to David and me in a few seconds. Almost immediately after a plan was given me, I was told to hug my brother and hold on tight and do not let go. Without another thought I obeyed. I took a quick step in front of him, turned to face him, and bent down to hug him. I had a quick thought I could weave my arms under his arms. That was dismissed as it would take too long, and the danger was to happen now! So, I flung my arms around David's arms and chest. I tightly squeezed his arms to his side. I noticed the surprised look on his face at what I was doing just before an exceptionally large rogue wave crashed over our heads. I held tight. The memory of us tumbling and spinning under the water remains vivid.

A few seconds later, Dad was there dragging us out of the frothy water before it carried us out to sea and drowned us. Mom was not far behind. To get there that quick they must have seen the rogue wave coming and started running towards us before the wave covered us. Both were reassuring brother things were okay as he was crying from fright. At the same time, they were praising me for thinking quick in reaction to the danger by holding on to him. I do not remember ever being praised for anything before this incident. They thought I wisely reacted on my own to the danger. I did not tell them about the impressions that told me what to do. I was enjoying the praise and I did not want it to stop as I thought it would if I told them the real reason, I grabbed

David and held on. They were saying I was so smart and I quickly reacted to the emergency. I was not that quick or smart. Plus, I did not understand where the help came from. It was just placed into my mind. That was the first experience of its kind. My world had just become much more complex.

As years passed, some of the memories did not fade but stayed as if they had a will of their own.

Right and Wrong. Mom took David and me to visit one of her friends around the block in Oakland. She had a son a year older than me. We were playing in the dirt of an unfinished basement with a bag of toy army men. Mom finished her visit. She and her friend opened the door to the basement and called us.

Then I did the unspeakable! My thought was that I wanted some of his army men toys. So, I stuffed some of his army men into my pants pockets. As I started doing so, I had a clear thought that taking the army men was wrong. I did not act on the warning.

Luckily, the other mom spotted two bulging pockets on my pants and asked, "What's in your pockets?"

I slowly started pulling the army men out of my pockets and handing them over to my peer. Both moms were saying I was too young to know what I was doing was wrong. Wrong, wrong. I knew taking the army men was wrong. The wisdom from the warning seemed to come from somewhere inside of me. No one had ever told me, that I could remember, but I just knew it was wrong. Where was my Grandma Linke to give me a full explanation of property rights, and why the violation thereof was a huge deal?

Most importantly, my conscience had warned me. At that time, I did not know the process had a name. As I did not heed the warning and I soon found out that my conscience is always right. It will warn me before I do wrong, besides allowing and even encouraging me to feel bad if I do not heed the warning and commit the wrong. Our conscience, what a wonderful teacher.

I would play with my kindergarten classmates at the playground at the local school. I loved the kids my age like brothers and sisters; they were always fun. A few of the older kids did not like me and were extremely mean to me. I was one of the only white kids in my class.

We moved from Oakland to West Sacramento soon after that.

Different Churches. I attended different churches from time to time when invited by neighborhood friends and classmates. Whenever an offer was extended to me, I anxiously accepted. We were a non-religious family. I remember one Sunday morning I dressed in my school clothes, ate breakfast, and started walking out the front door. My parents ask me where I was going. I told them a bus would stop down the street and take us to a church. An adventurous kindergartener. I loved the stories of Jesus and the Prophets of the Old Testament. I loved all the different churches.

Bad Dream. I had bad dreams. On occasion, I woke up crying from the terror of a bad dream. The occasions were getting closer and closer together. There were several dreams. But, as one bad dream started recurring, the other bad dreams ended. In this dream I was falling. I was falling and falling. As I was falling, I could see the ground. I was falling fast, and the ground was getting awfully close. As I got closer, I could see what would be the worst thing that was going to happen. It was bad enough that I was going to hit the ground after falling a long time, but this was not just ground. It was a swamp area with mud and shallow water.

The worst thing was I could see poisonous snakes on the ground, crocodiles, and man-eating fish in the shallow water. Worse yet, they were aware I was falling. They were watching me, waiting for me! Then I hit the swamp hard, but I did not die because the mud and water broke force of the fall. I was stuck in the mud, thrashing around in the midst of those creatures. Then I would awake crying, full of terror. Sometimes sleep was not so pleasant.

School. At school the teachers gave us things to learn. We did our best. Some kids were quick, some were slow, and most of us were somewhere in the middle. I was on the slower end. But at recess, we were learning other things. Year by year, our baseball and football skills were improving. But our social skills of finding status and establishing pecking orders were improving more rapidly. The harshness that went on during recesses in some ways overshadowed the in-class activities. At recess, the stronger and aggressive would bully the weaker, then the more profane would challenge each other to see who was the most profane. We kept getting worse and worse, as regular as the days of the week. I am not sure how much of the recess was carried into the class, but the weaker and slower ones could not help being further slowed in their classroom learning by their treatment at recess.

Fishing. was an activity I enjoyed. I could go fishing and the cares and harshness of the world were washed away, at least for a while. Fishing was a sport unlike the other sports. Competition could bring out our best, but often brought out the worst in us. When fishing, there was no lying, cheating, and no one had to be defeated for someone to win. A neighbor boy and I could enjoy fishing with no one getting hurt, except an occasional fish. Plus, the neighbor's cats sure enjoyed the fish.

Prayer. By fourth grade at West Sacramento Elementary School, some of my classmates were perfecting the art of how to be mean and how to gain status by hurting others. I would catch myself wanting status and thinking of how I could be mean to someone to elevate my position. Then I would grow more disappointed with myself. Sometimes, in defending myself, I would see I was learning the harshness to perform a successful counterattack. There were some girls involved in the verbal attacks also. The early school years were full of this "growing up" which seemed more like just becoming mean, aggressive and hate-filled. The years just showed it would get worse, and I was not immune. It seemed that, sooner or later, I must be like most of the others. Or, equally bad, become one of the floor mats that were to be stepped on by others to elevate their status. I could see no other choices. I had no hope for a happy future.

It was a clear sunny day, as most days in California were. I was incredibly weary of the meanness disease that infected us. During a recess, I was walking toward the far ball diamond with my back to the noisy playground. I put distance between the playing classmates and me. I was thinking how, in time I would be like the worst of my classmates as they explored greater and more advanced degrees in the meanness of life. I was not immune from the disease. There were some of my classmates staying farther away and were less affected by the sickness than me, but they were the ones belittled and bullied the most. What a choice: embrace evil or be the object of aggression. Most were going that direction, hopeless as it seemed. It was just a matter of time, not direction.

I was going to become what I did not want to become, and it seemed out of my power to stop the process. My hopeless appraisal of the future was that good would only happen in fleeting and transitory incidents that would quickly be overshadowed by a robust response of evil.

So, as my thought and walk took me farther away from the others, I decided to pray. There was no other possible help I knew of. I was praying to God as reverently as I could. I briefly explained my problems and my lack of hope. As I rehearsed my predicament, it seemed my state was so fallen it was hopeless of any salvage. There seemed only one option to my position. So, I started another prayer. My head was facing down and my hands were in my pants pockets and my walk was slow. My course of action and request for aid was clear. I asked God if He would let me leave this life. I did not want to stay here any longer. There was not enough love here. I asked Him if I could die and come back to live with Him again.

It was during this request I sensed a man was next to me on my right side. My eyes looked to the right, but because my head was hung down, I was looking toward the ground. At that moment, there was a very dark silhouette type image of a large person. He appeared to be coming into focus or in some way materializing. The fact that He was a man was more of a feeling and a response to the size, as it could not be determined from the direction of the gaze. From the proportions of what I saw, He was over six feet tall. (My dad is 6’2” tall, and He seemed a little larger.) He was walking beside me, only about a foot away. He was in mid stride with His hand swinging at His side. His hand was exposed at His wrist beyond a very wide sleeve. The clothing must have been a robe of some kind. He was in stride I could see there was no light between His feet and legs as there would be if He were wearing pants. The long garment covered down to the foot in stride, past his ankle. This whole view was very brief as it scared me. As soon as I saw the image I gasped in fright and took a startled first step to a run angled off to the left. My hands were out of my pockets and my head was coming up. My left arm was outstretched towards the direction I was going. As soon as the first step was taken reason returned and it was clear that whoever this was, He had not come to hurt but to listen and maybe help. He may have come to grant my request but probably more to listen to the request and reveal himself that He was listening. As I turned back, He was gone. As quick as He began to appear, He was just gone.

Everything I had been feeling and sharing in prayer was now in the back of my mind. In the space of a few seconds, I went from feeling hopeless and lost, to being stuffed with questions and the possibility of help. There was something else here on this earth, besides us in the flesh. Who was He? Where had He come from and where did He go? How did He come? At least part of His message must have been to fill me with wonder, as that is what He did. The fear that quickly left seemed only a byproduct produced by me in response to His appearance.

The one thing that was sure was there was an unseen world where He came from and to where He returned. This knowledge was far beyond my understanding. But this occurrence lit a fire inside me to find out more. It was obvious that answers were not to be found from the education of the day. Teachers never talked about spiritual things. It happened in response to prayer. So, for me, religion was the subject.

This occurrence was much different from anything I was aware of that happened to anyone else, at least that they talked about. I knew anything out of the ordinary you were associated with could be used to belittle you. So, I did not tell anyone. I wanted to try to understand the meaning of the occurrence.

I had been actively engaged with the alpha group from football and baseball. But now my path started to disengage from them. I became more content and comfortable being in the group out of favor with the aggressive crowd. My time was divided between the two crowds. There was predictability about the other crowd's degeneration as they became increasingly mean. Being meanspirited seemed that group's admission price that must be paid. High as the price was, seldom was it not eagerly paid. Peer pressure was as strong as gravity to so many, me included. This whole assessment may be worse than it may have been to others as I seemed to be more sensitive to the harshness to me and others.

TV. There were things to learn, and religion seemed the only place to start. I started getting up early on Sunday mornings and turning on the TV. There were religious broadcasts to study. Different religions had their own programs.

I would watch to see if they said anything familiar. Each week I would search programs for something I could recognize. A heavenly man can still come to us today. Some religions should know and share that knowledge. The only thing recognizable as coming from God was the Bible stories they told besides trying to apply those stories to us today.

Old movie. I watched an old movie about a young girl who lived in Europe. She had a vision of a heavenly woman. I was not sure if the story was true or just a script written for the movie, but it did seem true to me. To me, the movie highlighted the scorn that could result when a spiritual experience is shared. The young girl told some people and got into lots of trouble. At least she had one church leader who tried to help her. I could see no such help for me if I spoke up. At the time I wished I had a friend who was a Catholic priest, like the girl in the movie. My heart went out to the young girl for the troubles she endured. God bless her. There was one more big difference between our experiences: the young woman was remarkably good. I was just ordinary. So, if I told of this experience, it could be worse for me. At that time, the thought never entered my mind that people might just ignore me. Consequently, I was silent.

Foursquare. It could have been a couple weeks after the prayer and the appearance of the heavenly man. I was with the new group, playing foursquare. I was an athlete, and baseball and football were really fun games. But the admission price still was the choice I would have to put someone down or be the object of the group's scorn. As I did not actively participate in putting someone down, it was a sign I must be weak, and I would end up being the receiver of the aggression. This sub-game ruined the appeal of the sport. Consequently, as of late, I regularly found something else to do and others to do it with. This day it was foursquare, not nearly the sport, but the admission price was acceptable. There was a line waiting to play. I had just stepped in to a square and bent over a little in anticipation of the ball coming my way. The skill level was surprisingly high. It required all my attention to stay in the game.

Someone called me by name. It was a man that called. It was not through my ears, but the call came directly to my mind. Immediately, I knew this was not an ordinary person calling me. Who can speak directly to my mind?

My thought was that the call might be from the man who came in response to the prayer. Looking around, He was not there, but there were large, fluffy clouds floating over. My thought was He might be standing up there on a cloud. As they were far up in proportion to the distance, and He would appear small and hard to see. So, a thorough visual search of the clouds was started. The reality of the present soon came to me. I was standing straight up in a foursquare game, engrossed in looking at the clouds. I stopped and looked around. The whole group was staring at me. They were all quiet, waiting for my next strange move. Some of their faces showed a sadness, as if they suspected I may be coming unwound. So, swiftly, to the end of the line for me.

The game resumed. I mused that there was not one laugh or loud word of ridicule, especially given what I had just done. This fact was so strange that the gravity of the call was replaced with my pondering on the group's reaction to my strange act.

He called my name again. My attention was immediately focused on listening and I closed my eyes and bowed my head in reverence. Seconds later, He said, "Of these make thy friends." What words! I said the words over and over a couple times in my mind. *Of these make thy friends. Of these make thy friends.* The words sank into the center of me. I looked at the "these," the group that was playing foursquare. The ones just moments ago that quietly watched me and must have thought I was falling apart. But not one word of ridicule was breathed. Not one loud, pushy, or mean fourth grader. I started looking at the group individually. So "these" the humble, the kind I was to make my "friends." Well, it was not hard to see the wisdom in this. I was thrilled! The wisdom was thankfully received.

I did not know if the man who attended the prayer and the man who was the speaker were one in the same. But I did know that wonderful help was being shared by someone who cares for me. Someone from the unseen world knew and cared for me! If He cared for me, He cared for us all since I was nothing out of the ordinary.

I still did not know much about religion. But I knew God was not absent or asleep. He or His angel answered prayers and even spoke words. In His answers was His love evidenced by the help and direction to one drowning is the trials of this life.

The words were spoken in a calm and direct manner. The voice was not a loud voice, a little softer than conversational and softer than I would expect would carry God's words. The words were not demanding or commanding but issued in an instructive manner. The five words were said slow enough to be clearly understandable but not laboriously slow. When He spoke, I slightly sensed His presence. When the words were over His presence was gone also. I was alone again. However, I knew His presence was available and approachable yet incredibly exalted, far beyond me. Five small words gave a short, yet incredibly profound counsel on how I was to get through school without the gravity of peer pressure pulling me to the cell of meanness and despair. The instruction was so overwhelming I did not have the presence of mind to even form a response, I just accepted and was silent in the presence of the teaching. I did not even thank Him.

Something else needs to be shared. When I said He called me by name, it cannot be understood without more discussion, if it can only be partially understood at all. The name He called me is much more than what we normally mean. The name He called me was much more than what I would have expected. It was the truer more complete me, not just plain Stan. As it was given, I knew it was the truer me, a more complete and encompassing me. Further, it was given in such a way I could not know what the truer name was. It was not for me to understand as I am now. I could not repeat it or even say it the same way. I do not have the ability. But it was singularly me, only me. He knew the more complete me, not just the mortal/fallen me.

Sorry, but that is the best I can do with these words. There is so much more with the unseen heavenly man than with us. There is so much more, so very much more, to all of us than we now understand. The man who talked to me knew more as He spoke my name. We have forgotten most or maybe all of what we were. God loves us so and that love from Him makes all of us so very singularly special. He knows the real and complete individual that we are. Without God's help, we can only react to the mortal/fallen individuals around us that we know with their simple names and without the understanding of how very special they truly were and are now in our forgotten state. All glory to God our Father and His Son our Savior and Redeemer and the Holy Spirit forever and ever…

There is a pattern starting here. He was teaching me much with few or no words. The heavens are open and gave aid! So many questions, so much I do not know.

Evil. It was sometime later, maybe a couple weeks after the foursquare instruction. I was again on the playground during a recess. (So far, these occurrences had all taken place at school during recess, where the peer problem was.) I was off the blacktop area of the playground not far into the grass near the close baseball diamond. With no warning a violent blow struck me. It was as violent as if I was hit by someone taking a full swing with a baseball bat. The blow was not isolated to one spot but was generally applied across the front of my body, from my head down to my knees. The violent hit is hard to remember and explain because of the unexpected and suddenness of the violence and it was not understandable by regular experience. Suddenly, I was just hit! Immediately, I was in bad shape. The blow did not have the physical properties that would normally accompany such an act. I was not forced backwards by the blow as would have been the case if the blow had been delivered by a baseball bat or anything else from our physical plane. My legs buckled at the knees, and I almost lost consciousness. I was attempting not to fall, and my eyes were rapidly blinking as I tried to stay conscious.

Added to this, as soon as I was a little more aware after the blow, I recognized there was something like a furious pressure on the front of my face, more concentrated on my eyes and forehead area. The force was like something was desperately digging at me and wanted to move into me, passing through my skin into my body! I was still teetering, trying not to fall and blinking, trying to concentrate on consciousness when this furious pressure demanded all my attention and strength. As if by instinct, I knew this was a greater danger than the blow that had just struck me. The first hit was a distraction to disarm and confuse me prior to this activity. All my concentration turned to the effort to resist this force in front of me. It was my body, and something was violently trying to enter! An understanding came to me or was placed in my mind, necessary and timely information to help me survive this situation. It was calmly given with confidence to a favorable outcome, into my wildly frantic mind. The help, the understanding was, I was to stay forward in my body. Immediately, I realized my spirit was filling the back part of my body and the front half or more of my body was empty of my spirit. I tried to concentrate on being in the center, and then I leaned my spirit forward into the front of my body, trying not to be forced back by the evil force. This would not allow the other to enter. A couple seconds of this resolve and the evil force stopped. I was recovering fast. Before this I had no idea that there was two parts of me. Obviously, I knew there was a physical me, but now I knew there was a spiritual part of me that resided inside the physical part of me. What a way and time for me to learn this.

Then the worst happened! *he* spoke to me. (The small *h* in *he* is intentional) This was certainly not the same person who spoke at the foursquare game. With the words I recognized that it was a "he." *he* spoke with such great force that his words filled my mind. The force of the demand was not from the loudness, as the words were not spoken loudly, just conversational. *he* said, "It never happened." The words were said with a force and violence that previously I had no hint that words could be so spoken. I knew immediately the object of the demand was the spiritual things that had recently happened. I was at a loss the doubt the words forced on me was overpowering! *his* words forced and filled me. I was breathless for a few seconds. The third assault was more overpowering than the first two acts. What could I do? This was too much! I had no defense to this. I had great trouble thinking. The forceful words challenged my entire reality.

For some time, my mind felt like it was frozen and would not work. I could remember the two spiritual experiences and at the same time I was being forced to reject their truth, existence, and reality. I was defenseless to his force. After the words, I was filled with the force that demanded the spiritual things did not exist. I still remembered them, but the force was so strong it was as though they did not happen.

I could remember I existed. I exist and am real. Struggling to think I knew I existed. If I existed, then those experiences existed also, and they were part of me. Then my thoughts were, I exist, and they exist, then the words from the evil man are a filthy lie! Then like coming up and gasping for air after being under water a long time, the forced lie was not overpowering any more. The challenge to my entire reality was a lie! The two spiritual things had happened. As much as I am real, they are real. I was still reeling from the situation, much more exhausted from the struggle with the lie than the other two challenges. Now my thoughts were turned to: who had done this? An insecure feeling came over me when I realized the blow, the attempt to force entry into my body, and the assaulting and forcing words were evil and had to come from an evil source, an evil man. It seemed the evil source was probably the same evil one spoken of in the Bible…

What incredible power he used against me. And he did it all without raising his voice with no emotion in his voice. I had thought the things of my life were getting better before this. There was no question as to him being real or a fable. *he* was as bad as they made him out to be in the Bible. *he* knew who I was and what God had done for me. Before this I was insecure, now... I felt a little like a wild rabbit. But I had escaped. Other than the trauma that was now in the past and some lingering fear, I was okay. The pain was all gone. That night when I changed into my pajamas, I expected to see bruises to the front of my body resulting from where he struck me. There were none. With time I found if I did not think of the occurrence the fear stayed behind me.

At this point, I was not mature enough to reason out that each danger was met with help as I needed it. Now I understand, we are not left alone to face something beyond our ability to handle. God new I would be able to deal with the lie without His intervention. He gave me the opportunity to fight that battle with my limited abilities. At least that is how it seems to me, looking back at the occurrence. All these experiences should have and eventually did lead me to losing the fear of evil. I certainly did not think of the occurrence much, back then. It would be complete folly for me to think I escaped from that incident by my own strength.

I cannot adequately thank God enough for His timely instruction, to keep my spirit forward in my body and generally watching to make sure I did not lose the struggle with evil. Or, probably more correctly stated, He knew all the variables of the attack before the attack started and sent me the appropriate help by way of one of his angle servants before the attack started. The aid was then delivered at the time of need. All this to my wonder and to the glory of our God.

By the way, what kind of man is this evil one? Such great powers he was once called a son of the morning. Now he is the kind of man who would beat up and try to take the body of a weak ten-year-old who cannot even see him. It is no wonder Heavenly Father had him cast down for his rebellion in heaven!

Many years later, I was listening to a religious talk radio show when the two speakers were teaching that satan was not real, just a way of teaching us about evil. I wish they could have been there to experience the evil one's attacks. I suspect, then the radio conversation would have been a little different.

Hope. There has been a lot shared so far. I hope and pray you can understand these words as the spirit intends. The attempt is and will be to show some of my life experiences and God's love and direction. For me, this life would be a disaster if not for the intervention, direction, and forgiveness of God. The life struggle was never taken from me, but God was and is always available, never further than prayer, sometimes closer. The life struggle, if I can deal productively with it, is where much of my change and growth comes from. The past struggles have given me a little understanding and confidence to deal with the new trials of life. (The trials seem to keep getting harder.) I have tried to take the words given to us by Jesus into my life to help change and direct my life through the trials.

The Lord does not do for me that I can do for myself. He helps me and does the larger things that I cannot do. It appears plain that despite my struggle to be better I will die light years short of what Jesus' example and words calls for me to be. It is my hope and my testimony that, if I follow and try hard to do what Jesus teaches me to do, after I do all that, I can do, I will still be lacking, but the grace of our Lord will make up the difference and save yet another. Every part of His will and teaching is far better than what I can do or be. I have certainly learned at least that. Any change from my ways to His ways is a great improvement. God has given me so much, what can I give Him in return. It is the surrender of my will and accepting His will that seems my truest gift to Him. This turns into a desire to completely follow, keep his commandments, and love Jesus and all my brothers and sisters here in mortality that seems my only real offering I must give to Him and my best hope to be better.

Two Missions. It had been some weeks since the attack near the ball diamond. I was at school on a covered walkway near the cafeteria. I was quietly standing in a clam mood. Generally, school time was not spent on thinking of all the spiritual things that had been happening. They seemed almost overwhelming. Currently, my mind was on the edge of those thoughts. Peacefully, an understanding was placed into my mind. I immediately knew it was from God. It came much faster than talk or even thought. It all came in a second or two. Then it was just there. It was like receiving a memory, and it operated like a memory when I wanted to review it. I knew I was given two things to do. The first thing to do was to "attend law school." Law school was where I would learn things that would aid in and precede the second mission. The second mission was to "attempt to the presidency." Who else would give such missions to an ordinary ten-year-old? The direction was plain on what was to be done. This calling was for me as a servant or representative for my chosen master.

Who to Tell. There was nothing of what had happened that was shared with anyone? It seemed that by so doing it would be a great way to get into big trouble. The old movie of the young girl in Europe who had some visions, the Fatema saga, had continued to cause me to ponder, a little glimpse of what might happen if I said too much. As I mentioned before, in the movie the young girl had a Catholic priest as a friend. I still wished I had a Catholic priest as a friend, but sadly I still did not.

This whole activity was lonely. But there were important things happening. Maybe I could share some of them with just my parents. I shared the slightest of experiences with my mom and dad, an ordinary ten-year-old telling my parents I would go to law school when I was older. There was some sense of Mom not knowing what was wrong with her son. They had nothing to say, just wondering looks. Although we did not speak of this subject further at that time. A few years later, my dad told me there was a law school in Sacramento. So, obviously he had remembered.

A few weeks after my sharing, on a weekend we went to visit my dad's parents in Oakland. Not long into the visit, Grandma Warner called for me. With her raised voice and her fists on her hips, she boldly pronounced I was not better than any other member in the family, and I could get the idea of going to law school out of my head right now! It was with her mention of law school that I knew what she was talking about. Mom must have told Grandma what

I had shared with her and Dad. I kept my mouth shut to Grandma's scolding accusations. Soon her tirade was over.

This experience with Grandma brought questions to my mind of what things would have been like if anything more than a whisper of what had happened to me had been told to Mom and Dad. I was as insecure as a rabbit, not the type to think myself better than anyone. Grandma had to be blind not to see that, and she was not blind. For some reason, which was beyond me, she was terribly upset at the thought of law school and me. I could not figure out the reason for her anger towards me. That was the last of me sharing anything with anyone for about eight years. Then the experiences were shared only very little at a time with Bev and Grandpa and Grandma Linke. My first son, David, showed more interest in the experiences than anyone did until my second son, Joshua, came along.

Grandma Warner was the first in a lifelong list of those who became terribly angry when I would share some of the spiritual experiences God gave me. A few others have been very appreciative and uplifted when some of the spiritual experiences were shared with them. The third group had no interest in hearing them.

Sunday Mornings. I still watched the Sunday morning religious shows. Some shows highlighted how to make the best of difficult situations. In those days, there were lots of shows and old movies that showed the same. Sometimes you could even see the faces of courage portrayed in films. I still remember watching the Loretta Young show series and some of the teachings. But the Sunday morning religious TV shows continued to turn into attending church with school classmates. Talks with classmates at school would soon reveal who attended which church. From time to time, I would be invited to go with someone to their church. All the invitations were gratefully accepted. I thoroughly enjoyed all the different churches.

Churches. There were lots of different churches with lots of differences in what happened at the meetings. I could not find what I wanted in the youth classes. The Old Testament stories were grand, and the stories about Jesus were great. But they did not tell much of what was happening today. I knew the Heavens were open to us today. Someone or some religion should know that too. Soon I asked to attend the meetings with the adults. I thought maybe they were teaching something more than was being shared in the youth classes. I was told I could not attend the grown-up class. Then I started asking adults what happened in their classes. Not much was shared with me. I needed to ask more people more questions. In a Unitarian service as well as some other churches all attended the same meeting. Then I knew what was taught there. They did apply the teachings of Jesus to the common experiences of the day. That seemed much better than just re-telling the stories. That is one of the intended purposes of the scriptures. But none of the churches taught that angels would appear, and the Holy Ghost will talk to you and put understandings in your mind, plus all that unpleasant stuff about the evil one and the attack. There was probably much more taught but not to the young like me.

Hawk. A friend named Brad from school invited me to come to his house for the morning. I accepted immediately. His house was only a hundred feet or so from a large irrigation canal. His dad had a rowboat we were going to use and maybe do some fishing. He lived a few miles away, so it did not take too long to get to his place on my bike. Soon after I got there, he took me to see a white and gray hawk in a cage. He and his father had found the extremely sick hawk. They kept it in attempt to nurse it back to health, intending to release it later. The hawk had not been getting any better. That morning, Brad's dad had told him to put the hawk out of its misery and bury it. Brad did not want to follow the instructions in hopes that with more time the bird might still recover. He asked me if I would take the bird to my house in hopes that with more time the bird would get better.

We started carrying the cage with the hawk to the top of the levy to the blacktop road. At the top of the levy, we balanced the rather large cage on the handlebars of my bike. It was not far from where the road angled down off the levy. Brad went home and I walked my bike to where I could coast down the incline. This was a full-sized bike, and I was still small. As we coasted down the hill, one of my hands was on the handlebars and the other was holding the cage in place. Somehow, the cage moved, and we all went to the right as we fell. For some reason, I was not so concerned with my own pain from the fall, only the hawk's. I knew it must be painful for a sick hawk to be crashing like this. The hawk was silent and looking at me. I picked up my bike and then lifted the cage to my handlebars again. We were only partly down the hill, and it seemed we could still coast a long way if I could control the cage. Then we were off again. The cage was too large to control with one hand. We went only a short distance farther with the same result. As we fell, the cage rolled and I watched the hawk bounce around in the cage.

I was feeling terrible for the pain I was causing the noble hawk. This was a terrible situation, and I did not know what to do. It was too far to my house to carry the cage.

I remembered I could say a prayer. I got help when I prayed. I started a prayer with, "Please help me get the hawk home." As I was saying the first few words of the prayer, a thought came into my mind. I could take the hawk out of the cage and carry it cradled in my arm as I rode home. I quit praying and went and opened the cage. (I suspected the idea would not work as the wild hawk would fight me in trying to accomplish the task.) I learned how sick the hawk was as I reached in to take hold of the hawk prior to taking it out of the cage. There was not even an attempt by the hawk to keep away from my hands as I picked it up and took it from the cage. I got back on my bike, and we were off.

The hawk was cradled in my left arm and was always staring at me when I checked it as I rode home. It seemed okay, so I rode home at a fast pace. As I rode, I thought since there would be no cage at home the hawk could be put in our shed. As soon as I was home, I was quickly off the bike and checked the hawk. It was dead! My eyes filled with tears for the poor hawk. The bike ride was too much for it or the sickness was too far advanced. Then I became angry! I had prayed and God had let me down. I started into another prayer to tell God this was not fair! In effect, I said, "You answered all my other prayers, so why did You abandon me and the hawk with this prayer? You could have easily saved the hawk! I trusted You, and You failed me!"

I was in this attitude and had just finished these very words when I sensed God's presence. He was somewhere to the south of me; I did not know how far, Southern California maybe South America, I just knew the direction. (I would have expected His location would have been up towards Heaven, not south.) From where He was, He turned in my direction and took a step closer.

Even though I had no idea how far away He was, this was important. An understanding came into my mind. I knew immediately it was from God. The understanding was that - "I had received what I had prayed for." My mind raced. What did I pray for? What did I pray for? I had asked, "please help me get the hawk home." Oh no! I had received what I had prayed for! Oh no!

My mind was still racing. I had been foolish in my prayer and had not prayed for the health of the hawk, just to get the hawk home. *What have I done? What have I done!* It was me who cost the hawk its only chance for life when I was sloppy in my prayer that was given without much thought. And things were much worse than this. Beyond the feeling of majesty at His turning in my direction, I had sensed something when the understanding was placed in my mind. When I sensed God, I should have been overjoyed at His approach, but I was angry at him… His attitude towards me held among other things, a slight amount, or a hint, of disappointment, disappointment in me! Nothing strong or nothing like any bad feelings or anger towards me or judging me, just the slightest hint of disappointment at my attitude and angry prayer when I found out the hawk was dead. I had charged God foolishly! Then my mind raced again. *What have I done? What is wrong with me? I have disappointed my Lord.* The One who was there in my darkest hours, when I did not want to go on, He was there the instant I needed help. *What have I done? I have disappointed my God! Oh no, what have I done, oh no, oh please, please forgive me, I am so sorry, please…*

In my frustration over losing the hawk, I had forgotten the supreme goodness of God. I had forgotten what He had done for me. I was complaining about Him not helping me, something that has never been, is not now and never will be. I will try to pray differently and remember this lesson. Among His many attributes, I am thankful that Jesus is so very forgiving.

How far have we fallen, so far that only God can save us? After all that Jesus, our Christ, has done, how can we not worship Him?

When God teaches, He really teaches.

There is more to this teaching; have you understood it yet? I will discuss it further in another experience. I did not understand the further implications of Jesus' teaching here until decades later, if I will ever completely understand while in mortality.

My parents divorced…

Bad Dream Ends. I did not say a formal prayer requesting help with the bad dream. I guess my faith was not strong enough to lead me to ask for help. But I was thinking about the bad dream and wondering if God would help stop the night terror. I do not remember if it was that night, but soon after engaging in that thought, I had the same dream again.

The falling was the same. The creatures were the same. They were looking at me falling, getting closer to them. They were waiting for me. I hit the mud and water in a violent impact as always. But then I was not stuck in the swamp! The ground and water were only about two feet thick. My velocity was so great I fell right through the thin crust of earth and water. In the dream this greatly surprised me. But I was still falling at a great rate of speed. Then I saw another swamp with all the same critters waiting. I fell until I blasted through that crust of that swamp the same as before. Then I realized I was falling but I would not be stuck in the swamp and killed and eaten by the critters. I could fall but I would not be hurt, and the fear was gone. When the fear was gone the dream evaporated into nothing.

Thanksgiving. Our family never did have much money, but after Dad had to move away, we had even less. However, we were not lacking for much, except love was still in short supply. It was Thanksgiving time and Mom was really concerned we could not afford to have a turkey for the Thanksgiving dinner. It was not a big deal to me; food was just food. Pancakes in a happy home would be better than a grand dinner in a sterile house. But Mom was concerned, so there was a prayer for some relief in this regard. But we never did pray as a family that the family would stay together and be happy.

It may have been that day or soon thereafter I was playing on the railroad track near our house. For some reason, I had a handle from an old broken broom with me. A wild turkey came through the tall grass and appeared only about fifteen feet away. We startled each other. The broom handle was thrown with a baseball bat swing and hit the bird in the neck. We had turkey for Thanksgiving dinner, the answer to another prayer. But our family was still broken.

Missions. Years later and I am fifteen years old. It had been five years since the first prayer in the schoolyard. Five years since, I was given the things to do. Five years was a long time. Lots of things had happened since then, some of which I was not proud. I had spent lots of time trying to find and learn, but with little success. It seemed to me I was failing, failing badly. I was not learning much.

I was home alone one afternoon, wondering if my life had been such a failure to date that maybe I was released from the things I was given to do, the two missions. I was in contemplation of this when the admonition was given that I should speak out loud. No subject was given just speak. I knew where this inspiration came from. So, I opened my mouth and words started coming out. The words were a speech! I was speaking but not thinking the words. But I was listening with great interest to what was being said. I spoke for about three minutes. The speech was about the state of our present government, and what future awful consequences would result from abandoning Constitutional principles, and how to reverse the course to good. It was like listening to a Thomas Jefferson or Abraham Lincoln type speech. The wisdom was far above me, but I could understand a little. And the most incredible thing was this wisdom was being conveyed in such few words. Not to mention it was coming from my voice but not my mind. If only I had a manuscript of it. I finally thought/prayed "Enough." The words quit coming. The question had been answered with wisdom and love beyond what I could have dreamed. What an available, patient, forgiving, and loving God. All praise and glory be to the Father, the Son, and the Holy Ghost forever and ever and ever!

Prepare. How to prepare myself for the two missions was always in the back of my mind. I did some regular things like paying closer attention in school. I paid close attention to the politics of the local region, state, and nation. A couple years later, I helped a State Assembly candidate in his election. He did not win.

Chapter 2

Teen Years and Military Service

Card Game. I was seventeen years old. I loved my grandpa and grandma Linke; they were so good to me. I made frequent visits.

During one visit, although she did not tell me why, Grandma Linke decided it was time to teach me another lesson. All she said to me was we were going to play a game of double solitary. This double game allowed each player to play their cards on their game or the other player game also. I was not sure why she wanted me to play a game of cards with her. But being the grand lady that she was, I did what I was told. We each played with our decks of cards. I made a play, and she made a play, and the game went on. As I made a play, she asked if that was the best move. It sure was, I replied. She agreed it was the best move for me. Then she asked me if it was the best move for both of us. After evaluating the game, that move would not help her at a critical point in her game. It was clear I could play for myself or team up with her and we could both help each other. I changed the move to one that helped her. Her game needed the help at the time, and I was doing pretty well. Soon she was doing better than I, and at a critical point in my game she helped me. By the end of the game, with the help of each other we both passed parts of the game that would have stopped a single player. We both would have lost playing by ourselves. Playing together, for the benefit of both, we both won. A valuable lesson that cost me just a little time to play a card game, and it is still paying dividends in my life. Plus, I enjoyed the time spent with a grand lady.

I graduated from high school in June 1968. After graduation, I worked full-time and tried to attend college full-time. That did not work, and I was drafted in November 1968.

The study of religion was so slow. It was so hard to find anyone who knew anything more than the Bible stories. Some people had ideas about God, but they did not seem to know the heavens were open and God was approachable and anxious to hear our prayers and teach us. Bible stories were very good, but they were distant in time and customs. That is not to say they did not have application today, as they surely did. But there was so much that was difficult to understand.

Plato. As a nineteen-year-old, I was in the US Army in Germany. I had a high school diploma and was anxious to add to my education. (I just wanted to be smarter than I was.) There was limited opportunity for that until someone told me the US Army had a program where a soldier could apply for a correspondence class from an American university and the government would pay for the cost. I received the catalog of universities and the classes they offered; the choices were huge. I had just finished reading a book on philosophy, much of which I did not fully understand. So, I picked UC Berkeley and a philosophy class. I was sent the materials to complete as I read the course book. The class text was *The Republic* by Plato. What a mistake. There was no one around to talk with about the work. The book was difficult. I read part of the book and finally stopped. High school teachers had told me of the brilliance of that ancient Greek. Now I was studying him, and I could see little of that great wisdom. On the contrary, I was so unimpressed with most all except his questioning technique. I concluded that it must be me who was missing something. I let the academic world convince me I was the dull one for not recognizing the greatness of Plato. It was years later while studying the writings of Thomas Jefferson (highlighted by W.C. Skousen) that I found Jefferson and John Adams had made an exhaustive study of Plato. They did not agree with much that Plato wrote either. I was far too quick to trust academia and to dismiss common sense. I will not soon do that again. Plato did not follow God; he followed a different plan.

Transcendental Meditation. I was solidly Christian. But I wanted to know what this Transcendental Meditation had to teach. The meditation was said to be "pleasing to God." I practiced it for about three months. They taught little about God. There were some important things learned, but the meditation did not lead me nearer to God as directly as prayer and the study of the scriptures did. So, in a few months I was back to prayer and the search.

White Hair and Memories. I was assigned to a HAWK surface to air missile base in Germany. The base, where we stayed while not on duty, was a large WWII vintage military compound in the city of Aschaffenburg. The place where the missiles were kept was called a "tack site." It was located about ten or so miles away from the town in a clearing in a forest. We would be ferried to the tack site and spend our twenty-four hours on duty. Then, very early in the morning, a new group would take our place and we would ride back to the compound in Aschaffenburg.

Every early morning, on our way back to town I saw white-haired German women walking. It was as regular as the sun rising. Something was out of the ordinary with the women walking. I asked if anyone else noticed something out of the ordinary. What a mistake! The guys laughed at me for days every time they saw a white-haired woman. They said I could not get a date with a young woman, so I was checking out the old ladies. I guess it was funny. The question still begged investigating; the white-haired women still walked. They walked the same direction in the early hours. So, one early morning, upon returning from the tack site, I quickly changed clothes and was off investigating. I saw one walking a couple blocks ahead of me. Walking over twice as fast I quickly passed her. There were more several blocks farther ahead. Soon there were many to lead the way. I could see they would turn off the main road towards the river. Soon there were more to follow and pass.

A few streets off the main road they were streaming around the corner of a large walled area, nearly a city block in size. What was going on behind that wall? The stream carried me through a large, metal double doorway. Once inside, it was all clear. This was a cemetery. A large, very well-kept cemetery. It was being tended. It was not all white-haired women; there was an occasional white-haired man and some middle-aged men and women. I do not remember any my age.

As I walked, I read the headstones. Many headstones marked young men who had died during war years. Many had died so young. I was reading one headstone and a white-haired man handed me a small watering can. I took it and returned his humble half smile and nod. While walking, I watered some of the patches of grass or small shrubs that adorned the graves. The can was passed with a humble half smile and nod to a white-haired woman who gladly took the can and returned the half smile and nod. The tone was one of quiet reverence and maybe just a little wistful. I was left pondering on the almost overwhelming consequences that result when politicians embrace evil, and citizens follow them. How much pain can evil politicians cause us regular people?

Ted (not his real name) was about four or five years older than me, a lot smarter, and had a lot more life experiences. On the rare occasions when we were at the tack site together, he would talk of his experiences within his church. He told about going on a two-year, Spanish speaking mission for his church when he was my age. He had attended college and married. He had lots of interesting experiences. He told of another book of scripture his church had. I was not sure how or why his church got it. But his church seemed to have more than the standard differences from other churches.

A short word about race hatred in the U.S. Army in Germany. Most soldiers got along well. Some had deep-seated race hatred, and others were weary of each other. There were as many who were full of hate on both sides; it was obvious the numbers were small, but they were actively and successfully seeking recruits. It was so sad. One trio of friends allowed me a small part in their friendship they shared with a very few. They were led by a black man from U.C. Berkeley and two Latinos.

One morning at breakfast, a new white soldier came and sat next to me and one of the Latinos. He started using the N-word and carrying on. The Latino took his tray and left, leaving only the two of us at the table. I could have used his help. I started telling the young soldier his hate was going to isolate him to the group of haters that had nothing good ahead of them. Plus, most of the soldiers would shun him. Did it make him happy to hurt others? He should have left that hatred somewhere a long time ago, and on and on.

The next time I met the trio, the Berkeley psychology student started to accuse me of being a racist. Along with heated racist hatred language used by the worst of both sides. I seriously suspect the only cure for racism is the teachings of Jesus that can change our nature to a better. God bless all those who do not know of Jesus and get caught with the fishhooks of the evils of this world. Fishhooks are hard to get out.

This was another teaching moment lost. Not long after I left Germany without a chance to sit down and talk to my Berkeley friend and explain what really happened. He obviously assumed, since I did not leave the table, I enjoyed and agreed with the sad remarks.

I volunteered to go to Viet Nam, the most significant activity of that time. I wanted to see the war firsthand. I was an expert marksman, among other things, and should have a much better than average chance to get through the war. I had seen the good people of Germany and that was enough.

Good-by. Ted was interested in my study of religion. He asked me several times how my study of transcendental meditation was progressing, and he seemed interested with my findings. Before I left to go back to the US, Ted invited me to his home. Generally, he and his wife kept very much to themselves. After the dinner and some conversation, Ted wanted to read me some passages out of the Old Testament. As he started reading, a peculiar occurrence happened. While he was reading, I could not understand one single word, not one word. It was like he was reading in some unknown language. He continued and not one word made it to my understanding. But I did feel his concern for me. Ted asked me to remember his church when I chose another church to study. I told him that I would.

Back to the USA. I flew back to the US. To me, the flight back was most notable for two reasons. First, we flew over Greenland. It was huge and full of mountains all covered with snow. What a sight. Second, as I saw the US coast and flew over the land. I noticed a distinct change. There was a slight heaviness or slight darkness lifted from me when I was back in the US. There was lots of beauty and charm in Europe, but to me it did not carry the same feeling as the promised land.

Engaged. The Army gave soldiers a thirty-day leave before they sent them to war. During my thirty days, Bev and I were engaged. (We had been dating for several years, and Bev had graduated from high school.) We should have married, but it did not seem right to me to risk creating a seventeen-year-old widow.

Vietnam. I arrived "in country" at Cam Ranh Bay Airfield, and was immediately sent far north to Phu Bai, a base camp a little south of Hue. Phu Bai, what an experience. I was new "in country" and drugs, hard drugs, alcohol, immorality, bad officers, and race hatred abounded. Oh boy. What else could an army do to cause its ineffectiveness? An army needs a prophet to lead it, not even a good general (if there were any) and certainly not a politician. This war was not going well, and I had just arrived.

Zen. It was time to pick another study subject. I was solidly Christian, but I studied Zen Buddhism for a short while. I learned enough. Then back to the search.

Wrong Place. There are a lot of experiences of this time that are being skipped, mainly because they are dark stories of a dark time. I will share only one.

Tom, that is not his name, a soldier buddy, asked me if I wanted to go to a party. I thought he was joking. He insisted and we were off. Phu Bai had a swampy area not far from the Medi-vac heliport, along the green line (base perimeter). Tom said the party was not far, out by itself near the green line in a corrugated tin covered shack. Tom knocked on the door and a soldier holding his rifle looked out. Tom said, "It is me, let us in."

The soldier demanded "Who is he?" while looking at me.

Tom said, "Oh, he is from California." (Most soldiers had the idea anyone from California was at least a little crazy.)

The door guard said okay, and let us in. Instead of going in, anyone with two brain cells would have been running in the other direction. But, dumb me, I was from California. Maybe they were right after all.

We went in and the door was closed and the surly soldier with the rifle was sitting on the floor leaning his back against door. There were two rooms in the little, poorly lit hut. There were about ten soldiers sitting on the floor leaning up against the walls in the first room. Hard drugs… There were about four soldiers in a line leading to the doorway to the second room. I wanted out of this room, and the guard at the door was not in a good mood, there could be trouble there. So, I got in the line.

Standing in a line was something, familiar to a soldier. I noticed there was another soldier questioning the guys before they entered the second room. The questioner had a pipe with some white powder in it. The guy, two in front of me, had just finished talking. Then the questioner put his mouth over the fat end of the pipe and blew. A little white fog came out of the mouth end of the pipe and the soldier leaned over and breathed it in. I quickly asked Tom what the white stuff was. He said it was opium. My mind was racing. What a mess! How could I get out of this "party"? The guy in front of me was offered the opium and refused, saying that his company was going on patrol tomorrow and he could not get caught with a drug head. He went in and I knew what to say to pass the second guard. I said the same thing as the soldier before me. Would Tom tell the guard I was not going on patrol tomorrow?

I went into the second room. There were about twenty soldiers sitting on the floor. There was a chalkboard on the wall. Tom and I sat down and a buck sergeant walked into the room and started talking. He told us how to disrupt our company and talked about how some guys had succeeded in their companies. He was anti-war, and part of some organized group. At the end of his short talk, he pointed to two names on the chalkboard. One was a US Senator everyone easily recognized. The other name, we were told, was an attorney from New York City. They both had addresses. We were encouraged to contact them if we were somehow caught or got into trouble with the Army. The meeting broke up and I speedily got out of Dodge. What a crazy mess! Oh, by the way, do not go to any parties with Tom.

Book of Mormon. It was time to study another church. This time it would be the Church of Jesus Christ of Latter-Day Saints (LDS). I wanted to start by reading the Book of Mormon. So, I went to an Army chaplain's office. The chaplain was not there, so I asked his assistant if he could help me get a copy of the Book of Mormon. I was presented with a copy of the book and the time and location of the LDS meetings. I showed up at the LDS meeting. It was a quite different group from the regular soldiers. They were generally calm and settled, not the norm for this place. When I arrived, they seemed to know exactly why I was there, that Church mission thing. (A mission is where they spend two years sharing what they have learned about Jesus, with others.)

The weeks passed fast as I read the book. The book was filling me with insights about God. This was a companion work to the Bible. Each Sunday meeting the group was eager to ask me how the reading was progressing. Each meeting was filled with brief explanations of life's questions and simple explanations to the exalting teachings of Jesus. All of them could answer my questions and ask me questions I had not reasoned out yet, and then answer the question that would naturally follow the previous question they had just asked. There was a spirit to the meetings I felt. That feeling was so similar to the spiritual experiences from my youth. Plus, the feeling I had while running with my dad came back, when at the park he took me by the hand and ran so fast. They were taking me by the hand and running, so to speak. I was learning much faster than I could by myself. They told me the heavens were open. They told me angels still visited people on earth, and the Holy Ghost still spoke to some as in the time of the Bible. It seemed they knew all the things I had learned, and lots more.

After meeting with the group for about three weeks, I was transferred north to Camp Evans, the headquarters of the 101 Airborne Division.

Camp Evans. As I got to Camp Evans (101st Airborne base camp, also called Camp Eagle), I met the LDS church group there. I had read half of the Book of Mormon while at Phu Bai. Now this new group started inviting me to discussions about religion. I attended church with them for a couple months. Larry (not his name), a civilian who worked for the Red Cross and a second lieutenant with the 101st Airborne would regularly invite me to their hut in the evenings and we would discuss the Book of Mormon. I learned how their church got the book. I was told about the early life of Joseph Smith the young prophet.

Briefly stated, Joseph lived in upper state New York in the early 1800's. When he was about fourteen years old, he seemed somewhat confused about religion. He tried to understand a couple of the different creeds. Not satisfied with his findings, he went by himself into a wooded area to ask in prayer which church was right. As he prayed, a pillar of light appeared above him. In the light, stood two heavenly beings, Heavenly Father and His Son Jesus. Jesus told him he should join none of the churches, among other things. This is reverently and affectionately called "The First Vision." Sometime after that glorious event, an angel named Moroni appeared to the young prophet and told him a book written on pages made of gold was buried in a hill not far from where he lived. Moroni was the last prophet, over a thousand years ago, to write in the book and was the one who had buried the book in the hill. The book is a saga of two earlier civilizations. One of which traveled from Israel and lived on South and North America. Young Joseph was shown where the book was buried, and after some years, was allowed to take the book to translate it into English. The work was printed and is known as the Book of Mormon. The young prophet later organized the Church of Jesus Christ of Latter-Day Saints. If you want to know more about these remarkable things, you can ask most any active member of the Church of Jesus Christ of Latter-Day Saints.

I finished my reading of the book. At our regular meeting one evening, Gary suggested I pray to see if the Book of Mormon was true. Moroni, the last prophet to write in book, offered a promise that if the reader of the book would pray to know if the book is true, the Holy Ghost would manifest the truth to that person. Everything that they were teaching me was interconnected with the truth of that book. If the Book of Mormon was not true, their entire church was the same.

A day or so later, I went to my room in the hooch (tin roofed sleeping quarters). There was no door to my room, but no one was around. So, I said a silent prayer, as other soldiers could be walking through the hall in the center of the hooch, and I did not want any attention.

I did not have any specific expectations, though my experiences were that God answered all prayers in His own way, almost always in a surprising manner. Since this was of such importance surely, He would help me on this account. So, the prayer was a brief review of what I had learned from my reading the Book of Mormon and then a brief review of my feelings about the book. Then I asked if the Book of Mormon was true. While I was in the process of asking if the book was true, a small, warm feeling appeared in the middle of my chest. I noticed it, briefly wondered what it was, and then dismissed that line of thought as a distraction and returned to the prayer. I had not prayed much more when the warm feeling started to increase in size. The sensation started to increase like a solid ball getting larger in all directions, while the temperature stayed the same. By this point, the sphere of warmth went from my chest to my back, to the ribs on the sides, and to my shoulders. I stopped praying, opened my eyes, and looked down at my chest. My feelings were of a calm concern for what was happening, not of any alarm. A couple seconds after I quit praying, the warm feeling disappeared. I mused for a few more seconds on the meaning of the occurrence. I could not understand it, so I returned to the task at hand.

I started to pray again, covering generally the same review, but more quickly to the request this time. Again, the same results, the warm feeling started small in the center of my chest. It grew in size but not in intensity until the feeling filled my entire chest, from front to back, from my lower neck to my lower ribs. By this time, I was confused and thought to myself, *How can I pray when this is happening?* So, I stopped the prayer. I was very disappointed the prayer was not answered. Long ago, I had learned not to charge God with not answering a prayer (the incident with the hawk). I could not understand what the meaning of the warm sensation was. The lack of understanding turned to disappointment. My disappointment was enough to think this may not be the truth I am searching for. The book and the whole of the explanations seemed right, (I knew Joseph Smith was incredibly special) but this feeling was so strong it interfered with the prayer.

So, the next thought was not to try praying again, but to practice transcendental meditation for a while. I had just started to repeat the mantra when a strong, rapid, sharp pounding started in the middle of my chest. The force and speed reminded me of a kettledrum. But there was one more facet to the beating. The beat was at the same time strong, fast, and sharp and soft like the end of a feather. This could never happen in our existence. The end of a feather could not produce the strong, rapid, and sharp beating and at the same time be so soft. I knew in a second that this manifestation was from God. I did not know exactly what this meant but it happened in response to me starting to say the mantra, and it was definitely in opposition to the meditation. So, I stopped meditating. There was much to think about. Still confused, I soon gave up trying to reason out the events and went to sleep.

The next day I went to see Larry. The officer, a distant cousin to Larry, was there and they were talking. There was an excited anticipation when Larry asked if I had prayed about the Book of Mormon. There was still some disappointment in me when I answered that I had prayed. I explained the third experience about the pounding. The officer looked at me with a "this guy is weird" look. Then I looked at Larry. Larry looked confused at what I said, and then his countenance changed. In a serious and calm manner, he said the experience was from God. I already knew that. His statement surprised the officer. But the real effect of his statement was to let me know he could understand an uncommon manifestation of God. My statement, judged by the world, would be more than goofy. But Larry understood, he recognized the same God I did. His experiences or teachings in his church enabled him to recognize a complex activity of the Spirit. I knew then that he and his church, the Church of Jesus Christ of Latter-Day Saints, followed the same God that had given me so many experiences. That church was going to be my church for the rest of my life. I thought it was going to be easy now that I found the church I was looking for. Silly me…

The next time we met, Larry asked me if I wanted to join the Church. I said I did. He stated he would make arrangements for the baptism. As a side note, I was pleasantly surprised when I was reading and found out what the burning in the chest meant. For some reason, I did not associate the first two manifestations with the experience that Luke and his friend Cleopas received on the road to Emmaus. That is where the Savior opened the scriptures to them, and their hearts did burn within them. (The warm or burning in the heart is an affirmative conformation of truth given by the Holy Ghost.) If I would have made the association, I would not have continued to pray so intensely and the burning probably would not have gotten so large. Further, the LDS church has other scriptures that explained the burning in the chest and a lot more.

I did not share any of the spiritual experiences of my youth. I feel bad as so many of that group at Camp Evans shared so much with me. Maybe, in some small way, this writing will make up for being so reserved. Hopefully, better late than never.

Off to China Beach. It just so happened that there was going to be an LDS Church conference down south at a place near Da Nang called China Beach. Besides being a hospital area, there was a small rest and relaxation (R & R) area there also. Most of the small church group from Camp Evans wanted to attend. Larry thought this would be a good place for a baptism. Somehow, someone got orders cut for many of our group to attend the church conference. Larry was a Red Cross employee and was familiar with the casualties of our area. He expressed his concern for the danger involved in traveling by land that far. Finally, he stated that if he was going to get killed, going to a baptism was one of the better activities to be involved with at the time.

Raul (not his name) was a sergeant in the 101st Airborne. He was a member of the small LDS group at Camp Evans. He and I had become as close as brothers. We met and talked often. He shared his testimony of the influence of Jesus had in his family's life and much more. He had so many plans when he got home. Soon the plans that were for Raul and his wife now included Bev and me. He was assuring me that Bev and I should attend BYU with him and his wife when the war was over.

We had talked about the trip south to China Beach before we went. Raul asked me if I was going to take my M-16 rifle. I asked him what his thoughts were. He said he had no intentions of killing anyone, especially on the way to a baptism. I agreed, so we went with small bags full of some clean clothes, shavers, and toothbrushes, but no weapons. There was not room in the truck that was going to China Beach, so Raul and I found another truck that was going south, and we hopped in. The truck we started in went a long way, but it was not going all the way to Da Nang. So, when it came to its turn off, we jumped out and thanked the driver for the ride.

There was only one main road north and south. Everyone called it Highway 1. We started walking, sure another truck would come along soon. We walked into a small village of huts covered with corrugated tin roofs. The village was on both sides of the road. There was no one there. I was concerned. Something seemed wrong. I took out a camera and took a picture of Raul against the background of the huts. I put the camera back in my bag and my concern for our safety quickly returned. I could not understand why there were no people; there should have been, at least, chickens and dogs making noise. The area was too quiet.

We continued to walk in the dirt on the right side of the road heading south. I could hear a vehicle, not a truck, coming our way. It was coming from a dirt road through the village that crossed Highway 1. It could be a ride. We both turned to look. It appeared from between the huts. It was a brown jeep with a canvas top. The U.S. Army did not have brown jeeps. All the Army jeeps were green. A Vietnamese man, maybe thirty years old was driving. He did not have the passive look of a farmer. He was a soldier in light brown shirt and pants. The back and passenger seats were filled with about twenty or more enemy rifles. The driver crossed the street behind us and suddenly stopped. We must have surprised him. His right hand immediately went to the top rifle in the front passenger seat. We were about one hundred feet away from him. Highway 1 was the only thing between us. It was built up in a convex fashion, about a foot higher in the middle. Not much cover. My instinct was to turn and jump to the ground to lessen my target area then quickly disappear between the huts. But something was very wrong. Raul was not turning, and the man did not lift the rifle. I thought about pulling Raul, so I looked at his face to see what was happening to him. He was smiling! He was smiling a big happy Raul from sunny Concord, California smile. His happy nature was being shared with an enemy soldier that had his hand on a rifle. All the while Raul stood erect and seemed relaxed and calm. I suspect he was not seeing an enemy soldier but another of Heavenly Father's children. Thus, to Raul this was another one of his brothers. I took a quick look at the man in the jeep. He obviously saw we were unarmed. He must have seen Raul's smile and saw us as no threat. He released the rifle, still watching us he grabbed the gearshift and started moving. He quickly went between huts and was out of sight.

This encounter had lasted only a few seconds. Raul turned and continued walking. My concern was more than equaled by my surprise at Raul's reaction. Raul said nothing about it. It was no big deal to him. There appeared to have been no concern in him. I was at least confused. Again, I had lots to think about if I was going to understand what just happened. It was not long before a truck came along and gave us a ride. It did not have a canvas cover, so we had a great view of the ocean from the hills as we went south. We took some more pictures and got too much sun. Some of the scenery along the coast was beautiful.

Baptism. We attended the LDS conference. A tall, thin, white-haired man, the Southeast Asia Mission President, spoke at the conference. Then a few shared their testimonies and love for Jesus. There were maybe two hundred soldiers in attendance. After the conference was over, we went and changed into the baptism clothes. Larry and I walked out into the surf of the South China Sea at China Beach. Dion, Raul, and some others followed. The beach had a long gentle slope to the bottom, so we walked a long way to get into about three feet of water. During the walk, a Huey chopper flew low over us, probably wondering what two guys were doing dressed in white clothes. The door gunner on our side of the Huey had his hands on the machine gun and was close enough to see he was watching us.

I was being baptized by one holding the priesthood and having authority to baptize in the name of the Father and the Son and the Holy Ghost. I was quickly under the water.

Another experience... As I was under the water, at the bottom of the cycle of being baptized, for about one second, before I was pulled to the surface, everything seemed to stop, absolutely silent, dark, and calm. As calm as anything I could imagine. To me, baptism has several symbolic meanings. One meaning is the washing away of our sin. Going into and out of the water in the name of the Father and the Son and the Holy Ghost, is a washing or cleansing and forgiving of sins by the will and grace of Jesus. Another is the death. This symbolic is the death to our old life and not following the ways of the world anymore. The next symbol is the burial, being placed under the water. Then the last is rebirth, coming out of the water, as the birth of a wet child out of his mother's womb. Then we are into the new life, our life as followers and possibly even servants of Jesus.

While I was at the bottom of the immersion, I also felt the aloneness. I had always been a very private and withdrawn person, but this aloneness was far beyond anything earthly I had previously felt. It was as if nothing else existed in the universe. Only an intense silent blackness, and aloneness. It was as if I was dead in a tomb. It was as if everything had gone silent and alone. I was quickly out of the tomb and in the air and sunlight, with the living. In my new life. We walked the long walk back to the beach. In my mind, I was trying to fully understand what had happened at the bottom of the baptism cycle.

Not long thereafter, Raul placed his hands on my head and confirmed me a member of the Church of Jesus Christ of Latter-Day Saints and I was given the first gift/commandment after baptism; I was to receive the Holy Ghost. If I would stay worthy of the gift, I had the opportunity to have the Holy Ghost as a constant companion. Not just on occasion but constantly. Through the years, I have learned how hard it is to be "worthy" of that gift. But what a grand reward as I do follow all the rules.

All of us have the gift of conscience. If we will heed its prompting, we will be warned prior to doing something seriously wrong. We cannot do forbidden things until we have disregarded the warning. If the warning is disregarded and we do wrong, we then suffer the pains of our conscience along with other consequences. If we disregard the warnings too often, we may become past feeling and not recognize the gift of conscience. The gift of the Holy Ghost, given after baptism, as we always remember our Savior and kept His commandments, is for us to be close to or in other words receive a Revelator. This is the Revelator that teaches about our Redeemer, His will, and ways and so many other things concerning this mortal life. This is far beyond the activity of the conscience.

Hymn. Most Sundays we would meet in the little wooden chapel at Camp Evans. It was a little chapel painted white. I never saw anyone else use it. It somehow seemed out of place. The group had songbooks. I think it was Brother Lee from Hawaii who led the music on most occasions. One of the songs we sang at the closing of several meetings was "God Be with You 'Till We Meet Again." This song had, as all songs do, a particular feeling to it. At first, I thought the song was sung at the close of most meetings because we were in a dangerous war and the song was a plea to our Savior for safety during the upcoming week. In a couple more meetings of singing the song, I came to understand differently. Safety in a war was a concern but not the primary concern. We could be killed, but the more important state was that we could forget

God. We could walk away from Him, we could, not "be with" Him "'till we meet again." That was the great reason for us singing the song, to be close to God through the week until we would meet again and talk about the Holy Spirit, Our Savior, and Our Heavenly Father, repent of the previous week's shortcomings, partake of the Sacrament, and re-pledge our lives to always take upon us His (Jesus) name and to following Him and keep His commandments and have his Spirit to be with us.

Oh yes, some were wounded and one of, if not the best of us, was later killed (Raul), but God was with us 'till we met again. (Later, I came to know the only real tragedy is sin.) As for my great friend, Raul, 'till we meet at Jesus feet. I look forward to that day. I hope that my family and I will be worthy to be where Raul is. The world does not know what they lost in Raul. I only received one letter from Larry, and I lost track of him. But in his letter, he waxed very profound when he said, in effect, all those... hills of Viet Nam were not worth Raul. He was so right, may God bless Raul and his family, 'till we all meet again.

Fasting. There would be maybe eight to fifteen who would attend when we could. Some of the meetings were spiritual and others were even more spiritual. I started experimenting with information I had learned, how fasting coupled with prayer could take you closer to God than prayer by itself. Fast meetings were different, more spiritual. So, it appeared that every Sabbath could be a day for fasting and prayer. The meetings got more spiritual as I fasted. I suspected I was not the only one who would fast before each Sacrament meeting.

I tried a two-day fast. The two-day fast was as different from a one day fast as not fasting is to a one day fast. I tried a three day fast. In a hot climate the body really does some changing without water and food. The third day was surprising for several reasons. One of the biggest surprises was I did not feel any hunger on the third day. Maybe the body had given up trying to make me eat by using hunger pains. The weakness was very pronounced and there were times that concentration was difficult.

Speech became a little difficult. There was a difference in prayer. I could feel the life slipping away from the body, and I was also aware there was no life slipping away from the association I had with God. On the contrary, there was more closeness or an increased awareness of the closeness that had often been there. If my life would continue to fail, I would still have the closeness to God. I was not too worried about the weakness as water was available any time I wanted. My whole body lost a lot of its energy. Even walking and talking took concentration. None of the guys in my unit seemed to take any notice I had not been to any meals for three days. If you are not in good health, this would be a serious risk. I did not even attempt a four-day fast. There was no reason for the attempt, like a great need, especially not while being active, out of doors in that hot climate.

Food and water are our tie to the physical life. When we fast and pray, we turn away from the tie to the physical life and approach God in a more humble attitude, thus the spiritual closeness that accompanies the fasting and prayer.

The Spirit at a Meeting. There was one particular meeting that seemed to be much more spiritual. The Sacrament was blessed and passed, and the meeting went on. This could have been a regular or fast meeting; it is past my memory. At that time, I regularly fasted before attending church meetings as to be closer to the Spirit during the services.

Basking in the presence of the Spirit was very pronounced this day. I was really caught up in the closeness of the Spirit. How rare and wonder filled. I remember walking after I left the meeting. Thoughts were of how wonderful it was to be this close to the Spirit and the peaceful feeling that it carried. As I walked, it was almost like walking on soft powder snow and not sinking too much. Maybe a little like being partly carried while I was walking. The thought of being carried was somehow foreign. My thoughts were then turned to the present. With some concentration my thoughts were turned to what was I doing. In the middle of remembering that I was walking I stumbled, like missing a step down. I was not sure where I was walking. The next thought was, *If I do not know where I am going, then where am I?* I had to concentrate to remember I was in the military then I remembered I was in Viet Nam at Camp Evans, and finally I remembered where my hooch was at and that I was going there. The irony was thick, one of the most spiritual and peaceful feelings I ever felt was while walking back from a church meeting during a war. Oh, how

I wish and pray that there would be more meetings like that one. My prayer is that all brothers and sisters of this church and every other church may attend at least one such meeting. I have so many brothers and sisters...worlds are filled with us.

Sick. I got really sick. It started with some dizziness, some loss of hearing, and difficulty seeing. Then my thoughts became fuzzy and concentration was difficult. I do not remember just staying in bed, but another soldier said he was going to take me to the medics. He was helping me from falling over as we walked. At the medical evacuation station, I found myself sitting upright and hearing noises. I could hear "Hueys" (medical evacuation helicopters) coming and going. I could see a soldier with his shirt off across the room. It was hard to focus my sight, but as I did it seemed he was dead from holes in his chest. He was sitting upright and leaning against the wall. I am telling this very dark episode for an obvious reason.

To my right, there was a table, and some medical types were working on a soldier with a young voice. I could not seem to be able to turn to see what was happening to him. But I could hear his screams of pain and his crying calls for his "momma" repeatedly. He was fighting for his life in a foreign and distant war as his desperate cry went out for his mother. A great American tragedy. I must stop here, or I will begin with the great accusations against our rulers! I went to Vietnam to learn and I did.

Back to the USA, again. I applied for and received a two-month early separation from the US Army to make the fall semester at American River College in Sacramento. The "early out" of Vietnam was great on both ends, out of the war and not missing a semester at college, and especially seeing Bev sooner.

Fort Lewis, Washington. We arrived, got off the jet, and were given some temporary accommodations. We were directed to sit through a briefing, part of which covered not bringing drugs into the US. Some soldiers were bringing serious hard drug habits back, and the Army did not seem interested in helping them. They were just discharged out of the Army, and it was their own personal problem.

We were told there was great anti-war sentiment, and our uniforms would draw unwanted negative attention. We were directed to buy some civilian clothes and wear them when we left the base to go home.

Chapter 3

Back to Civilian Life

Back to Bev. As I landed at the Sacramento airport, Bev was waiting for me. Fashions had changed. My first thought was, why was I so fortunate. Bev had waited for me for nearly two years. She had written to me nearly every day.

Then, I watched lots of people going about their business as if nothing was happening! All the while Americans and others were dying in a foreign and distant war. I could not be convinced they did not care, nor did I think they thought the distant war was worth the cost. So, it must be they felt powerless to control the government. That "bad politician" thing again, like Germany, Japan, and so many others. Lots of people were dying because of bad politicians. But, to my recollection, not many of the deaths were politicians or their sons. I have always been a rock-solid patriot, but for years after returning from Vietnam, I had trouble singing the national anthem, as I remembered how bad politicians crushed millions of peaceful people.

A Bishop. Bev and I had planned to marry as soon as I got home. She wanted to be married in a church, so I convinced her we should marry in a chapel of the church I just joined. I was told we would have to get permission to use the chapel from the local leader. Bev and I went and met with the local leader, a bishop. He was the leader of the ward. He said he was quite busy and seemed most unfriendly. What a start. We told him we wanted to marry on a Saturday not too distant. He said that could not he had other commitments. He said we could go ask someone else, some other local leader. We had no idea who that person was or how to contact him. Then we were quickly dismissed. What a meeting.

Bev was shocked and hurt. She wanted to know what kind of rascals ran this church I thought was so good. She was right, and I could not answer her. I did not attend that ward too much. "Of these make thy friends," I could only find a couple of them in that entire ward. This did not seem much like the church I joined in Vietnam. There could not be two churches with the same name, could there?

Bev and I marry. Bev wanted to marry in a church building. Obviously, the LDS Bishop was of no help, so Bev looked for help from other churches. Bev contacted several other local religious leaders with a similar result to the one we had with the LDS Bishop. Then Bev talked to a presbyterian minister in Roseville. He said he would marry us in his church. He was the only nice religious leader I had met in the US since my return. What was going on with religious leaders? We were grateful for his help, and we had a genuinely nice wedding.

I got a job with the local power company. I trained to be a high voltage lineman. I started attending night college classes.

Another Ward. We moved into our first house. It was a small, cheaply constructed house, but we were thrilled to have a house of our own. It was in another area and another LDS ward. I wanted to go to the new ward. I hoped it would be a different experience from what we had in the first ward.

This new ward was about as different as things could be. It was filled with an assortment of people, most of whom were simply delightful. What a change! Bev and I were treated very kindly. Bev's heart quickly softened to the kindness. Most were anxious to teach us all they could about Jesus and His ways as fast as we could process the doctrine. If this was generally what happened to people after years in the church, I was happy to meet the future. I wanted a future like the one in this ward. In particular, in Bishop Warner I could see the effect of him living the Gospel of Jesus Christ.

There were too many kind people and nice things that happened to us to mention in specific. It seemed that sometimes Bishop Warner orchestrated the kindness, but later it was evident that the acts came from many different hearts. Bev joined the church. We were taught the Gospel of Jesus Christ as fast as we could comprehend.

Set Apart. Bishop Warner "set me apart" (gave me a job to do in the ward) and gave me a blessing at the same time. One of the things he said was my mind would be quickened. That is all that I remember of what he said. But that was enough! I had never been smart, but I tried hard, and I had an exceptional memory. Gradually, I could understand more things after the blessing. I was still average, but now I had a blessing from the Lord, through the bishop, to help me. I was not as average as I had been. (Why didn't he bless me to be brilliant and wealthy? Just kidding.)

Twins. About a year and a half after we were married, we had twins… No effort for their safety and growth was too much. We could not be too protective of the special little ones. They were fortunate because of the exceptional care received from such a wonderful young mother. Their safety and care were as secure as any infant I had ever known. We were excited and overwhelmed at the same time with the responsibility of having twins, maybe more overwhelmed. By the end of each day, Bev was so out of energy that she seemed like a marathon runner at the end of the race.

Fireside. The twins were a couple months old. We went to a fireside meeting on a Sabbath evening. As was often the case, instead of getting a babysitter, we took the twins everywhere we went. If they could not go, we generally did not go or at least went one at a time. The meeting was held in the home of a genuinely nice family. A councilor in the Stake Presidency (a Stake Presidency is a group of three men that are the file leaders of the Stake which is composed of about six to twelve wards - a bishop is the file leader of a ward) was the speaker. When we got there, the bishop and most of the ward leaders were in attendance. At the start of the president's remarks was a disclaimer he was not too close to the Spirit that evening. We should have taken his remarks seriously and evacuated the home immediately. But we stayed. Bev had been a member for about four months. We were still trying to take in all the new concepts of the new life.

The talk was started and turned into more of a class of instruction with questions and answers. The subject quickly turned to abortions. Then the class turned darker; how and why the abortions were performed in other countries. This was a subject for a conversation at the local bar, not in this good home. What a subject for a tenderhearted young mother to endure while holding one of the infant twins! I looked at her and tears were streaming down her face. Unfortunately, my response was anger. I had no time to correct my error in emotions. Bev was hurting and I needed to get her out of there, now! I turned to the Stake President and told him to be quiet until we got out of the house. As you can guess, most were startled as the words that came out a little (maybe a lot) stronger than I intended. We stood up and walked out as Bev quietly wept. At the door, as we left, the homeowner's look was one of concern and lack of understanding at what was happening. He had no clue, and I had no time to explain. What a teaching moment, lost. As we went out his front door, I mentioned something to the effect that I would throw the Stake President out, if this were my house. This only further added to the confusion.

The next Sabbath came, and we attended the ward meetings as usual. As I entered the foyer to go to priesthood meeting the bishop, and several other brothers were there engaged in conversation. With my entrance everyone went quiet, and all eyes turned to me. Most of the men there were not at the fireside. It was obvious there had been a week of gossip. The bishop immediately opened the subject of abortion. He is a to-the-point kind of guy. He stated that the president had suggested Bev and I were upset because we had probably been involved in the activity. My last response, the week before, was a failure as it was accompanied by anger. Anger ruins most reasoned thought. So many other things could have been said that evening. What was my response to be this time? The second concern was the bishop was having this discussion in front of several members that obviously had been involved in the gossip.

Well, the time to respond was now. I told the bishop the president was wrong. There was never the need or would never even be the thought of such an evil act. I managed the response in a conversational manner, with none of the heat I was feeling. Then I told the bishop, the Spirit confirms truth so you can know who is telling the truth. I had recognized that this bishop had been close to the Spirit in the past, probably light years ahead of me. The bishop stared into my eyes; I think; this was an attempt to discern the truth. It seemed to me that he was confused, not knowing, or more probably being caught between two opposing gravities. One gravity being the words of his file leader and the other gravity being my words. Since the Spirit will only confirm truth, any confirmation would have been my words. His stare ended, and he was still wearing his confused look. He was still caught in the middle. His file leader was of enormous status and me a new member of little or no status. To the good bishop's credit, he was waiting, not siding with the weight of gravity and status. The bishop may have filed away the conversation until he was alone and had a chance to pray about it.

The other men made their way to the opening of the meeting. That was the last I heard of the subject. I cannot say what direction the ward gossip took. But a new member saying the Stake President made up a lie and charging the bishop to check with the Spirit if he wanted the truth, must have provided a fertile field to plant more seeds of gossip. Again, to the credit of the ward, we heard nothing more on this subject.

Melchizedek Priesthood. Bishop Warner said it was time for me to receive the Melchizedek Priesthood. I had held the Aaronic Priesthood for some time. I did not have any particular feelings for the Aaronic priesthood, maybe because I did not have a chance to use the priesthood much. So, I did not expect the second or higher priesthood to be much different. I sure missed that one...

I was called to the front of the priesthood meeting. I sat in a chair, another brother and Bishop Warner laid their hands on my head to confer the Melchizedek Priesthood upon me. As the authority was stated, I immediately jumped from the sitting on the chair to a standing position. This was an involuntary response, I did not think of doing this, it just happened. Something was wrong, the movement took less than a blink of an eye! This movement was so swift and powerful. It was not something that could occur with our body. I opened my eyes and saw the brothers of the ward that were in attendance with closed eyes and bowed heads, all except one on the second row in the middle. He did not seem too involved in this activity, his head was up, and his eyes were open, looking straight ahead. As I thought about this, I realized I had left my body in the chair, and it was only my spirit that was standing. That was why I moved with such speed and power, no bulky body to move. I did not want to leave my body unattended and possibly vulnerable to being taken by an evil spirit, so I sat down in the same incredibly rapid and powerful movement. Still thinking about what had just happened and how I was not receiving the Melchizedek Priesthood with nearly enough thought and reverence. This priesthood was much more than I understood and suspected. I must not underestimate the things of God again and again, as I seem to always do.

I think most people would have more brains than me and would not share all the mistakes they made. But, without sharing the mistakes, as you can see, this would be a noticeably short record. Even though most of these experiences are an embarrassment I will endure the embarrassment as I have hope that, as you read of my shortcomings, you will be forewarned and forearmed when it is your turn to go through these same or similar experiences. You will not have to start from scratch as I have, in trying to make the best of these types of situations. You have my prayers for your success in life. You know God anxiously hears and anxiously answers your prayers in His own majestic way.

These experiences were not just for me but also for you. I am a very ordinary fallen mortal God is using as an example to show you and others how God deals with those in similar circumstances. Yes, I am the one to be used as the fallible example despite my embarrassment. This writing seems to be an opportunity for you to experience all this vicariously. God bless you.

A Name and a Blessing. It was time for the twins to receive their infant blessing. The blessings were regularly on the first Sunday of the month. I had missed the first Fast Sunday Sacrament meeting after they were born. So, Bishop Warner asked if I was going to be at next Sunday's Fast Meeting. His request was a light encouragement to me to perform my priesthood duty and allow the Lord, through me, to bless the twins.

Early on during the Sacrament meeting there was the announcement I should come forward with the first child accompanied by those asked to assist in the blessing. Our son was the first born, so I carried him to the front of the chapel. Maybe I ask too many to assist. There was not enough room for everyone to form a small enough circle that they could all reach both hands under and help support David. So, the circle was a little larger. They turned sideways to David, extending one hand under David, and placing the other hand on the shoulder of the brother in front of them. Brother Barnes, our home teacher was the last of this line, and he in turn placed one of his hands under David and his other hand on my shoulder. I was carefully cradling David with both hands, being very careful with his head, neck, and back alignment.

I was voice for the blessing. This was the first infant blessing I had ever voiced. I suspected that the faith of those in the circle and those in the congregation was somehow also involved in the blessing. But I was not sure how. I called David by name, stated I was doing this in the name of Jesus Christ. I stated by what authority we were performing the blessing, by the authority of the Holy Melchizedek Priesthood that we held. Then I stated what was being done.

With the first few words covering about five to ten seconds something remarkable happened. Where Brother Barnes' hand was placed on my shoulder, over my suit coat, something tangible flowed into my shoulder. It came through my suit jacket, white shirt, tee shirt. It was something not of the matter of this world. It could be explained like water from a hose that flowed from a specific point in his hand into a point right below on my shoulder, through the clothes. Then the substance spread out as it headed toward the center of my chest. After a few inches into my chest, it was to spread out much to feel it any further. But I could still feel the flow entering my shoulder. It was not an even flow, but more like the water coming out of the spout into a bathtub, but not in any way forceful or violent. What was it? Virtue was my first thought. I remembered that the Savior had said virtue had flowed out of him. I thought, if it is virtue, I may be worse than I thought, or than Jim, or maybe all the others in the circle, and possibly those of faith in the congregation, are well above me in the way they live and follow our Savior. These thoughts took a very short time to run through. At the end of the brief thoughts, I was feeling pretty humble. And at the same time trying to not mess up the blessing, as I was speaking.

David's blessing was still ongoing. I was given a couple things to say, and I said them. Then I thought other fathers had blessed their sons to go on missions for the Church. I was ready to voice my thought. The words would not come out. I tried to speak and again there was resistance to the words. So, I quickly realized this was not my blessing, and my own thoughts were okay for some places and times, but this was a blessing from our Lord and my will was not good enough. It was plain to me that I should start acting like a servant and not like this blessing was from me. I quickly dismissed my thoughts. I went quiet and still, opening my mind to what the Spirit had to share. Some things came and I spoke them. Then when nothing more came; I closed the blessing. This blessing was from the Spirit and not from me. One more addition, if I had tried hard, I could have voiced my will concerning the mission. I did not, at the resistance both times I stopped. With the first resistance I suspected the Spirit, but with the second resistance I knew for sure what the Spirit wanted to teach me.

First Blessing of the Sick. Dave, a ward member, and I went home teaching. Every time we went home teaching Dave would share one or two of his experiences in the church. He and his wife, Ann, were exceptional examples to Bev and me. Both for what they knew and taught us and for the way they applied their knowledge of Jesus to their lives.

The family we visited was a nice family. We talked a little and it was said the daughter was sick and wanted a priesthood blessing. Normally, the husband and father in the house take the lead in the administration. Here the father was not an active member. The wife was a regularly active member and had great faith in our Lord. She was the one who asked for the blessing of the sick daughter. Obviously, Dave was my leader here. He said we would administer to her daughter right now. The mother already had consecrated oil out and available. She handed the small bottle of oil to Dave. He said he would do the anointing. That meant I would seal the anointing and be voice for whatever blessing the Spirit would dictate. Dave was older than me and a long-time member, so he had done this more than a few times. Further, his faith was probably much stronger than mine, so I was surprised he did not reverse our roles. But, knowing Dave he wanted to give me a learning experience. He probably knew his faith was to be added to mine, somehow, and that would be sufficient when added to the faith of the daughter and this household, to bless the young sister.

So, with some hesitance, after the anointing, my hands were gently placed atop the young sister's head, followed by Dave's. I quickly came to the part of the blessing where I should add what the Spirit wants said. I started to say she would be well. As I wondered what the Holy Spirit had for this sick sister, my mind was given an understanding. It was like nearly instantly being given a memory. The next second, I knew she was not really sick in her body. She had been dating and did something she felt very remorseful over. She had been through great anguish of sole, and this was the cause of her present state. I did not want to know all this. But I did. I did not know what to do. Immediately, all the other information went far distant, as the words "thy sins are forgiven" were calmly pronounced by the Spirit. The words were given, and I felt the slightest part of the Spirit's affectionate feeling for the young woman accompanying the words. The Spirit shared love and compassion for this young sister. But my response was confusion.

My mind raced. In a quick and silent response in thought/prayer to the Spirit, "This is me, Stan. I am not worthy to say such a lofty statement. I am a plain and ordinary member. It would take someone great to speak such words and I am not great, just ordinary. Jesus said such lofty things but, how can I?" The last thought given back to the Spirit was, "Am I even allowed to say such words?"

I was lost, thinking of myself and not the young sister who, by inspiration of the Holy Spirit, needed to hear the words just given. What a mess! All the while an insecure young priesthood holder was fumbling with what had just happened, the young sister was sitting patiently waiting.

Dave recognized I was silent too long. He spoke up, in my place, and said the concluding words to end the administration. Oh, boy…

The young sister did not hear the words given for her by the Spirit. I failed the Spirit and the young sister.

You can easily understand what happened when I thought about this when I calmed down. I remembered the Holy Spirit only speaks the words and will of our Savior. Since Jesus lived, suffered, died, and lives again, He can do or say whatever He wants. He is our Law and our Lord. And whatever He does or says will be to our benefit, whether I understand it or not, because of the love He has for us. And if He feels to use such an unworthy servant as me, I will try to never again fear or be confused to speak His words. My experiences with Heavenly Father's will, through His Son, through the Holy Spirit, are there always is much more to learn. His will is always stretching me as I try to grasp the understandings. Further, a little teaching on the matter by my church file leaders or friends would have gone a long way towards helping me do things right the first time. They had taught me so much but, obviously, there was much, much, more for me to learn.

So, to this end, I am explaining another one of the strings of my stinging failures. The whole world can read and laugh if it wants. I probably deserve it. But after you are finished laughing, please remember these experiences, so when you get to that same or similar place you will not fail as I have, and another will not be denied their blessing and comfort from our Lord. May God bless you and forgive me.

Second Blessing of the Sick. A month or so had passed since the first administering to the sick. As is understandable the experience was still vivid in my mind, when another young brother in the ward called me and asked if I could accompany him to a hospital in Sacramento where a friend of his was being treated for cancer. My thoughts raced over the previous experience with the blessing of the sick. Next, he was telling me she wanted the Sacrament brought to her. Then, for some reason, as if he could anticipate my apprehension, he told me we would probably not be administering to her. I said I would go.

As we were getting off the elevator and almost to her room, an understanding came into my mind from the Holy Spirit. This sister would pass out of this life in two days. The understanding came in a calm and direct, to the point manner. There was not a hint of her passing being out of season or wrong. It was the time for this to happen, nothing out of God's order. It was not many steps until we turned right into her room. Before we entered the room, I was expecting an older sister at least in her 'sixties or more. The understanding was silent on everything except her being called home to God and when. So, I was greatly surprised to see a sister in her early to mid-thirties, sitting up in the bed. Further, she looked a little sad, not at all sick. She talked with my friend, and I found out she had several young children and lived at the far north end of the valley. Her husband and children were at home attending church that day.

Shortly after that, we offered the prayers on the bread and water, and we all partook of the Sacrament. She then asked my friend for a priesthood blessing. I thought, if I am voice, I will tell her what will happen. I do not know if I should tell her outside of the administration, I think not. I wondered if my friend had the same understanding given him. She asked my friend to give her the blessing, so I was to do the anointing with oil.

After that was completed, my friend sealed the anointing and started to pronounce a blessing. He said two or three times during the blessing "If it is Our Father's will, you will be made well."

I knew it was not His will. It seemed very plain that he did not know what was going to happen to her. He closed the blessing. They talked some and we went home. I did not share the experience with him either.

I guess this was another step of learning or at least failing. I fell on my face again. As the years go by, it has become plain that I should have mentioned to her the revelation given to me. The wisdom was not for me but for and about her. This understanding finally started me sharing experiences of the Spirit with others. To my consternation, sharing things of the Spirit in the wards has led to me being very unpopular with many a leader or past leader, as well as some members. I must sadly state only few recognize the spirit of some of the things I share as not from me but from the Holy Ghost. I try not to give too many of my own ideas and try to share what the Spirit has shared with me.

Now by sharing these things with so many who may read them I may become unpopular beyond measure... If that is the price exacted for the opportunity to benefit a single someone somewhere, the price is not too high. I know a little of how much Jesus loves us. He wants Father's will shared with His fallen brothers and sisters. I wish I were great so I could share much more, but I am just ordinary. I am sorry.

You have my hope and faith and prayers as you go through the trials of your life. I can understand some of your trials. I love you. May God bless you.

The Fly. It was a sunny day. I was working on our car in the garage. The twins were still infants. Both were in the playpen, in the shade of the garage, not too far from where I was working. Bev was gone, probably taking a break from caring for the twins. I was keeping a close watch on the twins. A large fly, maybe a horsefly, came and was trying to land on one of their faces. I immediately went to their aid. I tried to shoo it away, but it would not leave. As soon as I was done waving my hand at it, the bug tried to land on a face near the eyes. With fast reflexes, I tried to knock the fly out of the air, something that had been done in the past. But for some reason this thing was extremely fast and persistent in the extreme.

At this point, I became aware of a bad or dark feeling concerning this situation. At this dark feeling, I immediately decided to use the priesthood I held. I raised my right arm to the square, stated the authority by which I was doing this, and commanded the fly to land in front of me. Immediately, the fly started flying at one-half to one-quarter speed and flew to a spot in front of me and landed. My right hand went from the square rapidly to smash the fly that was now sitting on a ledge in front of me. My hand landed in lightning fashion, in a crash as it hit. To my surprise, my hand landed in a cupping fashion. The cupping form was not caused by me. Somehow, I was not allowed to kill the fly. The fly was safe under my hand. Then, to my further surprise, my hand moved, not under my power, about ten inches to the edge of the ledge. When my hand reached the edge of the ledge, the fly flew out from under my hand, still at a greatly reduced speed. It flew off to the northwest. I am sure everyone can tell me what I did wrong…again. Plus, what I should have done.

Apostle. We had been attending the Citrus Heights Second Ward for some time. A ward announcement was made that an apostle would attend our next stake conference. A sister made a comment later this is something we should plan to attend and see the apostle. She added her thoughts as to the importance of hearing an apostle. She emphasized the word *apostle*. The stake conference had not seemed too big a deal until our sister gave us the encouragement. So, we went.

The name of the visiting general authority was mentioned. But since we did not know much about them, the name meant little. It was a beautiful day, sunny as usual, for the Sunday drive to the Stake Center. We were most of the way there when the Spirit started feeding a talk into my mind. As I was driving, I could understand a string of concepts being unfolded. I was driving and my attention was divided between the two, like listening to the radio, except that this was coming directly into my mind not through my ears, and this was much faster than one could speak. I was most interested in the string of wisdom, and I started paying less attention to my driving. I did not start to swerve or anything like that. I came to the last stop light before the Stake Center and stopped in the left-hand turn lane. Then the information came at a much faster rate. I could not have driven the car as the information was so fast that it was all I could do to sit there and take in the fast feeding of the concepts. The string lasted only a few seconds. A few seconds later and I was clear headed again and the light turned green for the left turn. I was still musing on what happened during the time we waited for the meeting to start. We were sitting somewhere near the middle of the congregation.

He appeared to be not a tall man, rather ordinary looking from that far away. I did not pay too much attention to the speakers until he spoke. As he spoke, I knew right away this man was no ordinary speaker. He was giving the same string of concepts the Spirit had only minutes earlier given to me. I listened and he kept along the same line. The string was the same the whole talk. He voiced the whole talk that was given to me of the Spirit.

During his talk, the doctrinal concepts did not seem to be the most important thing being shared. Although they were important, to me, the important fact was that he did not deviate from what the Spirit shared. I was listening to one who was following in an undeviating manner a higher direction. I was amazed! What kind of man was this apostle? He was someone special. There was a long journey ahead for me in this Gospel. Besides the scriptures and the Spirit, there were mortals acting as signposts aiding us along the Lord's way.

(When I first wrote this experience, I put the name of the man in the account. There was another experience with another apostle covering another concept. I shared an early draft of this writing with high-ranking local church leader who shared it with a high-ranking church official in Salt Lake City. The official in Salt Lake City demanded I delete those experiences from this writing while threatening legal and Church consequences. I deleted about four pages covering the second experience and the name associated with this experience. Those four pages were important.)

Temple of the Lord. Bev, the twins, and I went to the Oakland Temple. Bev and I were married in the temple for time and all eternity. The twins were sealed to us for the same. The temple is where families can be sealed together through the generations and ages of time, not just, "'till death do you part..." As you can see, this eternal linking is of great importance to anyone who loves their family. We are all part of a genealogy like those of the Old and New Testament. We all have the opportunity to memorialize and link with them in the temple, for the living and those that have passed on.

Most, if not all of us, have a desire deep within us to find out about our ancestors; that "Roots" thing. Our wise and loving God placed that desire there and came with us to earth. Because of that, long ago I started researching my family history. I know a little about who some of my ancestors were, what they were like, and some of the things they did.

Great Compliment. It was in the Citrus Heights Second Ward. Our family showed up to the Sacrament meeting, as usual. There were extra people there at the meeting. The Stake President was in attendance, sitting near Bishop Warner. After the Sacrament was blessed and administered to the congregation, the president talked. Our ward was going to have a new bishop. I loved our bishop. He had a booming personality, but it was not too much of a distraction from his faith and testimony of our Lord. I hope everyone, at some time in their life, could have such a bishop. He was released by the Stake President with some less than kind words. One phrase that stood out like a sore thumb was "sometimes bishops get a little dictatorial." Who was he talking about? I never thought of him as being dictatorial in the least.

I looked at the bishop, and he was looking at the speaker. My thoughts were, *Does the speaker know this bishop at all?* Our bishop had expended considerable effort using all his knowledge and personality to teach us the Gospel of Jesus Christ. Well, there is probably more here than I know, but even so, this is an extraordinary bishop, end of discussion! So, the new bishop was Dave my home teaching companion. The exiting bishop gave a few brief remarks. Vivid memories remain of three of his remarks.

First, Bishop Warner stated, "With every fiber of my body" he knew this work was true. Second, he stated he "loved being Bishop," and I think this was not the first time he had served as a bishop. He went on to explain that he "missed being away from it."

I had been asked, previous to the meeting to give the closing prayer. The meeting was ending, and I went to the stand and microphone to offer the closing prayer. I closed my eyes and started the impromptu or from your heart prayer. Not much of the prayer is remembered other than it was from me on behalf of the ward to Heavenly Father and was given in the name of Jesus Christ. Except that, somewhere in the middle of the prayer, the Spirit whispered to me, "We are thankful Bishop Warner was a good shepherd to us."

My expressions stopped and I said, "We are thankful Bishop Warner was a good shepherd to us." Several questions raced through my mind then, and linger now. Did Bishop feel the words as from God? Not from me, but only through me? What did the Stake President feel? Did the Spirit confirm the words to the other members listening? Was this given in any way as a response to the "dictatorial" comment? The Holy Spirit using the words "a good shepherd" applying to a mortal may well be one of the greatest compliments that can be received here in mortality. Especially given the fact that one of the many names of our Savior is "The Good Shepherd."

By attending evening classes, I finished a degree at American River College. A law school in Sacramento offered evening classes and I was accepted. Construction work during the day and law school at night, plus Bev with the young twins, day and night. Bev and my time were filled to overflowing.

Church Conferences. It is the Citrus Heights II Ward, and I am in the Elders quorum meeting. A young brother a little older than me is teaching the lesson. He is teaching with the Spirit in strong attendance. He discussed briefly what is happening in Church conferences, prophets, and apostles teach us. He said if you read these talks, "I promise you a special experience." The Spirit confirmed the truth of what he had just said. I do not remember anything more he said. But, if the Spirit was going to abundantly confirm what he said as truth I was going to go there, to the conferences, and know what more the Spirit would share with me.

I found a copy of the most recent conference. I was not spending enough time with my family, so I had, very limited time to read. I took the conference issue of the Ensign magazine to work and decided that for a couple of days I would read it at lunch break instead of law school homework. I read the first conference talk. Nothing... I remembered the Spirit confirming the words of the Elders quorum teacher. I read the same conference talk again. No "special experience." I had read the talk twice and I tried to, and I think I did, understand what the speaker was saying. But the reading did not produce a special experience. I was promised a special experience by my young brother and by the Spirit. So, I would not quit. I read the talk again. This time the Spirit confirmed the truth of a concept that the speaker was teaching. The promise came true. Every communication with the Holy Spirit is a "special experience." A communication from one of the God Head, what more could I ask for.

In an effort, to try to understand what had happened, my thoughts were that maybe the Spirit requires that I read each talk three times before He will confirm a truth. Next the thoughts were of the conferences. At each semi-annual conference there are about five sessions, and each session has about six speakers. As soon as I found time, I read the next talk. The Spirit confirmed the truth of a point the speaker was addressing. It had happened on the first reading. As soon as I found some time, I read the next talk. The same results. Could it be? Could It Be. I read the entire conference in the space of a few weeks. Every talk but one had some part of it confirmed to me by the Spirit. For some reason that one talk is the only one I remember now. It was a talk about communication. And even that talk may have had some confirmation, but it was not a positive one. It seemed the speaker was trying to impress more than share to our aid. And it happened in front of the whole church and was memorialized in ink. What a great responsibility and opportunity to speak in a conference.

General Conferences. This part is being shared to express how important this subject is to me. While I was in law school, there was extremely limited time to study the conferences. But after graduation in 1980, I started an exhaustive study of the conferences. I do not keep track how many times the Spirit confirms truths, it just happens regularly, generally more than once per conference. For over two decades, I have tried to study at least one conference a week, most often it is more like two per week with some a little less or more.

When I read or listen to conferences, I have a special week. As the years have passed, I have a bookshelf full of conference audio tapes and CDs starting in 1980. There are some gaps when I could not afford them. But most are there, and I have listened to them over and over and over and over again. I still am thrilled to listen to the talks.

The Spirit has confirmed to me the truths taught in the conferences thousands and thousands of times. May God bless that young brother who taught by the Spirit. I did not get a chance to thank him. I hope his life has been filled with joy and happiness. I will spend more time on this subject later.

Get ready, the study of conferences and scriptures is filled with wonder, and we may approach God similarly to what happens in prayer. God gives us answers to life's challenges as we read conferences and scriptures.

There has not been much mentioned of the two missions. I always followed the politics of the day and studied the political history of the past. I studied and learned all I could. Studying history and politics may not be interesting to you, so it has been largely left out of this writing so far.

The traffic was heavy and moving fast. Bev and I were waiting in a line on the street sidewalk to get into a show on a Friday evening. There was a serious car wreck across the street. Knowing advanced first aid and more, I immediately started across the street to help. As I started the first step into the street, without looking at the traffic, my chest bumped into something immovable. Nothing I could see, but it was like some extraordinarily strong man put up his hand against my chest and I could not move forward. Just then, a fast-moving car passed where I would have been walking. I lost track of the traffic in the concern for the person in the wreck. Another in a long line of thanks be to God for His attention to my safety.

To Salt or Not to Salt. The high voltage lineman trade is dangerous. When I entered the trade, I did not know just how dangerous until I was along in the apprenticeship.

One day I had an impression I should stop adding salt to my food. I knew where that impression came from, so I stopped adding salt to my food. I did not know exactly why but it probably had something to do with the electrical trade I was in, probably a potentially 120-volt contact. Those types of contact would happen from time to time and more salt in the body would probably make my body more conductive and more at risk.

Months later. There was a high voltage power outage in the Sacramento. Several of us were called and we worked long hours at night to restore the power. Under those conditions, the power company supplies meals for us when we work extended hours on emergencies. After the power was restored, we went to a restaurant. Since we did not make much money the company meals were a treat. The foreman took us to an inexpensive steak restaurant. When my steak came, I thought it would taste much better with some salt. The memory of the inspiration about salt, lightly floated across my mind. I thought of skipping the "no salt thing" for just this one meal. Then the words, "do you remember why" you stopped adding salt, were given me. The impression was light and could have been easily disregarded. It came as more of a pronouncement and reminder than a question. Then I thought again and remembered who had given the understanding. God's will was always best. The saltshaker was not reached for.

Soon, a day or so later, our crew was working in the south area of the city. We were re-labeling and changing the 12,000-volt underground cables. We would de-energize the line and then work on it. Our crew had a particularly good foreman. We knew this could be dangerous and he was watching us closely. The foreman and I went to a new location. The foreman radioed another group to ensure this line was de-energized. This location was where additional lines were to be added. The underground splice box location had about one foot of water in the bottom. So instead of standing in the water, I pulled the lines out of the hole. I sat on the damp ground and started to dismantle and clean the connector. I heard a distant voice yelling as if someone was severely hurt. Then I noticed the voice sounded like mine. During this time, it seemed as if I were in a prolonged blink, everything was dark. I opened my eyes, and it was like looking out a square window that was getting farther and farther away. Everything seemed in slow motion. Out the windows I could see the tops of the trees were sinking. I realized the trees were not sinking, I was falling over on my back while I was looking straight ahead. I knew then what had happened. The line must have been energized from the other end.

I then thought to myself, *I am twenty-four years old, and they have killed me.* My next thought was of my wife, Bev. She would be left alone to raise the two-year-old twins. Next, I decided to pray to Heavenly Father. I sensed I did not have but a small moment left, no time for a final prayer. In my mind, I called loudly, *Father!* Then everything went dark and silent. I do not know how long the silent darkness lasted.

Sometime later, I opened my eyes. I could not feel or move any part of my body. I did not know if I was breathing. But I could see the foreman. He must have been kneeling his face was close to mine. From the look on this good man's face, I could not tell who was hurt the most.

I was transported to the hospital by an ambulance. The doctor could not understand how I had survived the high voltage contact since the voltage went in one hand, across my chest, and out the other hand and out through my legs. Next, he said the burns should be cleaned and wrapped and I could be released. A company employee protested, questioning if I should not be kept for observation. The doctor said, in effect, if that amount of voltage and amperage did not kill me, then he was not too concerned anything else would go wrong. There were prayers of thanksgiving...but not enough. How could there be? I still do not add salt.

Who Done It. There were some union problems at the utility company. Someone called another union to come and talk to us about representing the line crews. That union had a reputation of corruption. We all went and listened to the presentation by the other union. I was not convinced the new union was good for us. I was going to speak against changing unions. There was a concern on my part given the other union's reputation. I spoke with Bev, and she was concerned also. I told her I would pray about it. The answer came, if anything bad was to happen I would know, or I could find out. I spoke against changing unions and the whole incident seemed to fade into history.

Not long thereafter, my lineman's safety tools were fouled. Not the type of trap that would generally get me hurt. I easily recognized the problem and fixed it. It was more of a warning or something like that. As you can imagine, it was unnerving. I immediately went in prayer asking for what I had been promised, "I could find out." As I started the prayer, the Holy Spirit placed an understanding into my mind. I understood the whole incident. This incident had nothing to do with the union activity.

Some days before someone (the Spirit did not tell me who) took Ed's (that is not his real name) dirty magazine, placed it in my seat in the crew truck, and opened it to a raw picture. When I opened the door that morning, the picture and I had an unwelcomed meeting. I promptly closed the book and deposited it in the nearest garbage can. Ed found out I had thrown his girly magazine in the trash, so he then fouled my safety tool. So, I had the truth.

I went to Ed and confronted him with what he had done. Ed denied the whole thing with a face that seemed as truthful as an angel. My mind raced, I had just accused Ed of a terrible deed and I may have been mistaken. The next thought was the Holy Spirit told me one thing and Ed told me the opposite. I will choose the Holy Spirit, who cannot lie. I told Ed I knew he did the act. He was searching; he probably knew no one in the world saw him, so how could I "know" that he did it? He claimed innocence again. I boldly told him I knew he was now lying just as I knew he had done the act. His face turned to fear as he knew I knew. I suspect he thought I might go to the company management with the information. He never did apologize for the act, and for the next couple years he was cautious around me. I acted as if I forgot the whole incident. With time, we were casual friends again. The Spirit is indeed and always a Revelator.

Elders Quorum. John was my Elders Quorum file leader and my friend. It was a Saturday morning and John came by my house to give me a ride to where a quorum brother needed help. The brother had a carpet business. The building had partially burned and there was considerable damage to the carpets. When we arrived, there were half a dozen other brothers already there helping to carry the damaged carpet out of the building. The business owner saw John and came to welcome us and thank us for our coming to help. He shook hands with John and then me. As we shook hands we looked into each other's eyes. As we did, the Spirit whispered to me that the brother burned the building.

My looks must have changed when I received the revelation, as the brother's expression changed from pleasant to very distressed. He quickly turned and went back to his work. I was stunned, as always. I thought about it and decided this could be shared with John. I told John what was just shared by the Spirit. John paid close attention to what I told him. Next, his response was that of not being too surprised. That reaction surprised me a little, as I expected different. Then John's next reaction was to thank me for sharing my experience. I do not know what John did or did not do with that information. He did not ever tell me.

It was some weeks later at a quorum meeting, a police officer and quorum member asked if any of us knew where that business owner was. If we knew, we should tell him. He said the business owner was in hiding and there was evidence someone had set the fire that burned his business. I did not share with the quorum what I knew. I do not know what happened past that.

Falling Away. One brother came up to me between parts of our church meeting and said he had found another church. He wanted to know if I would go with him. He said the people were friendly and there was no harshness among the members. I talked with him about it for a while and then it was time for our next church class. I was working during the day and attending law school at night and trying to spend as much time with my family as possible. Is that a good excuse for not spending more time with one of my brothers who needed attention? No? No... I did not notice when he quit attending church. Oh, wherever you are, I am sorry. Please come back and forgive me. Let us talk some more.

Dan. Another area, Bev became a friend with a young woman in our ward about her age. She was active in the ward, but her husband was not. As our families got to know each other, Dan (that is not his real name) and I became friends too. He was a great guy, and he had a good wife and two special children. He started attending church. His wife was thrilled. Even though he was a great guy, the Gospel of Jesus made wonderful changes in his life and that of his family. With time, both of our families moved to other houses in different directions. I would still stop by to visit him from time to time. His new ward was reorganized and he became a ward clerk. I knew the new bishop and was apprehensive. It was not too long until things happened, and Dan said he would have nothing to do with anyone who acted like the bishop. He further refused to have anything to do with a church that allowed such a man to continue in a position of authority when everyone knew how he was.

I had known that man a few years before he became the new bishop. He was wealthy and expected everyone to jump at his command. I had never seen a kind act from him. In all fairness, I certainly did not know what was in his heart, and I could only see a limited amount of his acts. But whatever was in his heart, some of his acts were harsh enough to uproot young faith before it could get roots sufficient to survive the storm. What a tragedy. Dan's whole family was gone from the Church and the Gospel of Jesus. I would occasionally drop by his house and talk. His good wife also decided enough was enough. I attempted to go and get aid from that bishop's file leader. Nothing…

There is so much that could be said at so many places in this writing. However, as here, there is little value in going further with things that probably are well understood by most all regular mortal experiences.

President Kimball. Someone in our ward said we should seek to know for ourselves the President of the Church is the Lord's Prophet. The Spirit confirmed the truth of that concept when they spoke. So, I decided to ask the question in prayer and at my first opportunity.

I think it was a Saturday. Bev took the twins to see her parents, or something like that. I was doing law school homework but decided there was a time of quiet and chance to pray. The question was asked in prayer. No response. The question was asked again. No response. I thought there should have been a response, even if it was in the negative. I started to ask in another fashion, and in different words. I tried to pray with more intensity. No response. I explained how all my prayers had always been answered, even if I did not understand at the time. (The incident with the hawk and many more.) I told Heavenly Father I knew He was so occupied with all the rest of mankind, and I did not want to take up too much of His time, but I would not quit praying until I had an answer. (Oh, what an immature attitude I shared in prayer, go ahead, and laugh.) I suspected I had an hour or two before Bev and the twins came home.

I continued to pray... After some extended time while still praying, I heard Bev's car pull into the driveway. I mentioned in a few seconds the twins would come running through the house looking for me and would tackle me on sight.

If this prayer was to be answered, I was almost out of time. I was still so immature in my communications with the Lord. But He seemed so anxious to teach and to overlook a lot of my inadequacies as long as I was seriously trying.

Just before the twins came into the house, the Spirit gave me the answer. He shared the understanding that I would not receive this conformation until I had done my part. I needed to study, learn, and do all that I could before the request was made. Oh boy! How dumb of me. I should have remembered or reasoned that one out on my own. That concept is well-established in the scriptures. After all that I can do… After that instruction, I started reading the conferences, paying particular attention to the talks by President Kimball. I read two of his books. In the process of doing this, the Spirit regularly confirmed the truths of what President Kimball was teaching. The conformations came repeatedly. With some time, I did not need to pray to ask the question again. I knew over and over again that Spencer W. Kimball was the Lord's living oracle on earth, the only one authorized by the Lord to use all the keys of His kingdom. Spencer W. Kimball is our prophet, he is the prophet of our Lord to us, to me.

God is so patient and understanding in His teachings and can we be anything other than overwhelmed and thankful. Through the years that we had with President Kimball with us I learned so much from him. I learned more from him than any other prophet, except Joseph Smith. Jesus sure used those two to teach us so very much.

New Song. It was early afternoon. Another journeymen lineman and I had just finished hooking up the electric services to some new houses. While driving the truck to another location, I noticed I was humming a melody. It was a great melody. Then I recognized I did not ever remember hearing this particular melody before. The melody was now repeating. I became more aware of what was happening. The melody was starting to play a little clearer and louder. The melody was beautiful and not extremely complicated. It was much more complex than a blues riff and maybe a little more complex than a song like "Silent Night." The beauty was certainly comparable. Somehow, I could follow the melody as if it were an old favorite song. But that understanding was being given as the melody played.

I was dividing my limited concentration between driving the truck and trying to keep my mind on the song. It seemed clear that if my concentration on the song was lost, I would not remember it. The melody was going around again. It was wonderful. Then a young woman's voice started singing with the melody. It started as if far in the background and quieter than the music. It became stronger until I could recognize what she was singing. The voice was still softer than the melody. But I could tell she was singing a song of appreciation to her mother for the love she had received despite her disobedience and the pain she had caused. The song was as wonderful as the melody. This seemed like something that would be sung by an angel in the eternities, to a relentlessly loving mother by a repentant and thankful daughter. Now besides driving and humming along with the melody, I was trying to think of how I could capture at least the melody.

I had learned to play the guitar, a little, but I cannot read a note of music. I thought of trying to make circles and place a line like a clock's hand to a point higher or lower to represent each note. This was almost too much for my concentration. I could not figure out how to make the idea work and I could not spare any more concentration, or I would lose the melody. I was desperate I knew that I could not keep up the concentration on the melody too long. It was all going to be lost if I did not do something quick.

I saw a pay phone. I knew Bev had a small cassette tape recorder at the house. I thought if I could call Bev and have her start recording, I could sing the song into the recorder. After it was recorded, someone could make some sense of it and it would be saved. This review almost was too much. I barely was able to follow the melody. I am a little dyslexic, possibly a lot. It is enough that things like reading or dialing a phone takes serious concentration or I cannot do the tasks. I knew dialing the phone would be difficult, but it was my home number and that should make it easier. I parked the truck, not saying anything to the other lineman. I got some change and started dialing. The dialing took too much concentration. The melody was lost. Bev answered the phone and I briefly told her the sad story. I suspect she was again thinking what a strange husband she had. I wish I could share the song with you as part of this book. All I can share is the song's loss. After this life is over, I will hear that song again and maybe sing my own words of praise to God for what he has done for me.

Neighbor. I spent many a Friday night at law school. One Friday night I got home about 10:30. I walked into the house and was greeted by a tired Bev. She gave her all to loving and caring for the twins. The twins were long asleep. To me, her smile was the sunrise of the day. Then the Spirit whispered I should visit a neighbor that was a member of the Church. It was very late, but that was no excuse for not following the direction of God. I told Bev what I had just received. She encouraged me to go. Neither of us had any idea of why I was being sent.

I walked the distance of three or four lots and rang the doorbell. The sister opened the door and invited me in. I was a little surprised to find the entire family, including the little children awake and in the living room. Tod (that is not his real name) and I were friends and his wife, Ann (that is not her real name), and Bev were close friends. Tod greeted me. He was not in a good mood. Neither he nor Ann asked why I was there. They were packing and getting ready to move into a new house the next day. So, I started helping.

There was plenty of work to do and I did not know if that was not the reason I was there. I am not a big personality; actually, I am a little dull, especially given that the work and school and the commute made a long, long day. But as I recognized the tension between them, I tried to be happy and even funny. I was unnaturally funny! Me, the life of the party? I was saying lots of funny things. Tod and Ann and I were all laughing in a couple minutes. It is almost beyond words how we were treated with such laughter. Something was still seriously wrong here. But here I was, saying funny things repeatedly and making a fun game out of packing.

When I first arrived, Tod was in the early stages of anger. He was slowly coming out of his anger. The irony of the situation...the Spirit chooses a boring person to be the needed and only source of a jovial evening packing. Ann was so grateful for me being there and for me being so funny. She kept thanking me for stopping by to help. She should have known the humor was not so natural to me. Her gratitude should have been to the Lord, the author of everything good that was happening. God has a surprisingly fantastic sense of humor, something that previously I did not know. It was becoming a little clearer, but not all. We worked until well after midnight that evening.

As the days passed, Bev had conversations with Ann. She admitted to being beaten several times by Tod. She said that night had started towards being an awfully bad night. That must have been why the Spirit sent me. Poor little Ann; my heart ached for her. Ann, what a wonderful little sister with three little girls, one still an infant. Later they moved away. But they took the problem with them. Things got worse than ugly, and she finally left Tod after being seriously injured and seeing her little one beat.

Regularly, I tried to find good candidates and help in their political campaigns, an involvement in the second mission thing.

Politician. I have not spent much time discussing the evil one or evil spirits, as it is not healthy. If much time is spent discussing the subject, it tends to draw evil spirits as rotting meat draws flies. Please do not let interest in this area take you to an evil somewhere you will greatly regret visiting. So, I will type fast and finish these incidents.

I was in downtown Sacramento going to meet with a person who was going to run for a political office. I knew of this person, but I had never met the person before. My intent was to find out what type of person this was. I wanted to know if this person was good and had some wisdom and courage. If I found out this in the affirmative, I would help in the campaign. I parked and was walking into an office. The office was poorly lit. Only the person running for office was present. I introduced myself and was politely thanked for coming and invited to take a seat. With the first step or two I took toward the chair, something attacked me. The force was around my forehead. At the same time, something was interrupting my thought process. I was trying to concentrate on the force on my face. I stood still not wanting to try to walk as I suspected I would probably fall having little control over my body. I was rapidly blinking, trying to regain better control over my thought process and my body. This was similar but not exactly what happened to me when I was ten years old, and the knowledge of that experience was available and used. I was much bigger and stronger now and had a lot of experiences that had strengthened me some. With a few more seconds of concentration on control of my body, my head became clear again. The dark force was gone. My consciousness was such that my faculties were again operating more as usual, and I started a first and second timid steps walking again.

Now in the seat and calming down, I looked at the person. Something was very wrong here. The person did not ask what had happened to me or if

I was all right. The person seemed aware. As we talked, I learned much more than I wanted to know. This is a very clever and evil politician that had an evil spirit or spirits assisting or possibly controlling. I certainly did not help.

The person was elected. Oh boy…

Not all those who fully embrace evil spirits are as easy to spot. One incredibly sad note is the evil one and his minions have an agenda. The agenda is to associate with and then to control individuals and lead them to further evil. Equally bad is that they have a political agenda also, to control government thus leading the collective of individuals in greater and greater control (less and less freedom) and evil. To this dark discussion let me add to counter this almost unstoppable evil we have the Gospel of Jesus Christ, the only force strong enough and even designed to correct and control evil. We all have our God-given ability and freedom to choose good or evil, God Himself will not violate that freedom He gave us. Once evil has been chosen, however, we are not free to choose the consequences that follow those choices. No matter what the politicians and courts decree to the contrary. For help, all we must do is read the scriptures and history and then pray.

Warning. Our bodies are a temple of God where we can receive revelation from God. Evil spirits will enter your body if allowed. Please do nothing to allow that to happen. For those who do, the depths of the worst misery and evil will result, they become slaves to the evil one. The war in heaven was between God, that wanted us to be free to choose good or evil, and an evil one that wanted to force or enslave us with and in his evil. In our free state, we can choose to draw near to God, feel his love for us, and receive his promptings and revelation. I will share only a few examples of evil.

The Young Woman. A friend was thinking about running for a California State Assembly seat. My friend and his wife were loaded with talent; very smart, concerned, and good people. The type this state and nation needs. He and I were across the street from the State House in Sacramento. We had just come from a meeting with an assemblyman. We were walking back to his car. A tall, thin, young woman was walking towards us. She was about sixty feet away when I first took more careful notice of her. She had probably been beautiful, before.

She was in her early to mid-twenties. She had stringy, filthy hair of a blond, oily dirty color. She was wearing filthy, ragged army type clothes, and had only some of her front teeth, with those remaining in some degree of rot. She was staring right at me, approaching with some urgency.

Something seemed wrong or evil. She came and stood about four feet directly in front of me. I thought she might attack, so I took a half step back with my right foot to come into a defensive fighting stance. Her eyes were even more telling than her person. She was in trouble and had been so for some time. She declared the most obscene statement to me. Then she bent her head back slightly and laughed. She walked around me and on down the street. My friend quickly mentioned she was really "messed up."

We continued our walk. As you can guess, my thoughts were pondering on what had really just happened. Then the Spirit told me. She did things that had allowed an evil spirit into her body with her spirit. Now, at this point, she could not rid her body of the evil spirit by herself. I also had a sense of the pain her parents were in while she had been in this state.

I held the priesthood that could have commanded the evil spirit out of her. By then we were around a corner and she was gone. Then it was my thoughts that picked up the theme at that point. I prayed; could she have known I held the priesthood? Further, the response was that she could have recognized the priesthood. Then my thoughts were that she may have been trapped with and tormented by evil spirits partially in control of her body. Her cursing may have been all she could have said but her meaning may have been seeking help. I could have cast the evil spirit out of her, giving her back sole possession of her body. But, at the time, my concern was of a possible physical attack.

I felt terrible. What a time for one of my failures. My next thought was of what this state of the young woman had to be doing to those that raised and loved her. How exquisite was their pain in their love for her? I looked for her, but by this time she was gone. How could I ever make up for this failure? Maybe there would be another time.

Lost Law and Justice. An unexpected panorama occurred in law school. As we studied the different concepts of the law, we studied the law from old England Common Law to the present. The study did not include a review of the law given through Moses or Roman civil law, so I studied them myself. From the earliest recorded law up to the forming of the United States, I easily recognized the great struggle made by the inspired, the wise, and the courageous to end the rule by force and the special privileges of the few that caused the suffering of the many. It seemed to me that most of the history of this world has been, the few rule the many, the few devour special privileges they take from the many by means of conquest, slavery, serfdom, addictive substances or activities, taxes, operation of corrupt law, and the like. Most of the special privileges were ended as the first free people in modern time were protected in their God-given rights by a government guided by a God inspired Constitution! The United States government as organized under the glorious and God inspired Constitution that guaranteed freedoms. It took wisdom, courage, and hundreds upon hundreds of years and untold barrels of blood, courage, and tears from a struggling humanity to reach this nearly free state. We were almost there! The Native Americans, African Americans, and recent immigrants can say there was a long way yet to go, but we will get there.

Then, here in the US, just like the Romans, Hebrews, and other civilizations, the pendulum started to swing back to the rule of the powerful and their manipulating of the many. My continued study broke my heart to follow the corrupting of our God inspired Constitution by the ignorant and wicked in our judicial, executive, and legislative branches of government. Through the years the slide away from freedom and justice has continued and even increased in speed. If we continue this course our destination is absolutely fixed and terrible… Then, I will not have the only broken heart…

I will be very brief with this concept. One of the first things I learned in law school was how to lie, by use of confusion. "The truth is its own servant," is a statement I tell myself. I was taught that if the facts are plainly against you, do not use them. Go to the letter of the law and confuse the issue with an endless discussions of exceptions twisting them until the listeners are confused. If the law is plainly against you, do the same with the most detailed and confusing discussion of the facts that you can twist into further confusion.

Constitutional Law class in law school was a joy at first and later a heartbreaker. God largely inspired the Constitution. Later, it was being dismantled by our federal government. I made some very brief comments concerning the activist supreme court to class members during class breaks. I suspect a student shared them to the instructor. At the start of a class, the instructor called me by name and ask me a supremely complex question about the Constitution. This was never done before in that class. The instructor had worked for a very liberal mayor in San Francisco and was very much in favor of the federal government diminishing state's rights and the rights of citizens.

I was stunned at the question. I started giving thought as to how to answer when the Spirit informed me the intent of the question was a pretext, the instructor was going to use that answer to dismiss me from that class and the school because of my conservative beliefs.

I then decided to let the Spirit answer the question. I was in law school because I was following God's direction and I needed His help now. I had full confidence He would help in this time of need, so I opened my mind to what the Spirit would share and started to speak, not knowing what words would come. As I spoke, simple words gave a concise and comprehensive answer to the complex question. After the answer was given, there was a long period of silence as the instructor and the class were stunned, as was I, at the wisdom that was just shared. It was clear that the instructor thought that I was hiding a brilliant mind. We can all laugh at his misconception of me being brilliant. The simple fact was the answer was far more than brilliant, but not reasoned by me, just spoken by me. I was not the author, just a servant.

God is displeased with what has been and is happening to the U.S. Constitution. He gave us in the U. S. and the rest of the world a wonderful gift, but we are letting it be torn to pieces. The freedoms it once protected are God-given and not to be violated but, by so doing, we incur His rath. There will be eternal consequences to those that are doing satan's bidding by tearing down the U.S. Constitution including those in power and are doing nothing to stop this tragedy. The opposite is true for those patriots who have defended the Constitution in times of war and peace.

CHAPTER 4

After Law School – Time for a Deeper Study of the Gospel of Jesus

Dark Trial. This will chronicle a dark time. This is a brief review of my best recollection of this dark time. There certainly will be many different perspectives on this episode. I want you to know that these next incidents are added in attempt to be an inoculation for you, not as accusations against others. When your trials come or if they have come already, I hope and pray you do not charge the Lord as causing them. The Lord is our only salvation. After this life is over, we will again tell all these stories in the presence of so, so many and there will be divine reviews, teachings, perspectives, judgments, and compassions. There will be ages of instructions. I hope and pray you will receive this in the spirit intended. I hope and pray my intention is right. I wish we could sit and talk together. Possibly we will meet in this life. If not in this, then in the next.

Scam. One in our ward had mentioned there were some local church leaders offering an investment opportunity. Boggs (that is not his real name) made frequent mention of this great investment opportunity in priesthood meetings. One time he was talking to a potential investor in the chapel immediately after Sacrament meeting. This did not seem right, but he was much more experienced in the church than I. On another occasion he briefly talked to me about the enterprise. I took him up on his invitation to meet at his office in Roseville. We met and I received a polished presentation on the program from Boggs. As we talked, he told me he had been a Stake President and the other organizers of the investment group here in California were only high councilmen in various stakes or members of bishoprics. I knew several of the men. He said they were buying accounts receivable at a large discount and then quickly collecting or reselling.

I did not have much money to invest. He explained this was a multilevel program. If I convinced others to invest, I would share in part of their return. I knew lots of people who were financially well off, so that had possibilities. I was encouraged to contact those I knew with means and talk them into investing. The potential financial rewards seemed great. Before I could ask friends to invest, I needed to further investigate.

I wanted to know more. I went to the California Corporations Commissioner's office in Sacramento. I started asking questions and found out that some time back that state agency had ordered this group to stop their activities in California. All the while the group was going full speed ahead. If it started good or bad, I did not know. But now the promoters knew it was now a scam. I called and confronted Boggs with the information from the state officials. He was furious with me for talking to the state officials.

I spent some time thinking on the ramifications of exposing the group. If I did nothing, many more would pay a terrible price. If I exposed the group, they could attack me in some fashion. There were so many who would be hurt so badly if I waited or did nothing. I decided to pay the price and expose the rascals. I was not sure how and when, but the opportunity would present itself or I would choose an appropriate time.

The next Sunday morning during priesthood meeting, Boggs started advertising his investment scheme. I was amazed. He knew I knew the scheme was a scam, and I was there in the meeting. He must have figured his status in the church coupled with that of the others involved was far too much for an obscure member to challenge. I asked to speak and then told all in attendance Boggs' investment scheme was under investigation by the State of California regulators, and they had been ordered to stop all activity. As you can imagine, the members were thunderstruck. An obscure member was, in effect, calling President Boggs and all his group, thieves. Word traveled fast and soon most everyone knew. In that area, at least, the scam was greatly reduced.

I was a ward Sunday School leader at the time. I spoke with our bishop about the persecution of our family. Our family was not welcome at church. I asked for his help. He laughed at my request. He laughed! Then he refused the request. He worked for the Church Education System as a seminary teacher. Oh, boy... Things in the ward were getting worse.

I talked to the elder's quorum president. He was definitely antagonistic too. He knew the church regional representative, and I asked for the rep's phone number. Sometime later, he gave the number to me with a comment I would probably not get a meeting with that church official. I called and could not get a meeting with the regional representative. There had been and still was a lot of venomous gossip.

Our family was really hurting. Most of our closest friends, at least we thought they were our friends, from other wards would not talk to us. A new bishop was called in the ward. Not much change for us.

A member of the bishopric was assigned to sit in the Sunday School class with me and monitor my class comments. About the same time there was a new Elders Quorum president in the ward. He came to visit us. He said the ward leaders sent him. He talked with us some. Then he stated he had come to tell us if we did not agree to do what the bishop told us, he was there to take our Temple Recommends from us. Some discussions followed as we asked him why he was doing something so obviously wrong. He stated he did not want to do this, but the other ward leaders forced him to. He finally realized what he was doing and why. The weight of his misdeed reduced him to tears and he left in a shower of apologies.

A new counselor was called in the ward bishopric. He and his wife invited our family to their house for dinner. Obviously, they knew what was going on in the ward. At the end of the dinner, he discussed the persecution. He said that "no one" could remain active in the Church under these circumstances. He said there would be no help from any local leaders. He went on saying, "no one is that strong;" sooner or later we would have to leave the Church or receive what was planned for us. There were plans to deal with us.

My youngest brother, who lived in another area, said he had a message for me from a member. A family with few means, with a son on a mission, had been ready to invest the value of their home in the scam. They told Mark to tell me "Thank you" for exposing the scam. They would have lost their home, which was about all they had, if I had not spoken up. Mark said they were afraid to tell me themselves. They were afraid the wrong people would find out they had associated with us.

I have only shared a small part of the trial.

After all the years that have passed, this episode was still hard to write. However, it was much easier to write than live. Courage and wisdom were in such short supply. Perhaps they always are. I think the term is ravaging wolves in sheep's clothing. President Benson further explained this concept in a conference address.

There is so much here for us to learn from. It is my hope and prayer that those who so eagerly embraced a position in the persecution, repent of their acts and do not carry their miss-deeds into the next life. Now is the time for us to repent and give away all our sins. The Lord has already paid the price for us if we will repent. We need to recognize our faults and walk the life path that leads to our Lord. Those who are persecuted heal and grow only as they give away their hard feelings towards their persecutors. What a sad irony that the one persecuted, as they become bitter at those who persecute them, become infected with the same hatred that directed their persecutors. They become like the mean ones. What a clever and poisonous trap! So, it is of monumental importance that we, that I, not embrace the hatred. After all is said and done, Jesus will cleanse and heal all that follow Him! Repent and forgive with love.

There is another concept that is operating here. It may sound strange, but an opportunity for growth can always be found amongst our trials.

Brother Swisher long ago said to me, "We cannot change others, we can only change ourselves." Through the years I have learned how right he was. So, if any growth is to come out of this experience, I must find all those things that I could have done better and resolve to do them better next time.

As I review this sad chapter, I see so many things I could have done better. It was hard to think during that time, I suspect I was just reacting. Maybe that was the biggest mistake I could have made in those circumstances, and I made it. I should have spent more time looking for someone who could have interceded. If I could have found some help, maybe the additional resistance to their activities would have resulted in some of the bad stuff not materializing. Further, it is always wise to be patient in afflictions. Further, you probably see the things I did wrong easier than I do, as you have a different perspective. It is my hope when your trials come, this volume will be of some help to you. If nothing more, at least do not do things the way I did. I am sure you will be able to do things better, much better.

If my family and I had left the Church because of the bad things that happened to us, we would have probably lost most or all the rest of the experiences in this book. We are not the first followers of Christ who had bad things happen to us.

There has always been a fire inside me to fulfill the two missions. The first mission was complete; I graduated from law school. There was still the second mission. A campaign for a community college board of trustees was started. The choice was clear; the community college board was letting staff operate without the oversight that was needed. Many departments were being run for the benefit of the staff and to the detriment of the students. I offered a choice and a change to the voters. I did not win.

Another Blessing. Our church activity was gone… I left the power company after thirteen years and started building custom homes. Two large construction contracts were breached, and I could either sue or walk away with nearly nothing. I walked. What more could go wrong? So many trials had really, really hurt us. Many of our supposed friends were gone. Bev's dad was gone. Her mother was blind and so frail. Bev's grief for her dad ran as deep as a river. It seemed I could do nothing to help her. Our business and life savings were gone. I had no job. And more... There was bitterness on my part.

My dad was the only one trying to help. May God bless him. One day, Dad told me I was losing weight because I was not eating. That was new information to me; I had not recognized either the loss of appetite or weight. I was just reacting to my circumstances, not thinking. Depression was crushing me.

I was home alone one day. I knew there was a door that led to our God. But I had such trouble trying to get myself to pray.

It is a humbler posture to pray on your knees than standing or sitting. Then it seemed there was an even more humble posture than kneeling. In the scriptures during exceptional times some would pray to the Lord lying face down. This seemed an exceptional time. I went into the living room and lay face down and began to pray. I asked for help. Immediately, the crushing feeling from the depression was gone! It was just gone, completely gone! It was like some huge weight on me had just been taken away. The weight and crushing pressure were just gone. I was left with the most peaceful feeling. As usual, I was surprised. What other emotion is there? Of course, being thankful should have been the first thought, but, sadly, it was not.

How could this happen? Where did the crushing depression go? Where did this great peace come from? That answer was easy; from God. I went to my feelings to see if I could sense even a small amount of the crushing pressure and weight. It was not there. Where was my immediate gratitude that should have overflowed? I was trying to analyze the blessing instead of giving thanks. Science instead of religion. I then tried to make the depression come back so that, maybe I could learn to control it and make it leave by my command and control. Possibly this could be shared with Bev and others… It did not come back, and I quickly realized this was a blessing, not a tool for me to use. It was then easy to understand, that all the time the depression was from me. It could and would come back the next time as it did the first time. If my thoughts were too much on the dark, bitter, or troubling things, they would start adding together and become crushing again. If I did not allow my mind to spend too much time with those thoughts the weight from the troubles would not start adding together and become crushing. Count my many blessings and do not count the problems or they will grow.

My path was clear. I should use what few talents I had, one day at a time, to rebuild our lives. My thoughts and choices one day at a time would lead me where I choose to go. I started making choices again instead of reacting to the bad things around me.

This whole incident had taken only a couple minutes. Prayer, oh prayer. Has there ever been such a door? Not in the hour of need, but in the minute of my need our Lord was there to respond. Oh, how He responds, what peace he spoke to my mind. All praise be to the Holy One of Israel!

Through the years when the depression starts to return, I often recognize I have forgotten to give thanks for the good things in my life. I have forgotten to count my many blessings. Even if some things are not going well in my life, there is still much to be thankful for and no room for dark or bitter thoughts or too many thoughts on troubles. There are always good things to fill my mind and choose the right and let the consequences fall where they may. Sometimes the depression comes very quickly and powerfully. At those times, I need to sing the hymns of the Gospel and pay close attention to the things in my life that are too demanding. If any mean or bitter thoughts appear in my mind, I do not let them stay, I think of better things. The life choices are always mine, even though they may be hard.

Time passed… Things got better.

Campaign for Congress. Since I was ten years old, as previously mentioned, there has always been a burning desire in me to do whatever I can to stop the slide away from good government, orchestrated by those who would rule over us, not represent us. Consequently, I started a second political campaign, for Congress this time. I shared the best wisdom I could find on this earth, most of which was inspired by God, and much of it came from our Founding Fathers. The offer was for me to be a servant not a ruler, to follow those principles that would help us to be a happy and prosperous people, and the freest we could be…

Again, much came from the Founding Fathers and the God inspired Constitution, most of the rest from the scriptures and those like Smith, Lincoln, and Benson. One issue I highlighted was our free vote, one of the great foundations of our republic. I warned it would not stay free forever. In the direction our country is going voter fraud is becoming more common. It will not be too long before it will be easier to get a candidate elected by using voter fraud than debating issues and trying to persuade… Especially using computerized vote tabulation and mail in ballots. (This was predicted in 1989, and look what we have now.)

I did not win but at least the voters had a clear choice between two quite different directions. Plus, the warning about the precarious position of our free vote.

Washington State. There was a strong impression, without explanation, to move from California to the Seattle area. I had a good job, the family was settled, we had a very nice home with a pool, and with not much debt. So mortal reasoning was against the move. But...

When I mentioned to Bev I would like to move, she agreed. I took a high voltage lineman job in Seattle. There were some genuinely nice people I met there, and all the rain made it a very green city.

I preferred to work construction rather than in management, so I transitioned to blue collar. On the job some of the language could be categorized as "raw construction." One day, a helper and the lineman I was working with were involved in an exceptionally foul conversation. Then it got worse. They started profaning the name of our Lord. I had made some requests of them in the past to keep the foulness to a dull roar. Maybe they were doing this to joke with me, I did not know. I asked them to make a deal with me. I agreed I would endure, without complaint, their most foul and obscene language if they would agree not to profane the name of our Lord, Jesus. At that request all went very silent for a while. No agreements were made. The raw language continued, but the name of the Lord was not taken in vain as much after that. How could anyone knowingly profane the name of our Savior and Redeemer, the Anointed One? The One most full of love and concern for us. Jesus is the one who gave His life to ransom us.

Argentina for Two. Our oldest son, David, received a mission call and was readying to go to Argentina for two years. We went to the Stake President's office. The president talked with David a little. Then he set David apart as a missionary. At the same time, David was given a blessing. One part of the blessing was that his father would be safe at his job until David returned. Many times, I learned what that meant. I will share only two incidents.

Knife. Joe, the foreman, a good guy, asked me to help a lineman with some work he was doing. We went up in a bucket truck to work on a line energized at 26,000 volts. The lineman told me what he was going to do. A rope was sent up from the helper on the ground. A pulley was put on the pole and a grip was used to attach the rope to the energized line. The helper on the ground was going to use a powerful power-take-off roller on the truck to pull the rope that would in turn pull the conductor so we could transfer it to another position on the pole. This is not the way I would have performed the job, but I was assisting and maybe this is the way the other lineman was trained and the only way he knew to accomplish the task. With care the job could be done safely this way, so I did not want to confuse him with another plan. The helper at the truck had years of experience and everything should have been fine.

The Spirit whispered to me to take my lineman's knife out of my tool belt. So, I did without a question. I was standing in the basket of the bucket truck beside the other lineman with my knife in my right hand. There was no use for that tool doing what we were going to do, but the Spirit is the Spirit. I learned long ago to trust that a certain Someone who knows the past, present, and the future. God's knowledge of the future was my concern here. The helper on the ground started making the line a little tighter and we would tell him when it was tight enough. Then, the worst happened. The helper on the ground slipped, hitting the truck controls. The rope became tangled and was rapidly getting far too tight. In a couple seconds, the 26,000-volt line would be pulled enough to cause a loop that would cause a line-to-line fault. We would both be severely burned or possibly killed. In a couple seconds, the knife cut the tight rope and the pole shook violently from the release of the force. We were okay.

There were prayers of thanksgiving. Later that day, I mentioned to the other lineman the impression I had received to take the knife out of my tool pouch. He attended another church, but he could not help but recognize this was an impression from the Holy Ghost. We talked of saying our evening prayers of thanksgiving for the aid we had received that day. The next day, the other lineman mentioned he had said a prayer of thanks for me saving us. At this I was greatly distressed. He did not understand. I only cut the rope. I was not much more involved than the knife. The Holy Ghost is the one that orchestrated our safety. The thanks should have been directed to God. I should have had more discussion with the other lineman on that point, but his church taught that the church I attended was a congregation of bad people, or at least deceived. Consequently, he was weary of me, concerning religion and had not been interested in listening to much I had to say.

Two Towers. Another incident happened on a 400-foot-high tower near Lake Union along Interstate 5. We were changing the 115,000 and 26,000-volt conductors on the towers. A company engineer and the crew foreman told us how they wanted all the conductors put in rollers in preparation to pulling the old wires out and pulling the new wires in. We went up the tower and started doing the work. After working on the tower, I was assigned. I had a warning (the warning did not give me much information to go on; it seemed the Spirit wanted me to figure this problem out more on my own) that this activity was not safe—life or death safe. I watched all the workers on this tower and thought about the overall effect of what we were having on the structure of the tower. There was some slight recognition of a problem.

I told everyone this was not safe. I did not fully understand what was unsafe exactly, but… The foreman, Joe, a great guy, took my act as insubordination. He was confident I was a smart lineman, so he was caught between the two gravities, his position of a supervisor where he represented the best interests of the company and his knowledge that I was a very good lineman. The company gravity won, and he told me if I did not shut up and go back to work, I would be fired. He went to the department supervisor; I suspect to get me fired. His boss, Bill, was a smart and reasonable man. Bill also knew I was a smart lineman, and his first act was to get the engineer involved. I was over my head; I did not know exactly what was wrong, but I was putting the pieces together and my job was on the line. So, I requested to see the tower engineered plans. Except for Bob, a particularly good lineman from San Diego, the crew had abandoned me. A couple were outwardly critical of me, the rest were just watching to see if I knew what I was doing or just getting myself fired.

A meeting was held at the office. There were about fifteen employees working on the two towers crossing the lake who were in attendance. A couple of other company foreman who had heard what was going on were in attendance, along with the supervisor and the engineer. I was the only one complaining. I was on the spot! Old plans of the old towers were brought, rolls of them. I opened them and found the tower base. There were numbers in the large; I think well over a hundred thousand. This must have been the compression weight that the towers could support. I fumbled through the large old roll of blueprints to find the top section of the tower. There were two numbers. One still in the tens of thousands range and one was two thousand. Okay, the large number must have been the compression supportable weight. And the two thousand? Was that two thousand the supportable weight that the tower could support from a side pull? I asked and the engineer said that my understanding was correct. It was all becoming clear. There were very uneven angles on the tower. I started to explain if the heavy conductors were all put in rollers, as they wanted, the uneven angles would place cantilever or side strains on the tower many times in excess of the two thousand pounds. The engineer did not agree and started to argue with me. The supervisor and the foremen were just watching.

Another foreman, not working on this job, understood, and picked up where I left off. He asked the other linemen working on the project what angle the two rollers were in after they were installed. Most agreed the rollers were pulled at about a thirty-degree angle. A light came on for the engineer and the supervisor. They understood their plan, if followed, would collapse both towers and killed about ten of us from both towers.

The supervisor quickly ended the meeting so as not to have more discussion on the engineering error. The plan for the work was improved to a safe manner. Some of the linemen still did not understand. One lineman said to me that I had saved our lives. That "me" thing again. It appeared to me the Lord knew this would happen and well over a year earlier had me start rearranging my employment to serve Him to stop this disaster. He only shared the impression of the safety problem at the last minute.

After all that happened, the project was accomplished, we were all still alive and David was still on his mission. This was another fulfillment of the blessing given to David before he went on his mission.

Besides the tower incident, there were several other similar situations that seemed to have also been the reason I was so anxious to move to Seattle. The Spirit obviously wanted me there to help change the course of all the events on the towers and the other near misses. What love and concern for our safety from Father, Jesus, and the Holy Spirit. All praise be to Them! Forever! And ever!

Second Campaign for Congress. I started a second campaign for Congress. I met two men who had both intelligence and courage that helped me with the campaign. Dave and Joe, such a rare combination. The campaign went very badly. National political leaders put pressure on locals to steer clear from Stan as he will not "go along" with national leaders and that he will never convert to the "pro-abortion" position. Plus, I was very dangerous to the national political establishment as I explained how they were looting the social security system. If the American public ever understand what the national politicians are doing, there will be at least a voting revolt.

I withdrew from the campaign and withdrew from the Democratic political party as that party demanded that support for abortion was the first and most important issue for any party member. The political leaders did not have any love or even respect for the God inspired Constitution and so many of their leaders were solidly against so many of God's laws.

I took a job as a high voltage lineman working for the power company in Oregon. Not quite so much rain, a little more sun. We lived in Salem.

The song "I Believe in Christ" is one of the most moving pieces of music I have ever listened to or participated in singing. It is a song with a melody to fit a simple straightforward theme, the pronouncement of a belief in Christ. The first time it was sung in a Sacrament meeting I was stunned. I could not sing the whole song; the words were so touching on my belief of Christ that my eyes were so filled with tears that I could not read the words to continue singing. The next time the song was sang in church it had the same effect on me. I noticed another brother had the same reaction and I guess I did not feel so self-conscious. Again, and again, the song did not grow less moving with time and familiarity. Again, and again, I never sang the song all the way through, the spirit that accompanied the song was remarkable. The song aided me in praising my Lord. I love my Lord. He loved me first.

Serving in a ward would require me to sit on the stand during the Sacrament meeting and take notes on who spoke and briefly what they said, as well as counting the Sacrament meeting attendance. This would make me very conspicuous when the song was sung in the meeting. I did not want to be belittled by some of the ward members, so I asked, in prayer, if I could keep my emotions in check when that song was next sung. My prayer was granted in a few weeks when the song was used in the meeting. I did not shed any tears. But I did not feel the spirit of the song as I sang, that "I believe in Christ." It was a lonely feeling compared to before. (Again, my prayer was not well thought out and again I received what I prayed for, which was not really what I wanted but, because I asked in an unthinking manner, I lost something very special.) It was a sterile feeling as compared to before. The song was over, and I felt empty. I missed the chance to sing with my heart, praises and my belief to my Christ and my King. There was a quick repentance on my part and a realization that I would endure the looks and comments in the ward rather than not have the experience of the closeness of the Spirit that accompanied singing the song. I quit sitting on the stand during the meetings. My seat would be in the back of the chapel.

With the next singing of the song, the feelings were back accompanied by the spirit of the song. I sang, "I believe in Christ He is my King with all my heart to Him I'll sing…." out of the LDS songbook.

Gospel Doctrine Class. A noticeably confident sister was teaching the Gospel doctrine class in Sunday School. She also filled an important position in the Portland, Oregon Temple. When she taught, she spoke with great boldness. At this time, I was helping in the ward Sunday School organization. For a few weeks, all the teachers were there for their classes, so I attended the Gospel doctrine class instead of filling in for an absent teacher. The Spirit seldom attended her teachings, maybe less so than any church class I have ever attended. She did make a point of letting everyone know she was important. Others may be important, but only as they were behind her in that order. Pride? Yes, pride. Pride is such a loud noise that it keeps us from hearing the Spirit or in another view it insulates the person with pride from the Spirit. Then one Sunday the class was on the temples. At that meeting the Spirit was strongly felt. I was surprised and thankful. Hoping that was going to be the new direction for her class I visited it several more times.

The next several Sunday classes were as barren as the previous classes. I mentioned this to the Sunday School president at an organizational meeting. He wanted to attend the next class with me. We sat through most of the class, and he leaned over and mentioned to me, "I don't feel anything."

I told him it was because the Spirit was not in abundance in the class. The Spirit was confirming nearly nothing she said and was mostly absent from her class. Further, comments from class members were very few. The comments could have helped, but they did not seem to be welcome.

The Sunday School leader came up with a plan for another teacher. That teacher was released, and another was chosen, a young humble member. The Spirit attended the teachings of the new instructor. What is so sweet as the presence of the Holy Spirit sharing the will of Jesus?

I tried to help some good people in their political campaigns. It seemed that the best people seldom were elected to office.

Face Down. One Saturday morning, I was wondering what the Lord wanted me to do, and I was feeling a longing to be nearer to the Lord. I decided to pray face down. I had not prayed in this way since the bout with the crushing depression. This was not an extra special occasion, so my thoughts were, maybe this is not an appropriate time for this. Then, after a little thought, I decided/hoped that the humbler posture should not be so restricted. I so prayed.

Not long into the prayer, the Holy Ghost gave me something to do. I was to visit a family where the husband was suffering from a debilitating disease. I went to their house that day. The wife was surprised and concerned why I was there. I talked to both a little during a brief visit. In a couple weeks, I was called to be their home teacher.

Look. As usual I was listening to a church conference tape while commuting to work. A general authority was speaking about missionary activities and his grandson. It seemed to me the talk was more of his pride than humble instruction. I quickly pulled my thoughts away from that subject. He was a general authority and that was his business. It was my opportunity to look for the concepts he was sharing and try to understand them. The Spirit regularly confirmed the truths that I found, or that He identified for me to learn. The Spirit has generally opened concepts for me to learn that I would have passed over and not recognized. I never claimed to be brilliant, but brilliant does not even start to cover the intelligence of God's will, so as I align my will with His I can have access to wisdom far greater than brilliance...

The Spirit said, "Look."

I knew He was talking about, the pride of the speaker. Almost as a reaction I responded, "I don't want to look."

The word came again, "Look." This was not in the form of a demand, or in any way harsh, pushy, or impatient. It was given as direct instruction almost conversational.

I turned my thoughts to ponder the speaker's words. Yes, it was clear that the general authority had lost, at least part of his focus on sharing his understandings of the Gospel. He was speaking so he and his family would be seen as elevated or of a higher status. That talk with his pride was memorialized in a general conference. I guess I am not the only one that makes such big mistakes.

Obviously, that incident has application for all of us in general and specifically for me, and readers of this book. I am guilty of the same serious offense of pride if my motives are to elevate myself, instead of to share and possibly help. It is my hope and prayer that the reason for sharing these experiences is to encourage us in our desires towards God. As we are all spirit children from one Heavenly Father, we are only one generation from God. He is our Father, our Father which is in heaven. If it were not for the fall, we would see our glorious Father, and there would be no confusion on that point. Therefore, we are truly brothers and sisters, no matter what race or religion, we are family. Does Heavenly Father not love us all? He really loves and thankfully He forgives!

Further to the point of "Look," this is also a teaching about pride and our relation to it and those that embrace it. About sixteen years ago, a church leader read this book. He was incensed I would put this episode of "Look" in the book. How dare I do such a thing! Obviously, I was given this instruction to show how pride infects and is manifested in all of us, including leaders, not new news there. It was also to show how those with pride try to cover it up in others also, to cover the entire concept of pride. The brotherhood and sisterhood of pride.

Why am I sharing most of my spiritual experiences? So, you can have those experiences also. I hope you have felt the Spirit as you read the experiences. If so, then they are your experiences as well as mine. You have read how God has dealt with me in many circumstances. Will He not deal with you in some divine way? Of course, He will with all His Devine variations of His teaching circumstances. You will have your own spiritual experiences specifically crafted and orchestrated by an omnipotent and omnipresent Father, just for you. If you have not recognized His dealings with you yet, a fertile place to start is to read the New Testament, especially the first four books that carry the words of Jesus and The Book of Mormon, another testament of Jesus Christ, especially the part where He visited the Americas, and then the Old Testament. Read with an open heart with a desire to know the truth and the Holy Ghost will confirm truths to you. Further, a byproduct of your readings will be that you will understand and believe the Holy Scriptures and how they are crafted for you (us) specifically as well as generally.

In this writing, you can see how God has responded when I have prayed. I am very ordinary. If you are ordinary too, is there any reason God will not respond to your prayers? I have faith and hope that Heavenly Father, and His son Jesus, given their absolute love and wisdom, will respond to you in an exciting way so specific to you. You will be filled with wonder and hope in your approach of Jesus. So, open your mind when you pray and be as humble as you can so you can recognize God's responses. The opposite of humble is pride, or thinking we are better than others. Pride is an insulation from the influence of the Holy Ghost. If, for some reason, you are extraordinary then so much the better. You have my faith and prayers to add to yours as you pray or in other words as you approach His presence. He is anxiously available; He will answer in His very own marvelous way. His answers stretch and challenge us and help us grow.

There is one other concept to mention. Briefly stated, to one is given something and to another is given another thing, that we may all be profited. If we have love for one another, we will all use our individual talents to aid each other, that we may all be profited. That is my intent here. May God bless us all.

Teaching Moments. The intent is not to discourage but to inoculate. I will share only a couple more incidents of this time period. Again, the intent is to give you incidents to review before you are personally involved in one of your own. If that is too late, maybe you can view this and relate it to your experiences to possibly view them from another perspective and not be so hurt beyond your ability to endure and understand. Remember to look at the things I could have done better.

If you are going to make a list of my mistakes, be sure you have lots of paper. I have made a lot of mistakes. For this very purpose, Jesus gave us Baptism and the Sacrament, so we can repent and be forgiven as well as learn along the trek through this fallen life.

This was a Sunday priesthood meeting. The back row near the door was my seat in this high priest group. There were scholars in the class. The teacher had taught religion at Rick's College and BYU. Two members of the bishopric were in attendance and the Stake President had just walked in and sat next to me. The instructor was reviewing a New Testament incident recorded about an apostle. His discussion was about a time when the apostle went to some group to teach them. They would not listen, and they treated him roughly and threw him out. It seemed we were studying a printed or dead story. There seemed no life in the story as opposed to when the Spirit accompanied teachings. Teaching the printed word instead of the living scriptures was not new for a meeting. So, sadly, sometimes it seemed it was the general rule, not the exception that it could and should be. I may be a bit jaded here with this, or maybe a lot. But I was not going to try to chance the order of things. I was just an obscure member.

Just at this point the Spirit called me. I said, "Called me," further explanation is needed. I was on the back row with no one behind me. Someone unseen tapped me on the back of my head. This was something physical that I felt on my head, not the normal activity as most things come directly into my mind. Immediately, I knew what was wanted. The calls had happened, at times, before. I was to offer comment to the class for the Spirit. The Spirit wanted something to be shared and the direction of the class to be changed. Even before I knew exactly what the Spirit wanted me to say to the group, my immediate response in prayer back to the Spirit was, "Oh no, not again. Why me? Every time You do this, they become angry with me, and I become more unpopular in the ward. They won't listen. I am the least of all here in this group. Why not choose a leader? There is no courage here." This phrase, sharing so many of my thoughts took only a moment of thought/prayer to respond back to the Spirit. During this string of my whining, I realized I was issuing the Spirit a "Jonah" response. I needed repentance, so quickly I thought/prayed, "I'm sorry. I'm sorry."

The next part of the repentance process was to do as directed. I raised my hand to do what I was supposed to do. As quick as my hand was raised the instructor called on me. I did not yet know what I was going to say. But that was not my worry. This had happened, at times, before. Every time the wisdom came, even in the second that it was needed. Sometimes the wisdom would come when I started to speak or sometimes just before I spoke. The Spirit would give me the words directly or the concept to be shared. If it was the concept, then I would be left to fumble for the words to try to convey the meaning intended. It was much easier when the words were given.

Just before I spoke, I remembered or was just given the memory, I am not sure which, of President Kimball talking about perspectives. I briefly shared the concept by way of a quote from him. Then my comment was a quick review of one of Jesus' parables, the two men praying, a Pharisee and the Publican.

Something wrong was going on in the class. We were all sitting there, seeing ourselves as the apostle we were reviewing and having only the perspective of the apostle. We were not reviewing the story with the additional perspective of the mean people because we saw ourselves as better than them, elevated above them. This single and superior perspective was a sign of our pride. It seemed clear the Spirit was accusing us of thinking like the Pharisee.

That was all, and I quickly ended. My comments had lit a short fuse for some tempers of class members. A member of the bishopric forcefully spoke, started by saying he was tired of me interrupting the class with these meaningless comments. He further stated all that was being taught was an apostle tried to teach the gospel, the people would not listen, they roughed him up, and tossed him out. He further stated I was making things up that were not there. The instructor then fully agreed with all aspects of the last comment and stated I was making things up from nothing and causing problems, again. These were light reviews of the mean words. The instructor was looking at me, expecting a response to such a spirited chastising. He waited for my response.

The Spirit was silent. To make a response in my own defense seemed to be a short road to contention. Contention is not where the Spirit resides. A response may help to soothe my feelings, but nothing good would come from it. It seemed better to endure the words than further chase off the Spirit. We had plenty of harsh words already. I was waiting for someone in the room to look past the harsh words and recognize the wisdom in the concept that had been shared. But that did not happen.

The instructor smiled at me with the glee of having told me off in front of the group. My next thought was to whine. I almost let the thought/prayer, "I told you so," slip through before it was discarded. I did not want to whine anymore. I was getting so weary of these...

Sometime later, when my feelings were not so tender, I pondered on the activity to better understand. I was in my pickup commuting to work in Portland. I turned off the conference tape I was listening to. It seemed to be my opportunity to ask God for the brothers to be forgiven for the harsh words. I was always asking that Jesus' life and death and life atone for my sins and misdeeds, so it is my charge to forgive others as Jesus taught.

As soon as I started the request, a concept taught by Elder Maxwell came into my mind. In one of his conference talks, we were taught to look for the irony of the situation to help us understand situations. Look to the perspective of the situations, recognizing the irony can help teach us. Next, the Spirit explained the irony. I am thickheaded, or I would have realized it by myself. The group had been seeing themselves as the ancient apostle they were studying. In the class they were teaching traditions and the letter of the law without the life the Spirit gives to the scriptures, as the ancient Pharisees did. But the irony was they thought they were like the ancient apostle, but they did not act the part. They acted like the ones the apostle tried to teach, the ones that would not listen and treated the apostle harshly.

Part of the problem for the class was the Lord did not send someone great or important to the class, He used me. Paul could teach with the voice like a lion, my voice is low. Further, the class obviously had problems recognizing the teaching coming from the least of all in the group. The Holy Spirit, the incredible Unseen Instructor!

Harshness. The harshness of some in the ward was bothering me to the extent I was spending time pondering on the concept of harshness in hopes of understanding more and becoming less bothered by it. An unexpected result occurred while pondering on the subject. I was given a vision, almost dream-like, certainly a metaphor, that started as if I were viewing the experience.

The vision was in black and white. It happened faster than real-time. It started with the leaders of the ward asking me, a terrible singer, to sing a solo in Sacrament meeting. My poor singing ability would, at the very least, detract from the spirit of the meeting. Worse yet, I was asked to sing "I Believe in Christ."

To be obedient to the duly called leaders, I took the stand at the podium and started to sing. At this point, the vision changed from me watching to me being in the experience. It was me with my natural voice, with no divine help to my voice, as I had hoped. I was singing the great song with my poor and untrained voice. The sound was not good, but the spirit the song carried soon arrived and my feelings for my Savior reduced me to tears, only half able to see the words and sing them. The glee of some, at my plight, soon turned to snickers that soon, for some, turned to light laughter. I resigned myself to the humiliation.

At this point, I was still not far into the song. Then I saw a friend, a Samoan brother from that ward, stand up. He started to sing the song with a strong, talented voice. Then another member stood and started singing. Then another, then another, soon nearly one third of the ward was standing and singing. Standing with some others singing our love and praise to our Savior when the vision ended.

The pettiness and harshness seemed captured in a temporary spot of time and of not much eternal significance of its own. To me, the importance of the harshness was it produced a reaction from me. In response, would I become harsh or humble?

After that, I did not spend much more time pondering on the harshness of the ward or reacting to it. Another thought was, I must have temporarily forgotten, "Of these make thy friends."

Later, I found out it was not just me. A wonderful Samoan brother mentioned how he enjoyed our conversations. Further, he stated I was the only one in the ward who would talk to him. I had not noticed that. I am so dull to have miss that. I was heartbroken to hear his words.

Accused. From time to time during a Gospel doctrine or priesthood class, some things would be taught or commented about that was plainly not true. Sometimes I would comment and try to correct the errors. As part of my church experience, I would often share my testimony on a fasting Sunday.

The first Sunday of the month, we skip two meals, or fast for two meals, and give the money saved by not eating, to our church to be given to feed the poor. It feeds the poor and probably as importantly, it should help humble us from our pride.

At one point I was called into the bishop's office. He wanted to know where I was getting all the stuff I was speaking about in the meetings. Further, that many "leading members" of the ward were terribly upset with my comments and wanted me to stop making them. It was more of an accusation than a question. I did not respond. Most of my comments were quotes or explanations from things the Spirit confirmed from church conference talks. He stated I was probably part of some study group that was or should be outlawed by the Church. I was then dismissed after he stated I was forbidden from sharing my testimony in that ward, and I should keep my comments to myself. He did not stop me from teaching the high priest group as he had no authority over that activity.

I was part of a study group of two. The greatest sermons you will ever hear will be to an audience of one, said Elder Maxwell in a conference talk. I have heard some of those sermons from the Spirit to an audience of one, me alone. One such sermon lasted about four wonder filled minutes. For more than a decade I would generally spend three hours each day listening to audio tapes of church conferences and the scriptures. Often when something wrong was boldly asserted by a class member or the instructor, either the Spirit or my memory would bring part of a conference talk or scripture to mind. I would share it...too often to the anger of someone.

Old Lady of Sorrow Corvallis, Oregon. It is about mid-day, and I am walking west on a street not far off the old main street. I am on the south side of a street that runs towards the college campus. There are three people walking the same direction as me about fifty feet in front of me. About a block ahead, heading towards us is an old woman shouting the vilest of curses. She is dressed in rags. The failure, years before in Sacramento has immediately come to my thoughts. The three in front of me, getting closer to the old lady of sorrow, quickly cross the street in mid-block, I suspect to keep a distance from her.

The old woman continues her shouts, and she sees me. She recognizes me for some reason. There is an evil in her, not just a confusion. I am looking directly at her, and she is looking directly at me. She is about one hundred feet from me, and we are closing on each other. Our eyes are intent on each other. If she gives me the slightest reason to think she is seeking my help, I will raise my right arm to the square and in the right name and by the right authority, command the evil spirit or spirits to come out and away from her. She can later re-accept them again if she chooses, but at least she will have that choice. She does not have that choice now.

She stops cursing at about ninety feet from me. I do not know what else is going on, but I am calm and ready to act as a servant of my Master, Jesus Christ. She is quiet now. She quickly crosses the street, watching me all the time. The others in front of me and crossed the street, I suspect, to get away from her are now walking way around her.

That was not the last time I saw this old lady of sorrow. Some weeks later, I was in Corvallis again. I stopped at a mini mart to buy a pint of milk to have with lunch. There were about four people waiting in the checkout line. As I went to the check stand line, the old woman was quietly standing in front of the person in front of me. She turned to face me and was nervously watching me, saying nothing. Where were her filthy shouts? There was still an evil with her. She looked at me with fear, as if she thought I was about to attack her.

While standing there, my mind raced through many of the considerations of the circumstances at hand. If she gave any hint there was a need for help, I would immediately raise my right arm to the square and cast the evil spirit out of her. In this setting with people around, if the act caused her some pain or discomfort or especially if the act of the evacuating spirit was violent, which it very well might be, the people would point to me as the cause. They would probably have no reference position to understand what would be happening. My thought was they would probably call the police and I would probably be arrested for the act, even though I would have never got close enough to physically touch her. Oh well, if that is the price, I am ready to pay it.

Anyway, she was standing there quiet, facing forward for a couple seconds, and then turned and faced me for a couple seconds. While facing me, the look of fear was obvious. The look was so obvious the man between us in line seeing her also turned to look at me. He was obviously satisfied I was no threat to her as he soon went back to his own business. She made no other actions and said nothing. I could take none of her actions as a plea for a release from her condition.

The Melchizedek Priesthood I hold is to be used as a service to all mankind. It is not an offensive activity of my choice; I am only a servant and wish not to do something contrary to His will with His priesthood. It is my hope I did not fail her, as I failed the other young woman on the street in downtown Sacramento.

Jesus' example was never to tread on the choice of a person. There are no forced changes, no matter how badly it is needed, no matter how good the change would be. If it were just evil spirits or the evil one himself, there would have been not a second of hesitation. They gave up their rights when they stood in opposition to Father's will in the pre-mortal existence life and were canst down. But here, one of my sisters was living her life, as she chooses, no matter how much I disapproved. All I needed was her slightest request to help or something close thereto.

The thing I do regret or maybe learned is that my thoughts were not more filled with more love for her and compassion for her plight. I did not speak to her; I did not even speak to her. I could have, at least, asked her if she was in some distress. I was acting more like a firefighter ready to toss water on a fire. I should have used my limited ability to gather and process more information to make a better decision, all the while knowing that the Spirit will add to or confirm the wisdom of how things really are, not just what I can gather or how things appear to me. The Spirit did not say to cast the evil spirit out of her, and I could not reach that conclusion from what I knew. Speaking to and asking questions of her could have resulted in receiving valuable information. Another failure! Oh, boy...

Please remember, if we do something to allow evil spirits to enter our body we will suffer horribly. Both women were suffering more than I could understand. Please be forewarned and be very careful.

Sermon by the Prophet Joseph Smith. Joseph Smith was and is a wonder filled prophet. Just from his first vision, he taught volumes about God the Father and the Son. Please study him. If, with an open heart, you study his life and teachings you will know he is an incredible prophet of our Lord,

Jesus Christ. He never claimed infallibility, although he is plainly stellar among us.

Twice a year, in early April and then six months later, the leaders of the Church of Jesus Christ of Latter-Day Saints meet in several meetings. Each semi-annual meeting is called a "General Conference."

The King Follett sermon was given by the Prophet Joseph Smith during the April 1844 General Conference. This sermon was and still is my favorite of all conference talks plus, I dearly love brother Joseph. Much of his life effort was to directs all towards Jesus. I had read or listened to the talk many (at least five possibly up to eight) times before. This time, when I started to listen to the conference talk, it came alive! I was hearing brother Joseph as I was listening to the audio cassette. Soon I was hearing him more than I was hearing the reader. He was speaking with such power and authority from the Spirit that at about a third of the way through the talk I stopped to see if it was Joseph speaking or the Spirit. As I stopped, I came back to the present. I was listening to a cassette voice; but the words were from Joseph Smith the prophet being confirmed true by the Spirit. I started listening again, the words of the recording were turning into the voice of Joseph. There was so much emotion in his words (emotion is not the Spirit but can be a byproduct) and the Spirit was confirming so much so strongly I thought again this may really be coming from the Holy Ghost. I had never heard or even supposed a mortal could so speak.

There were several themes going on at the same time. At the same time, he was speaking to those of us who love him and to those who hated and wanted to kill him. At the same time, he was opening a door to our further understanding. He was speaking to the advanced and us that were slow but trying. And maybe, most of all, he was speaking words so closely paralleling God's will that I could not distinguish between his words and the confirmation from the Holy Ghost.

I stopped listening a second time to see if this was coming from the Spirit or Joseph. It was Joseph's words and God's will. Then I was alone with the cassette again. I started listening and the talk came alive again. I finished, basking in the wonder of Brother Joseph's love and wisdom he had learned from Jesus and was sharing with us, all as he was teaching other concepts! Added to this in an overflowing way was the confirming influence of the Spirit. The words to a song written about him come to mind, "Praise to the Man that Communed with Jehovah..."

I wished I could have lived in his time, then my thought was that this dispensation, prior to the return of our Lord, is his time. Joseph Smith is the prophet of the restoration of the Gospel of Jesus Christ. His words are still helping prepare us to receive our Lord. May God bless brother Joseph and his family.

Please do not let me be misunderstood. I DO NOT worship Joseph, or even have faith in Joseph. My worship and faith go only to our Heavenly Father and our Savior, Jesus; no one else, certainly not to a mortal. However, my love for Joseph is great and I am so thankful Joseph did God's will in such an understandable way, teaching me so much. Joseph certainly has earned my "praise."

A year or so later, it was time to study that conference talk again. I started listening to the talk. The words stayed words of the cassette reader this time.

Sister. A sister was in distress. The details of the distress are not the issue and will be skipped. The Stake President and I were her home teachers. Most of the time I went with my little boy as the Stake President had lots of other people to look after. The sister called us both to come and give her a priesthood blessing. I did not know that until the president arrived that he was coming. There is a solid concept - the Spirit will be restrained if those in a prayer circle have unkind feelings for the others. This same concept is probably transferable to other situations, like a blessing.

This good sister needed a blessing to comfort her during an exceedingly difficult time. This was not a time to chance the feelings of the Stake President toward me. He had been conspicuously quiet during some harsh times in our ward and stake, times that he had the authority and ability to act, one way or another. His silence was, or at least seemed, an acceptance and even a light approval of the harshness. If he still harbored some of those same harsh feelings towards me the Spirit would be restrained, and our good sister would not receive the purer words of the Spirit. I was determined to do all that I could to make sure the Spirit was not restrained. If I had known that the president was to come, I would have offered the most appropriate excuse not to be there, to allow the Spirit to be less restrained. But we were sitting in her living room and she was sharing some of her difficulties.

My heart went out to her in her difficult time. My mind was drawn back to the issue of the Stake leader. I was trying to think of a way to get out of the situation. I could dismiss myself and just leave. This would look like I was weird, but I would endure that if it would help the sister. But that may have a disruptive effect on the situation. I was in a quandary; what to do? To add to my lack of action, a chair was now placed in the center of the room in preparation for the blessing.

The Stake leader asked her who she wanted to voice the blessing. To our surprise, she chose me. My thoughts were racing. What could I do to have the Spirit in attendance and unrestrained? The thought came that we should have a prayer first. I had forgotten that teaching of Nephi in the "Book of Mormon" where he teaches that before using the priesthood we should always pray. I made the request of the leader to say a prayer before the blessing, and then I kneeled. Everyone followed to their knees and the Stake leader offer the prayer.

The effect of the prayer was to invite the Spirit. The Spirit was then in attendance, so the blessing would be good if I did not get in the way. I opened the blessing as usual. Silently, I opened my mind to what blessing the Lord had for this good sister. I can remember only two parts of the blessing. The first was a little startling. I was to say, "Breathe in." So, I said, "Breathe in." I had learned, long ago to say whatever the Spirit wanted said. I was afraid she had stopped breathing and there was some medical emergency.

Then the Spirit said, in effect, as easily as you breath in your need for oxygen is met. You never worry about your need for oxygen being met so do not be overly concerned that your other needs will not be met. Be thankful your breath meets this need. Your other needs will be met in a similar way. I was relieved there was no medical emergency and surprised at the beauty of the concept, all at the same time.

Next came an impression to say, "Breathe out." I thought, *here we go again*, but at least there was no medical emergency. I said, "Breathe out."

Then the Spirit said in effect, as easily as it is to breathe out you can, with a very little added effort, add your vocal cords and breathe out music. The music will lift your mood. The good mood will surround you like a fragrance for you and for all those close to you.

Some other things were shared, but I do not remember them. The beauty of God's will always surprises and inspires me. The Spirit blessed the sister. Probably more important than anything said was the feeling that was easily felt. The Spirit was close. She was reminded God loves her and is concerned about her. God had helped her, was helping and would continue to help her through this life. All praise be to the FATHER and the SON and the SPIRIT! Forever and ever! Has there ever been such a Love!

PS: I will start adding "PS" to give additional information. I have tried to be very brief, if not this would be double the pages. This is the "small pages of Stan Warner" or the "Reader's Digest" version of the occurrences.

This is now out of the time order; we are in 2019.

I gave a copy of the book to a religious leader. He gave me a review of the "Sister" experience. He explained why it should be changed. He was right. He explained the inference carried by my telling of the incident seemed to say I was more correct or spiritual than the Stake President. This is the same Stake President who was sitting next to me as explained in sad "Teaching Moment." Yes, the comment I was placing the Stake President in a poor light was preceptive and correct. My perception of this incident is as accurately recorded here as I could make it.

So… I was going to change it as suggested. I woke up at six on this Saturday morning and gave some more review, thought and prayer to the change I would make.

The Spirit shared something more. I am leaving every word of my original account, every word. Now I will share a few of additions.

I was hurt by the events in the "Teaching Moment." As mentioned there, such a bad set of occurrences. From there, the hurt clouded by reasoning. I should have known better. I do understand, from teachings and personal experience, that when we are hurt, we need to follow the teachings of Jesus and forgive and give the hurt to Him. (If we do not give the hurt away with forgiveness, we will pay a terrible price as we go forward.) Jesus paid the price for all sin, hurt feelings, and all the other bad things that happen to us. He paid the price by His life and death. He will make all things right in the next life. I should have forgiven more completely if I wanted to follow Jesus.

One of the by-products of not forgiving is the dark haze in our minds mingled with that memory, surrounding those who could or even should have acted with some resistance to the bad acts. I did not completely forgive the Stake President for what I witnessed him do or not do. This left me with that dark haze that clouded my best reasoning and perception. The ability to perceive and reason is of such great importance in us as we try to be better children of God, it is hard to overstate the importance of forgiveness.

With that concept out in the open let us look at the incident again. As is so often the case I made a mistake for all to see. I suspect the Spirit wanted all of you to see my mistake. So, here is the same incident years later, hopefully without my hurt and resulting pride, and clouded thought process.

I was concerned the Stake President was still harboring poor feelings for me based on what he had not done in the priesthood meeting, that would in some degree insulate the Spirit from this activity. Well, that could have been but probably was an error on my part. His lack of engaging in the activity could have been concerned for the brothers who were so harsh. He could have thought, *This is bad, but Stan will be okay.* He may have thought commenting in class would only make things worse. His telling them of their harshness could have been too much for some in the class. Further, he might have been pondering these statements and asking for help from the Spirit as this was a "way over the top" action in the Lord's meeting.

As you can probably understand, a dozen more things could have been going on with the Stake leader. I am sure he wanted to not make a mistake and to do the best. In that heated and contentious atmosphere a quick response from the Stake President might not have been the best course. I now suspect the Spirit, the Spirit that teaches all of God's spectacular will and only God's spectacular will, may have left him wondering what to do, giving him an experience, and giving him time to reason out the best he could, what to do, and only then giving him the best course of action to bad occurrence. To go much further with this reasoning is possible, but to be brief only one more thought. To help the situation, private conversations, and reviews of the acts with those involved could have been the best, which would have been something I was not aware of, and on and on…

Briefly stated, I should have known better and gave more thought and prayer to the situation. Not fully forgiving, and even worse, not recognizing I had not forgiven, even if there was nothing to forgive, left a dark haze that obscured by reasoning. That left me thinking something that may or may not have been the case at the home of the sister that needed the blessing. Or better stated, it was probably not the case. In any case any poor feelings towards the Stake leader were a hindrance to me (can you see the irony?) in being close to the Spirit. I should have dropped those thoughts like a hand full of molten metal.

More Understanding of the Bad Dream. For some reason, I was thinking about the bad dream that had filled me with terror when I was young. I remembered and reviewed the dream, a little slower than real time. This was done to try to see if there was anything more to the dream I missed as a youth that might show up now when reviewed from a perspective of a little more experience and maturity. I was reviewing the dream without the terror that accompanied the dream in my youth. This was like a classroom review. During the review, it seemed almost like I was having the dream again. I went through the falling and seeing the creatures watching me fall and getting closer to the swamp. This now turns to a slower motion viewing. The dream was just flowing as if I was having the dream again. I hit the swamp and got stuck. I did not fall through the swamp as when the dream lost its terror.

I never got this far in the dream before. I would always wake up crying before this point. I did not thrash around trying to get unstuck. I looked around and to my surprise the snakes and crocks and piranha were just looking at me. They were not trying to kill me and eat me. They were just looking at me. They were not dumb animals, they had intelligence, and they were self-aware. They knew of their fallen condition. They were not happy that another had joined them. They had sad eyes. They saw me with sadness and pity I had ended up in the same fallen condition as them. I was stunned at the possibility this review of the dream had opened...

As always, Bev had found the special ones in this part of Oregon and became friends with them. There were several extraordinary ones, they used such ordinary names.

The company I worked for moved me to Utah. We moved to American Fork. We lived near the temple.

Discern. Brother D, what a great guy. He was the high priest, group leader of the ward. It was the first Sabbath day to meet with a new ward. He greeted me as I entered the building and quickly introduced me to the bishop. The ward was being split into two wards that day, so the bishop was busy. But he shook hands and looked into my eyes and did not release my hand. He did not move or divert his gaze. I became a little uncomfortable. My eyes water very easily when I stare into someone's eyes. I then sensed he was discerning who I was. He wanted the Spirit to help him know who I was. I suspected, as a shepherd, he was concerned for his flock.

At that point, I silently mentioned to the Spirit, show him my whole life if he wants, and open my heart to his understanding. About that time, he seemed content, getting what information he wanted. He broke eye contact, let go of my hand and he went to his other duties. That was the first time that had ever happened so plainly to me.

A Three-Year-Old. A father and his young son walked to the stand during a fast and testimony meeting. The father held his son up to the microphone. The little one reached out and took a firm hold of the fixed microphone. The little one started speaking clearly in a rapid pace. The boy was talking about his love for Jesus.

I recognized some but not all the words. At first, I thought it was because the boy was little and was not speaking clearly as he seemed excited. But as the words came it was plain that some of the words were not English. I was astonished and thrilled with the little one. So many words, from the Spirit. The little one rapidly spoke for over a minute. The longer he spoke the less and less English words were used. No one stood and interpreted. The boy finished at the urging of his father.

At the last of his testimony, I had no idea what words were being said. I guess that is an admission that I was not as close to the Spirit as I could be. If I would have known what was being said, I would have interpreted. However, I could feel the abundant presence of the Spirit.

The little one finished, and he and his father walked back to their seats in a silent congregation. I am thankful I was there to hear and feel his expressions.

A brother was the next to share his testimony. His first comment was, "How can I follow that!" May God continue to bless the little ones. May God grant us the love, wisdom, and courage to help Him to so do.

Wanted, A New Song. I was setting on the last row of bench seats during a Sacrament meeting. Joshua, my son, was being good as usual with a couple of crayons and a coloring book. The Spirit shared an understanding. There should be another song. It should be a congregational hymn. There should be a part for male voices and a part for female voices, changing often. The voices should celebrate the differences in opportunities or responsibilities in our service of our Lord and Master. I was not sure if the females sang what the male's opportunities are or vice versa. The tempo is lively, the melody is simply beautiful by itself. There will be smiles on the faces of those that sing, and happy glances will be shared between family members. The song will have different meaning to us as we go through our lives and our understanding of Jesus develops. The female and male parts will be sung spiritedly, with each doing their best, maybe a little to inspire or encourage each other. It may partly be of that which we endure to help other family members have opportunities to help us. It seemed that it might also be a chronological review of different periods in progress through mortality. The singers will voice their understanding that the direction of their lives is towards Jesus our Christ.

Oh yes, before I forget, along with the deeper voice parts for the men and the higher voice parts for the women, there in another part… There would be a part for an angle or angles to sing with us. There would be different words for them to sing. The first word or two would be left for the angle to sing. If we hear nothing, then a member would pick up their part a couple words into their part and sing for the angel. Angels could still sing their part even if we could not hear them. Their part would be encouraging and aiding us to continue, in doing good, no matter how hard the path. (Try, try, try.) I started writing down some words, but help was needed. I found a melody…

To Share or Not. There is so much I want to share. I hope this desire to share so much is not based on a desire to become elevated in some way, which would be pride. That would insulate me from the Spirit. I am not anxious to share these experiences and be the object of scorn, either. But I am anxious to share these experiences so you can have this testimony from a common, even obscure individual, your brother in Christ.

If God has loved me this much, He has also loved you this much. If God has dealt with me in wonderful ways, He has and will continue to love and deal with you in wonderful ways. So many things are happening right under our noses with us not knowing about them; remember the white-haired ladies walking. It is our opportunity to recognize and try to understand His ways. Remember, His ways are not our ways, as much as the heavens are higher than the earth, God's ways are higher than our ways.

Friends. We met some special people through the years. As usual, Bev finds them first and I follow. Mention will only be made of some, but that does not mean there are not many more. Brother and sister R are evidence of where living the Gospel of Christ will lead. (Those last fifteen words were given me directly from the Spirit.)

D and D and their children are a wonderful family. D is a physician. I was sick, a bad cold with a respiratory infection. My eldest son was living near but was not available to come and administer (give me a priesthood blessing for my sickness) to me. So, I asked D if he would come to our house and give me a priesthood blessing because of the illness. He lived a couple houses away. I felt a little awkward asking a physician to come and heal me, not using his training in medicine. He came over and administered to me. Immediately, I was much better. I was not completely healed but I was much better, maybe halfway or a little more there. I guess that was the limit to my faith. But I was grateful for the change.

Joshua the Prophet. While pondering on the life of the Prophet Joshua, it became clear there were at least several things being taught. I will highlight just one. His life was filled with fighting the war against the others that lived in the different parts of the land God gave to the twelve tribes of Israel. The struggle of Joshua is a type or example of how we should fight or war against our personal unrighteousness and weaknesses. (It is better if you read the account.) Your discovery of this is more important than my words.

Joshua was at war with the help of the Lord. Are we not in a struggle with our faults and weaknesses, with the help of the Lord? If we are not at war with our faults, trying to overcome them then we will be in opposition Joshua's influence on us. The bad parts we do not fight will end up being a weakness in us and keeping a place, an undeserved place in us here and now and after we die.

As Joshua followed the will of our Lord, he was successful. Are we not the same? We need to find the Lord. Have we sought Him, have we heard about Him? Have we read about Him? Do we pray?

Sometimes things did not go well for Joshua. Then he would try to find out what he or his people were doing wrong and change it. Even in his failings, he was learning. Are not we the same?

He fought until he died. We are fighting to rid the ungodly in us until we die. He fought until he died but did not finish the war. We will not finish our war either. After we do all, we can do, it will be the Grace of God that makes up the differences between where we end up in this life and where we need to be to go back and live with Our Father and His Son and the Holy Ghost and those near and dear to us.

Joshua started the war when he was older. Many of us learn of the Lord when we are older. It is not until we are older that many of us become aware we have weaknesses and imperfections that MUST be changed. Somehow the straight path and an iron rod will be discovered. Then we must find the courage in us to follow them.

Enough, that was possibly too much. The process of discovery is wonder filled. The three testaments are filled with these types of discoverable concepts. If you are a seeker of the Lord, please read and ponder and pray about the teachings in those books.

We moved back to California.

I took Joshua to the place where the hawk incident started. The old house near the canal, the old house where Brad lived, was still there. To our surprise, we saw a white-tailed kite (the same type of hawk) near the house. We drove the road where I pedaled my bike with the hawk those many long years before. I showed him where I lived and where I made the mistake by charging God foolishly in the prayer. We drove to the old West Sacramento Elementary school, the site of several spiritual experiences. The school had been torn down and a chain link fence surrounded the grounds. Fifteen years after this, I took Luke, our youngest son, to the sites and we traveled the same paths.

A Gateway. For me, prayer is a gateway or door through which I approach Heavenly Father. I pray to Heavenly Father in the name of Jesus Christ because I cannot approach Father except through His Son Jesus, who is our Christ.

Remember, it takes an act of faith to pray. It is with additional faith that we share our thoughts, hopes, and desires with Him. It takes additional faith for us to be specific in our prayers. Then it is with even more faith that we wait and listen and feel for a response especially if the response takes some time or even a long time.

It is my experience with prayer that sometimes things will happen fast and obvious. Other times it seems nothing happened, until I spend time thinking or pondering all the surrounding circumstances. Then I see a greater thing or order of things has happened. Sometimes, as with the prayer for the hawk, I have prayed and receive what I prayed for, even though there was something better that could have been asked for in the prayer. Then, sometimes it takes considerable time to understand how the divine intervention was manifested. And then sometimes, to understand what happened, I must spend time in concentrated thought and prayer in the search for Heaven's response. This effort is a stretching, the same as hard work builds stamina and muscles. Except here the work causes a stretching or increased understanding of the workings of God. At times, possibly even most often, the answers come while we read the scriptures or conferences.

When we pray to God, the future changes. Not by us but because a loving Heavenly Father hears and answers our prayers. As He, who holds the universe together, He who acts or speaks, those actions or words are eternally operative. His answers to our prayers, those acts of His will changes the present and therefore ripple through time and the universe. His answers and changes are for our benefit even if only slightly or even if never understood by us in mortality. But as He acts the future changes.

It bears remembering that the Heavens are higher than the Earth, and God's understandings are much, much higher than ours. We are asking help from the Father, in the name of Jesus the Christ, the Creator of worlds without number. So, we see the will from an exalted Father is, from time to time, more than a little hard for us to understand, especially while we are in this mortal condition. His answers always show me that I cannot anticipate how He is going to deal with me. Lastly, we cannot be too thankful to a loving and kind Heavenly Father. When we pray Father hears... His response changes things in the world for the better. And ditto again and again.

Old Testament. I have so many audio tapes and I spend a lot of time commuting to work. The construction projects I help with require even more time driving so I can review safety, quality, and productivity. So, I spend lots of time listening and learning. The contents of the tapes make an enjoyable event out of a stressful drive. Some time back, I went through the entire Old Testament series of tapes in about five weeks, maybe less. This was the fifth or so time I had listened to the Old Testament on tape. But the previous times took substantially longer. This time the whole work seemed much more familiar. The types of things that went on in the volume seemed capable of being categorized. There was so much that was duplicated of sorts, if not only in the stories but also in the concepts explained.

I was pondering on the subject ready to ask in prayer for some help towards that end. Finally, I asked if I could write an abbreviated or readers digest type review of the Old Testament. As soon as the question was asked, the Holy Spirit placed a statement in my mind. It was "Oh Israel, Israel, how often I would have gathered you as a hen gathereth her chicks, but you would not."

I knew this verse or words close to it. Words close to the above statement are in the New Testament, the Doctrine and Covenants (book of revelations given to Joseph Smith), and in The Book of Mormon, Another Testament of Jesus Christ. I thought I had, before this, understood those verses. But, obviously not after this. The verse came as an incredible review and summery of the entire Old Testament composed by using twenty simple words. Incredible, the entire Old Testament reviewed in twenty words! In thinking of the totality of the meaning, I responded back to the Spirit in prayer, "No, it does not fit. What about the creation? The creation does not fit."

Immediately, the response from the Spirit came. "The 'I' represents the creation."

After a brief time in thought, it was obvious one of the reasons the creation was shared with us was for an example and review of the total majesty of Jehovah/Jesus as He organized this Earth, under the direction of our Father. This was done as part of His incomprehensibly large heavens, for our own small planet or place to experience the mortal fall, our separation from Father so we could be tested and tried to see if we would follow God's will. This is a place where we are tempted from one side and loved and taught by the other. Can we have faith in the Holy One of Israel who creates worlds without number? Yes, of course we can.

That point was settled.

Then I pondered on the phrase again. In a couple seconds, I again responded in prayer, "No, no, it still does not fit. The genealogies do not fit."

Immediately, as before, the response from the Spirit came. "The 'you' represents the genealogies."

Then, with a little pondering on the concept, it was plain the lists of who beget who was to show more than just lines of certain families. It was to show how we are all linked by blood, which makes us all mortal cousins. We are also linked by our characteristics, strengths, weaknesses, and by our reactions to His teachings. Finally, and most importantly for me, there is a Father of all our spirits, in heaven. Thus "our" Heavenly Father, making us all brothers and sisters and His heirs. Jesus taught us to pray, "Our Father" in Heaven... Jesus did not say "only My Father in Heaven." Our Father, the Father of all of us is Our Father in Heaven.

Oh, how we are taught. No need to categorize the Old Testament, Jesus already did it for us with His usual unrecognized greatness, so long ago. And who on Earth understood this, besides Jesus? I had no idea of this until the Spirit taught me. Anciently, as recorded in the Old Testament, Jehovah wanted to gather us, to love us and teach us and save us. But, most often, we chose that we would not.

Anciently, as recorded in the New Testament, Jesus Christ wanted to gather us, to love us and teach us and save us. But, most often, we chose that we would not.

Anciently, as recorded in The Book of Mormon, Another Testament of Jesus Christ, in the Holy Land and in South and North America on this and other worlds, Jesus wanted to gather us, to love us and teach us and save us. But often, we chose that we would not.

So, sadly, today Jesus Christ wants to gather us, to love us, teach us, and save us. But often, we choose we will not.

We have one continuing saga recorded in the three Testaments. The three books offer a wealth of experiences all available to help us today. Those that chose not to gather to the Lord left us with the instructive results of their unrepented disobedience. Their recorded failures as well as their successes all proclaim the consequences of those choices in days past. Today, today is our day, our life. This is where we add our life choices to the great saga of mortality. Today there is still just one decision. Near the end of his life, the Prophet Joshua framed the life decision in simple term when declared, choose you this day whom ye will serve...but as for me and my house, we will serve the Lord. I am thankful that the Lord has offered so much help for us in our choices, our great choices that have such eternal consequences.

There is one last note concerning this episode. I was not smart enough to recognize and respond to the Spirit both "No, no's." The Spirit placed the quick response into my mind as I was still pondering. The Spirit wanted the two questions asked, and I could not understand the issue fast enough, so the Spirit aided me in the thought process as He obviously wanted the questions asked so He could answer them.

Did I mention that our sincere prayers are not just lost, nor do they just fade away? They are kept, saved in the Eternal Realms.

Childhood Friend. As a child, Bev and her friend V were like sisters. Then Bev's parents moved from Tennessee to California, and they lost contact. They searched for each other for decades. Bev had, for years, told me of her love for V. Decades later they finally found each other. What a reunion for the two near sisters. Among many other things V wanted to know was what church Bev attended. She said she knew they would belong to the same church. (This reminded me of the story of Ruth in the Old Testament.) Bev told her she was a member of The Church of Jesus Christ of Latter-Day Saints. V wanted to join, so she started reading The Book of Mormon Another Testament of Jesus Christ. Bev and V would meet once a year. On about the fourth yearly visit, V flew from her home on the East Coast all the way to California to see Bev and be baptized into the Church.

The Spirit was very much in attendance at V's baptism. I wish the Spirit was that strongly felt every day. I was to give a talk on the Holy Ghost. Just before the talk was to be given the Spirit informed me it would be more pleasing for Brad to sing than for me to talk. He had a particularly good voice, but more than that, his songs seemed to be sung to the Lord, and we got to listen too. I did not know if the Spirit had given the same understanding to Brad. I quickly walked over and asked him if he wanted to sing at the meeting. He said he had not prepared for that. (By the way, what a humbling thing for the Spirit to tell me just before I was to give a talk. Oh well, it seems that truth is its own servant.) I mentioned the impression from the Spirit to Brad. At the conclusion of the talk, Brad decided to sing. The Spirit was felt much stronger after his song.

After the song, something even more precious happened. (I hope there is someone like Brad in your church group when you are involved in a baptism, or anything else for that matter.) The Spirit very lightly touched my mind. It would have been easy to dismiss the light impression. Thankfully, I stopped and opened my mind and concentrated on listening. Then the Spirit placed an understanding in my mind concerning V. It was of a time in the distant future if they stayed on the path. She and Bev would be much older, both with white hair. They would meet at a house. The house would be filled with family and friends. People in the front yard, backyard, and in the house. It seemed like a quarter of the ward members were there. From old to infants and all the in-betweens. There was a little one running through the living room. There was a large man in the kitchen or nook with his strong good-natured laugh. Everyone there was excitedly happy. Bev and V stopped for a second and talked in a hall or somewhere like that.

V asked Bev, "Have all these come just to see us?" She then smiled knowing the guests had not. That day they were anxiously waiting for a visit from a relatively young apostle of the Lord. This apostle was one V had known and loved, and he had known and loved her. The family and friends had found out about the visit and decided today was a good day to visit this home.

I was thrilled at the tender scene that the Spirit had shared for the new member of the Church! The service was just about to close. I started to share the understanding with V. There was resistance when I started so I was not to share it at that time.

The next day in our ward Sacrament meeting, the bishop asked me to briefly share the story of V's conversion. I started to share the vision then, but I was led not to, resistance. V flew home and I shared the understanding with Bev. A few days later, V telephoned Bev. V had a dream. The dream was that V came to Bev's house. Bev greeted her, opened a screen door, and V walked into the house. They both were old with white hair. The dream ended at point. V did not know the meaning of the dream. Bev then related all the information the Spirit had given to the delight of both. Obviously, it was the will of the Spirit for V to have the dream before she was to hear the further information. Oh, how many ways our Lord shows His matchless love for us...

Prayer by Joshua. I was sick and in bed. Six-year-old Joshua had a captive audience and was talking to me. I know that Heavenly Father really loves him. At times, he has shown a surprising closeness to the Spirit. So, I asked Joshua to offer a prayer that I would be well. He did. At the end of his prayer, I was a little surprised, all the aches and pains were gone. I wondered if I was well, I remembered all the pains of seconds ago and they were gone. I thought I must be completely healed, and the next thought was I should get out of bed. I hesitated a few seconds to think about what had just happened. Then all the aches and pains came crashing back in a flood. I suspect that my faith failed when I did not immediately get right out of bed when the prayer was over, when I realized the aches and pains were gone. I felt fine but I did not immediately act, the act of faith. Plus, I did not offer a prayer of thanksgiving. So, I was left in worse condition than I was before the prayer.

Besides the aches and pains, I knew I had failed to achieve the health Joshua had asked for in faith. If I would have been more faithful, Joshua could have had a surprising spiritual experience. What a failure on my part, again. The next day, I explained the whole story to Joshua in the hope to salvage some of the experience for him, including the response to his prayer of faith and my lack of a faith filled act.

Not long after the last experience, in the evening we were ready for evening prayer and bed. I was not feeling well. With the last failure/teaching still vivid in my mind, I asked Joshua if he would ask Heavenly Father in his prayer that I would feel better in the morning. In his faith he did ask. In the morning,

I awoke to the alarm and immediately out of bed, feeling fine, and did not remember I was feeling bad that night until I was already out of bed. There was then time to offer a morning prayer of thanksgiving for the little one's faith and prayer and my good health.

Sacrament Meeting Prayer. It is rare where someone says something, and the Spirit simultaneously and strongly confirms the truth thereof. Mostly, I have experienced this when listening to or reading church conference talks and the scriptures. On occasions, the confirmation will happen when someone is speaking in a ward or stake meeting. Most often the manifestation is not a direct response to a few specific words but a general good feeling that accompanies part of or the entire talk or hymn. It is most rare where someone says something, and the Spirit confirms the truth by saying the same words at the same time. I do not fully understand it yet. The first time this happened was the experience hearing Brother Joseph give the King Follett sermon. (Previously discussed.) The second occurrence happened during a Sacrament meeting closing prayer in Rocklin, CA.

A recently returned missionary had just finished giving his homecoming talk. He shared some great experiences from his mission to a foreign country. Unfortunately, he was also caught with pride and had boldly pronounced his folly during his talk. The bishop sitting near the speaker let the untrue doctrine he asserted slide by, possibly disregarding the words as a folly of youth. A humble sister then gave a closing prayer to the Sacrament meeting. Her words carried a humble supplication of thanksgiving and request for the Spirit to attend us. She later mentioned something to the effect, we are thankful "our son" returned safely from his mission. The words were our son, or the son of every mother and father. Of course, the young man was not in the physical sense her son, but her nature made no distinction she was as thankful as if the young man was her own son, and in a larger sense our own son. What a powerful pronouncement of love. What a sublime pronouncement of unity and acceptance. The Spirit confirmed her words and more strongly confirmed the two word "our son."

To me, the effect of her two words and the operation of the Spirit was as if fireworks quietly went off. As is always the case when the Spirit strongly confirms something, my senses came to full alert and of focused attention. These were her words, but the Spirit confirmed the words at the same time, they were our Lord's words. The confirmation was as strong as her sounds, maybe more. It seemed as if God had spoken them. May God bless this humble sister. Both, she, and her husband were examples of humility that we sorely needed in that ward.

There is so much I have not said. There is so much doctrine I would like to share with you, but you do not need me for that. With your faith and intellect, you can have the joy of discovery and approach our Lord.

Family History. There are many things I have found out about my ancestors. Lots of the findings warm my heart and I feel a little closer to them. The way they loved their family and dealt with their life struggles gives me encouragement to try to be better. I will share only a couple stories.

Wesley Warner, my grandfather, told this story to me, in the twilight years of his life. My best guess is that this would have happened somewhere around the year 1916. Matthew took his young son, Wesley, salmon fishing. Smoked salmon was an important food storage for the coming winter in a tough Humboldt County of northern California. Mat and Wes had finished fishing and were walking a trail back to their home. (At that date, the local Indians were still being shot and killed when they were found alone. Mat was strongly opposed to the killings.) Two men with rifles were walking towards the river and confronted Mat and Wes. Mat knew the riflemen were looking for Indians to murder. They demanded Mat tell them if there were any Indians at the river. (Two Indian men had been fishing on the other side of the river from Mat and Wes.) Mat lied. He told them there were no Indians fishing at the river.

The two men knew Mat was against killing Indians and did not believe him. They said, "Matt, you are an Indian lover." The riflemen went on to the river.

Mat and Wes were now in fear for their lives and hurried up the trail and on home. Not long up the trail, two rifle shots rang out. The two Indian men had been murdered. Ten-year-old Wes saw them from the ridge. Law was late in coming to that area.

Law was important to my mother's side of the family also. My mother's, mother's, mother's, father was "Egbert" Williams from New York. As a youth, his father had died in the Civil War. Some years later, he became a lawman in Dodge City, Kansas. He later moved to Tombstone, Arizona and became a sheriff. He moved to Tombstone about the same time as his friend and fellow lawman Bat Masterson. Marshall Williams must have been thrilled when old friends and fellow lawmen Wyatt, Morgan, and Virgil Earp arrived. Shortly after the Earp's arrivals the Clanton gang did some more robbing and killing. Marshall Williams formed a posse with his old friends from Dodge City, the three Earp's, and Bat Masterson. They caught and arrested Luther King of the Clanton gang and the rest of that war is history... Law came late to Tombstone too, but it came. (More family history later.)

Maybe that was too much of my family. Your family is full of interesting ancestors just waiting to be rediscovered and recorded for family yet unborn. Please, spend some time recording the information your older family members can remember. With each passing, so much is lost to us left here and future generations.

Before this volume is closed, I want to share some things that help me to receive revelation from the Holy Spirit. First, receiving revelation is never a common or ordinary thing. In most respects I am common and ordinary, but never revelation. Inasmuch as we are all spirit children of the same Father, we are not ordinary at all. Our Heavenly and Eternal Father is God. Our Father loves us and is anxious to encourage and inspire us during our semi-blind mortality. Do we have a desire, deep within us, to be closer to the loving Father of our spirit, our Heavenly Father? Of course, we do. Then we should pray. Ask, seek, knock, remembering that in so doing we are approaching the Throne of God. And God said He will answer. So, we need to do it as humbly as we can. Our prayers reach God. It does not take long.

Further, God is all knowing. He lives with the past, present, and the future constantly in front of Him. He knew what would happen to us before we were even born. We are the ones being tested and learning here, not Him. We are away from Him, here on Earth, going through our mortal experience. How long has our loving Father yearned to hear us? Our prayer to Him is a great act of our faith in Him. Faith is powerful. What an irony that the great act of faith takes such little effort on our part. When we pray with sincerity and faith our prayer will be answered.

Prayer. Our prayer is a one-way communication. The response to our prayer is revelation, or the two-way communication. Do we see, hear, or feel His responses? It takes faith to send communication or in other words pray. It also takes faith to receive the divine communication. As I have shared with you, the return communication or revelation, takes many different forms. Seeing something with our natural eyes seems exceedingly rare. It can happen depending upon the will of our Lord. (The Heavenly man coming into focus with the first prayer at the school yard.)

Having words come, the same as we talk with each other seems rare also, depending on the will of the Lord. ("Of these make thy friends," "Thy sins are forgiven," "Look," and so on.)

Our hearts can burn within us. Luke, in third person, testified this form of revelation happened on the road as he and Cleopas walked with their Risen and unrecognized Lord.

CHAPTER 5

The Holy Ghost Just Keeps Teaching

On occasion, I take a problem to the Lord, in prayer. Before I do, if I have received an answer that has similar circumstances, I try to use that wisdom and apply it to this situation as much as possible. If there is no previously received wisdom, then I run through my memory of the teachings of the prophets, present and past, which includes the scriptures. If still nothing, then I try to make the best decision I can, and then take my decision to the Lord. Try to be calm and free from the trappings of this mortal world. I try to explain my reasons for making such a decision.

There are generally three types of responses I receive. If the answer is positive, most often I will receive a small warming or burning feeling in the center of my chest and sometimes a very calm and peaceful feeling. If the answer is negative, I generally go into a "stupor of thought." That means I lose the mental grasp of or forget the thing about which I am praying. Often, I try to concentrate harder and start the request/ prayer again. If my mind wanders again, despite my increased concentration, I know the answer is no.

The third type of response is, nothing now. I must wait and watch and think more on the subject and try to understand more and often wait some more, possibly stretching my faith, before I finally comprehend the answer. (Did I reason out my best response or action, or did I use enough thought on the subject? Did I do all I could to try to understand? If not, a non-response is my fault.) One thing I know for sure is that our Lord, through the Holy Ghost, is anxious to answer our prayers, but not more anxious than He is to teach us to learn and grow in the ways of Heaven.

There is another not now response that means this is an answer I should be able to figure out myself and the Lord has confidence I will be okay with it. I try to never give up on His answers, His answers always are given, according to His timetable, reason and will, not mine. It is important to want to do the Lord's will and be willing to do whatever He directs, whatever. It does not do any good to pray if we will not follow His promptings or if we will only follow a response we want. Sometimes, or maybe most of the time, His promptings are not too easy to follow. He wants us to change, to grow not just act.

My will is at times okay, other times it approaches good, other times not so good. His will is spectacularly and absolutely perfect/complete/finished, all the time and through all eternity. He has a complete understanding of the past, present, and future. He answers our prayers, knowing what is more than good or even better for us, He knows what is best, eternally. Whose direction that leads to which future do you choose…

If we want our will too much, we will probably not feel His answer. Whatever the answer is, it is the best for us, even if we do not understand the "why" for a long time. We must listen during and after we pray. On occasion the answer will come when I first start a prayer. Sometimes it takes long and concentrated prayer to receive an answer.

Some things will distract from our ability to feel or hear revelation. Obviously the "Thou Shalt Not" things will keep us insulated from the feelings of the still small voice, which is the promptings of the Spirit. Obviously, a bad attitude should be shed before prayer. Drugs, alcohol, tobacco, tea, coffee, and other similar things insulate us from feeling or hearing the Spirit of God. Another mentionable is thinking we are better than others - pride. Remember to be thankful, express it – tell Him, tell our wonderful and loving Heavenly Father. I have said too much, most all this you already know this or could have reasoned it out by yourself, sorry.

Holy Spirit. I have been tenderly blessed to have had many thousands of promptings from the Holy Ghost. What a wonderful Spirit. He shares wondrous things that lead me to better understand our Lord, His will, and ways. But the Holy Spirit shares nothing of Himself. Through my life the Holy Spirit has brought the love of our Lord to me during troubled times and good times. He has shown me how the Lord loves those close to me, thus encouraging me to better understand how much more I can and should love them. He has shared so much more. Thousands and thousands of times he has confirmed truth or error, or otherwise shared things with me.

Through all this, He still shares nothing of Himself. I do not even know his name. Several times, I requested to know His name. Of course, no response. He will not be sidetracked from teaching about Jesus. I have never found His will or His personality, it is always the will of our Lord Jesus that He shares, that is His will also. He embraces Father's will through Jesus so completely that nothing can cause Him to deviate from His task. He points the way and encourages us to seek and to know of our Great Jehovah. The Holy Spirit shows us with exactness the will of our Lord Jesus, nothing less, nothing more. He exposes the difference in the Lord's will and the doctrines of devil's as plain as day and night. Jesus teaches us how to live and how to be, little by little until we begin to understand that we have a perfect and loving Father in Heaven and His Son that is so much like Him and the differences from me and them. That difference is where my changes should be made. A life's work I will not succeed in accomplishing. But each step towards that goal is so important.

To me, the Holy Spirit is such a supreme example of absolute humility. Right now, He is probably a little concerned I am talking of Him instead of Jesus. And He is right, discovery for the sake of discovery is to miss the point. Jesus teaches us to be different, to be better, to be more like Him. As mentioned, I have asked the Spirit, several times, what His name is, and He dismisses this request to focus only on the things of Father through Jesus. What an example of humility.

Even though we can and do disregard the promptings of the Spirit, He is still constant in his availability and willingness to teach us the perfect word and will of our Lord, in every possible set of circumstances. Only if we do really bad things and disregard the promptings will we have too much trouble receiving His return communication. If that is the case, then there is some serious repenting to do. After all that has been written and said about Jesus, much of which is so confusing, who else should we believe and rely on to give us the absolute truth that ends all confusion, if not the Holy Spirit? The Spirit teaches us, point by point, line upon line, that Jesus is the Anointed One, the Christ, the Holy One of Israel, plus all else that is important. He is my, He is our Savior. His will and ways are the perfect example for us to learn from and follow.

As we follow the Lord's will, we will become unpopular in this mortal world. If we look around us and at history, we will not be alone in this status. Ironically, by following the teachings of Jesus, even the bad things that happen to us can turn to our instruction and benefit.

As we consider our life and future death, we can remember that our Lord has already broken the bands of death and stands as Lord of Lords not just here and now on Earth but in the eternities as well. We need only choose whom we will follow and be gathered by. Oh, if there were only words to share my love for and worship of our Heavenly Father, His only begotten Son Jesus our Christ, and our Holy Spirit...

I have shared with you some of my experiences. It is my hope and prayer that there is some little something somewhere in this volume that is an aid or encouragement to you in your journey and that the Spirit will confirm to you, truth. I hope we can all pray knowing, or at least strongly suspecting that every single word of our prayer is being anxiously received and processed by God. Our sincere prayers do not dissolve or disappear. They are recorded and kept. And further, as a result of our prayers He will change the future and all eternities for our benefit. Part of the great change will be to our nature and our will.

Jesus is not absent or preoccupied with other duties or interests. He is not alone in His work; the Holy Spirit is here for us. In our day, Jesus has sent prophets and apostles, Evangelists, teachers, and ministering angels to help us, as he did in days long past. Often, even most often He even enlists the obscure and average among us to help each other for His purposes.

Please remember, God is anxious to gather us, to love us, to teach us and to save us. We can approach Him in prayer. He will hear and answer our prayer. Will He accept us as we learn and see the need to repent and draw closer to Him? Of course, He will. As we learn of Him, we cannot help but love Him. He loved us first. I hope that our faith will not be in each other, no matter what the status that a person holds.

I have mistakenly thought more of individuals than I should have only to be disappointed. I have never been rightfully disappointed in God.

Most Grateful. I am for the opportunity to share this work with you. Sharing some of these experiences is like explaining a great painting using only crayons. At times words are so inadequate to share some things from God. This inadequacy is all made up and more when the Holy Spirit confirms truth, as we receive absolute truth, at least a small bit at a time. But now I must return to the second mission given to me so long ago. If I have breath left in this body, it will always be the time for me to try to stop the slide away from the governmental principles that God inspired. Evil is seeking to take full control of the nations of the Earth to try to frustrate the will of God as the second coming of the Lord approaches. But in the end God wins and I hope we will all be on his side. But so many will not be on his side, I am heartbroken to say.

It is my hope that in the future we will choose representatives not rulers. Representatives follow the principles that inspired the American Revolution that made us the first free people in modern time. Great wisdom was given us in our God-inspired Constitution. I have seen many politicians want to bend, twist, or even break our God-inspired Constitution and the principles that it represents. It is my hope when our Lord comes, we will be found defending God's principles. When the great tribulations come and so many want evil practices instead of His will (Is that now?), will we be deceived and persuaded that bad is good and good is bad? We do not need to wait to see Him coming in the clouds of glory for us to bow our knee and give great thanks for His return. We do not have to wait for Jesus to be our law giver to follow His great Will. We can hope and pray and have faith to follow Him and repent of our sins to strive and search and study to know Him… Until we meet in this life or the next. May God continue to bless you.

This is the end of the experiences I was going to share in this book. There are some experiences that seemed too hallowed to share. So, a line was drawn on what to share and what not to share. After further review, I was persuaded to redraw the line adding these following experiences.

Some family and friends, from time to time, bring a dream to me to help in understand the meaning. Most often I have no idea what they mean, until I ask for help from God. There is a process to follow to receive the meaning of dreams. I will share the process I use a little later.

Driving past the temple in American Fork, Utah had daily taken me by a hospital specifically for those that were severely handicapped. So often I would see them being transported in their wheelchairs in a group caravan outing during good weather. There were prayers for them. Finally, with a plan, God was asked if He would allow some or all of them to be healed completely or at least to have their condition improved. The request was, would God allow me to go and heal, to His glory. A touch to a shoulder a hand or top of the head should be all that was needed if God would allow the request. Further, I mentioned that Father knew my heart and my faith and with His aid and if it was His will this could happen. (Please do not think I was asking for anything more than to be a weak and anonymous servant for our glorious God.)

Further, let me share... I and possibly all of us, covenanted, before I ever came to Earth, that during this life, I would not remember the life with God before this mortality, our pre-mortal existence. So, you do not think I am breaking my covenant, the Holy Spirit opened this memory. During the supplication, a memory was opened. The memory was of a brief part of our life with God before this mortality.

There was a huge number of us sitting on gently rolling hills. We were all spaced near, about two feet from each other with just enough room for Father (Our Heavenly and Eternal Father) to walk between each one of us as He taught us individually. Though there were vast numbers of us there we all knew Father would spend time with each of us individually, so we left room between each other so Father could come to each of us. We all wore white robe type clothes. It seemed we looked and felt fresh and young, an equivalent to here, of late twenty or early thirty something. But we were fully grown and incredibly old if this earth time could be used to measure time there. What a contrast to here, we were young and fresh and very aged. We were all brothers and sisters, but our attention was not on each other. We did not look at or talk with each other, we did not want to miss a word or expression of Father as He taught. We were anxiously listening to God, our Father.

He was so patiently teaching us His great will. As He spoke to one, we all accepted His wisdom as pertaining to each of us individually. Here He was teaching us about our earth lives to come. He would speak to one of the specifics of the next life in great detail, then move to the next one of us and do the same. We could all hear Him, even when He was far away. As His walk and teaching brought Him closer, I was even more thrilled.

He was in conversation and teaching a young woman, our sister, not far from where I sat. She was one of the great ones, she had progressed far more than most of us. They were a little to my front left, only about fifty or so feet away. The teaching was about how her life would affect her earthly family. We were being told about and discussing our future, with so many possibilities that it held, long before it would be lived by us.

Then the discussion progressed to what the consequences to her and the rest of her earthly family would be if she accepted a position of serious restriction of her mortal body. (Severely handicapped.) In her family the members could progress to a greater state of love, compassion, and humility because of their service to her needs... It seemed there would be pride affecting them during mortality, a serious obstacle to their successfully overcoming their mortal weaknesses. That pride would only flower when they/we were out of His presence.

After some length of Father sharing His great and complete wisdom the instruction was complete as to so many possible choices of her mortality. Because of her love for those that would be her earthly family, she chose a life with a severely restricted body. This would be so serious for her but of great aid to her family.

I am impetuous here in mortality. In this memory I found out I was impetuous there also. However, to a much more restrained degree there due to our tremendous respect we had for our Father.

After Father was finished teachings our young and very advanced sister, I ask for and received Father's attention. Then I asked if I could also have a similar circumstance for my mortality. (Briefly stated) Father in a most loving and instructive manner called me by name, and then He called me by name a second time. He smiled knowingly at me and started patiently explaining that my sister of the previous instruction was one of the great ones. She had progressed further than me (and most all of us). She had learned so much. Consequently, this upcoming mortal life with all the choices and resulting consequences was more important for me so that I could grow from those experiences.

Did I remember His teachings to me, that I would have so many and varied experiences that were most necessary for me to progress through? There were weaknesses in me that would not flower until I was in mortality, away from His presence. These weaknesses were to be lived and overcame in mortality, something that would not be as possible with a severely restricted mortality. The life experiences could change those weak parts of my nature I could not yet fully understand. As Father taught us individually, He was teaching us all collectively. This is where the memory was closed.

I have never looked at one in a wheelchair who could barely talk and move, the same way after this gift was given to me, to us.

Finally, I better understand, in a small way this lesson. Away from and without a direct memory of Father's glorious and joyous presence, I can be tempted and given the opportunity to choose between good and evil. There are those that will share their God-given experiences that may be an aid and encouragement to draw us closer to our Father and His Son and the Holy Spirit. Of course, the choices are clouded by those saying there is no God. There are those calling good evil and evil good, as well as those with flowery words trying to confuse and convince us to do those things that inhibit our ability to recognize and choose good over bad.

For sure, we have our free will to choose, and if we have done bad things our Lord Jesus is available to teach us to repent, be baptized, and receive His forgiveness and change from our fallen nature. For me, the greatest miracle, the miracle of the atonement, is offered by Jesus to all who recognize they are fallen and seek salvation from Him!

We discussed baptism. Jesus was baptized, not because of sin, He had none, but because He was leading by example. After repentance and baptism, we are washed clean. Being fallen humans, we still fumble in our attempts to follow our Lord, we sin. For that we can repent and every week, take the sacrament, to repent, to always remember him, to keep his commandments so we can be forgiven of our folly. Each week we can review the previous days and repent and start again. As we try, with our prayers for His help we can slowly (for me) or even rapidly (for others) follow his will and change our fallen nature to a better. Each Sabbath we can start again and by the force of our faith in and association with Jesus and His forgiveness, we can be different, a little at a time. What a great plan for us with the extended "start over" opportunity.

This life is short, and we will not overcome all. But as we repent and make Jesus our treasure, we can have faith in asking for Him to make up for those parts of our lives that fall short and apply His grace to our life choices and save yet another.

By the way, Jesus gave us the example to be baptized. He went to John, someone who had the authority to baptize. Besides His example, did He tell us to be baptized? Will we not follow His example and His words? In the next life, what will be our excuse when we are asked why we were not baptized...

A brother in a priesthood class in Utah County was complaining and upset because one late and very cold and snowy winter night while driving back to his home, his car hit a deer. Consequently, the serious damage to his car caused that he had need of help. He did not receive help from other motorists that just drove by without stopping or calling for assistance. As he had expected help from the other motorists and received none; he had anger. He shared his experience in a church meeting the next Sunday. From that time on, his anger continued to increase each week. I did not understand the severity of his bitterness and went in prayer to inquire.

The prayer for more information about the incident was framed poorly, that is, that the question I was attempting to ask was why he was so bitter. But the words were: can I have some more information about this incident? The Spirit answered the prayer and give me much more information than I expected. The prayer about the hawk, that I asked as a ten-year-old and the answer I received is still so very valid as a prayer guide. God deals in specifics and specific meaning in the words we use in prayers.

A wonderful understanding came to my mind in a vision. I was given a brief glimpse of a glorious and exalted Man sitting on His throne. I was about a hundred feet away, or maybe a little less, on His right side. The view was somehow filtered and not crystal clear, I suspect this was the case to allow me to see in an area that was probably incredibly bright, filled with the fire of His glory. The throne on which He set was a large chair not overly ornate. The throne was sitting on a raised floor about sixteen inches higher than the rest of the floor. The raised dais was in a circular configuration about twelve feet in diameter with a type of handrail atop small supports. The height of the handrail was below His shoulders and near chest height to those that were called before Him. There was an opening in the handrail in front of his throne. This glimpse was of the recent past, given in black and white. There were many glorious and exalted people, probably ministering angles surrounding Him. They all stood twenty or so feet back from the railing, anxiously waiting to be called.

This glorious Man, in a conversational manner, acknowledged a specific man. The one selected eagerly went to accept instruction. The one selected was told Ed (that is not his real name) would be driving his car home on a late night of a specific date, time, and location. The time given was soon. It was further explained Ed would hit a deer with his car and the accident would be of such violence Ed would die. There would be resulting consequences to his family... Because of Ed's wife and children, circumstances were going to be changed. The one chosen was instructed to go the point of the future accident and be ready to reduce the severity and consequences of that late night's accident. Ed should not die at this time... The glorious servant, or angel, went and did as he was instructed. The severity of the accident was changed. Ed did not die, nor did he know someone changed the natural course of the accident. This was where the vision closed.

Despite all that had happened, Ed somehow became bitter at the lack of help from the passing motorists that night. The irony was thick, as he was completely unaware and consequently not thankful for what was done for him that night. His life continued with his family...

May all glory and thankfulness be given to God. His glorious will and ways are extended to us here in our mortality even if we do not understand them.

It was somewhat interesting it was not because of Ed that the natural events and consequences were altered. It was stated, because of his wife and children, the natural events and consequences were altered.

When I finished the second draft of this book, many years ago, I was sitting in front of the computer. The end of the book at that time did not include all these extra additions and was only about one third of what it is now. But it was the end of the book then. There were still spelling and punctuation errors in the book, as well as unclear areas, but all the writing was generally complete. This work was done, ready to share with others, as so many others have shared with me, what they had learned of God's will and ways. Further, I was directed to share the experiences, as the experiences were not given just for me, but to all who would hear or read them, if they so choose. So, the feeling was a little thankful that the work was getting accomplished. Then, most unexpectedly, I sensed God; He was facing toward me; His attention was directed at me, and He took a step towards me. Although he was still a great distance away, somewhere to the south, on Earth. He took another step in my direction. Of all the other experiences of my life, the closest that I ever felt to God was quickly passed by this present experience of God approaching. This new closeness surpassed the other experiences by about four times. There was nothing in my past that was much of a reference to His presence this time. I was weakly sitting in a chair at the computer table. There was a sensation as if a great tide of His glory, presence, and majesty washed over me in increasing intensity. A great wave of his glory would pass through the room. The wave was of spiritual matter; it was a great wave like in a circular ripple in a pond, but this was great in size and was passing through the entire neighborhood, possibly recognized by few or maybe only one. The wave started from Him in the south. Shortly thereafter, another wave of increased intensity would rapidly wash through the room heralding His interest. About four of these waves left me extremely overwhelmed. I did not have the strength or presence of mind to get out of the chair and kneel before my Savior's distant approach and attention.

Although still at a great distance away, He was close, and I was not so insulated from His glorious presence. I do not know if I could have survived any additional waves of the increasing intensity of His glory. He accepted this work, as far as it was completed at that time, as weak and feeble as it was, and is because of my involvement, He accepted this frail and unworthy work.

It is my hope that you see all these experiences are and should be your experiences as well as mine. As the Holy Spirit confirms the truth of what you read, the experience becomes yours as well as mine, ours together. In such a small way, I am trying in this work to share/proclaim His love, His will, and His glory! His love, His will, and His glory forever and ever, worlds without end...

Trials for Joshua in His Youth. Some local church teachers and leaders turned aggressively hostile to our youngest son, Joshua. (Since then, we have an even younger son, Luke.) Other ward and stake leaders seem to be without courage, you know, that path of least resistance that leads to crookedness like rivers and other stuff, where some say – your cause is just but I can do nearly nothing for you. This has happened with some regularity to Joshua for age eleven to age fifteen. Finally, we left that ward. (This was all I was going to share on this topic. However, there is much more I will now add, as directed by the Holy Ghost.)

Most of the pain is gone as I share this. The hostile treatment of such a wonderful young man is still appalling. Most of the perpetrators were still unrepentant at my last contact with them. I hope they reconsider their actions and repent and not carry those bad acts into the next life.

To be brief – Joshua as an eleven-year-old made the mistake of correcting a couple primary teachers that would get the Old Testament prophets mixed up in their lessons. Joshua and I studied the scriptures every evening for years and he had a surprising understanding, especially of the Old Testament. After one class, he mentioned how upset the teachers were at his correcting comment. One of the teachers was a high priest and the other an elder. From that point, the high priest started becoming more hostile to Joshua as time went on. Joshua and I reviewed the circumstances and he decided not to make any more comments in the class.

The hostility increased with time. Finally, I had a meeting with the teachers, and the elder was apologetic, while the high priest stated he had the right to treat Joshua the way he wanted. Discussions with the local leader produced a "oh well" response. Soon after, as a twelve-year-old Joshua was with a new class of young men, things became worse as a couple of the young men in the group were the two most filthy students in his junior high school. (One was a son of a local leader.) The new leaders became overly aggressive as Joshua did not want to participate in scouting activities where the two were allowed to "run wild."

Briefly, several past leaders tried to push Joshua out of the church. I will skip much and give just one more group… The youth went to the temple to do baptisms. The two took small music players with headphones. While in the temple, they were listening to the filthiest music! Joshua would have nothing more to do with the group. The leaders started telling the other students Joshua was unworthy to be around and would laugh and point at him as he passed the Sacrament. The area leader told us he could do nothing, so go find another ward and attend there…

Well, there are pages more, but you have a flavor of what went on.

As his parents we were fighting mad at the acts of the "leaders." But the real concern for us was what this had done to Joshua. Would he leave the church, or become aggressive against the leaders and his fellow students who told him he was "unrighteous" because their leaders told them that he was?

Since he was put up a grade, he was a young seventeen when he graduated high school and went off to a university and escaped some of the trials.

Well, not much good so far. The trial was so harsh I missed some of what was happening. Only years later can I look back and understand, at least a little. The Lord said he will have a tried people. That means more to me now. Although we have endured many trials, the trials of our children hurt us more, much more.

The Lord speaking to Joseph Smith during some of his worst trials and to all of us said things like, all these things will give thee experience and these trials will be but a short time.

Joshua has passed through some extreme trials as a young man. As more things happen in his life, he can use these as a reference and see that he can endure and overcome filth and evil, while trying not to be infected with the wrong. Do not give too much of your thoughts to the bad of the past, let it stay in the past and live in the present and know that difficult times will pass as we choose to follow our Savior. Have patients and forgive and let go of the bad that happens. Jesus has already paid the price of all sin, what we must do is try not to be the cause of the hurt and forgive those that do and move on in learning of and following our Savior. I know it is easier said than done. But being unforgiving is cancerous. Plus, when the trials come to you, will you walk away from the Church and learning about Jesus? If so, they win, not you.

Disappointing Experiences. Several times I went in prayer and asked if I need to continue to study religion and the associated concept of government which directly relate to my second mission. As mentioned earlier, my study of living oracles and the scriptures has been exhaustive, coupled with unreasonably high expectations I place on myself. Further, some church, and most government leaders, have led me to great disappointment and sadness. I expect too much of too many, mostly myself. I cannot accomplish the second mission without help. I cannot recognize any mortal help to date, but serious resistance is always there not far away. That, in itself, is a tell. I should be much more patient. However, I am old… I further suspect some who live by a greater faith than me and live with few or no visions and such might say, "Stan, what is wrong with you? You are blessed so richly. Now quit whining. Go do the second mission without any help, if that is the circumstance."

Here is where I kick myself.

Some evenings later, a vision... In the vision I was sitting down, in a disappointed mood, a man came to me and sat next to me. It seemed as there was a slight haze or fog around us as I could not see him clearly. Couple that with the fact my sight did not stare directly at him. An understanding was placed in my mind that he was an apostle. No name was given. It was easy to sense he was a great one. He was ancient in his presence and wisdom. Further, at the same time and in contrast he was fresh or new in his voice, form, and energy, though he was very patient in his task. He knew me, of my calling (the work I should yet attempt to do), and of my recent serious disappointments. He briefly informed me I was to continue the study. My calling or task was in the future. I would need the additional wisdom that will be given, some of which will be given during my studies. There was an additional concept I did not understand previously and, for some reason, he did not share it at that time.

In the next few days, I aggressively went back to the studies. Within that week, while listening to conference talks, the Holy Ghost took my attention away from the recorded talk and explained that during the time in study seeking wisdom from God, besides placing myself in a position the Holy Ghost could aid me beyond my own limited ability to gather wisdom, often by highlighting a word or phrase for me to pay extra special attention to...besides the learning process, there was another activity at work. The choice to continue to learn more about God and placing myself, ready and anxious to learn, near the source of new or different wisdom, is of itself a second process. That second process is one that is humbling to the soul and molds one's nature into a more teachable or humble being. By the force of regular and prolonged association with higher wisdom/life we take on some of that difference... (Please, no laughing. Maybe everyone on Earth understood that concept but me, but it was discovery for me and maybe for another someone somewhere.) Let there be no misunderstanding, I have far to go in this changing of my nature...and every aid is welcome. All praise and glory belong to our God! Who is like Him in wonders and miracles, love and compassion, forgiveness and wisdom, mercy and justice and grace!

A couple more experiences and I will close.

A Man Named Joseph F. Smith has given us a wonderful glimpse into the next life. He saw and recorded a vision of the good place where people who were obedient to God's teachings go after this life. It is a beautiful and even stunning view of what the next life is for so many who have made the life choices that led them closer to our Savior and Redeemer, our God. And, of course, repented of the bad choices and acts, plus baptism and receiving the Holy Ghost. This is not to be the final destination, but the next step in our trek through the eternities. It is recorded and available for all to read and study in Section 138 of the Doctrine and Covenants.

The Dark Place in the Next Life. I will share something, so much less than Joseph's vision, that covers what his vision did not give too many details about. This is a rapid vision given during the day, so many years ago. I was leaving after a Sacrament meeting and someone said something to me; I do not remember what the comment was exactly. Then the vision opened.

It is of the area where the disobedient and unrepentant go after this life. This is not the final life destination where they/we will be assigned. It is the temporary holding facility, so to speak. It has been called "spirit prison." The word "prison," meaning confinement, is correct, but to me the word seems to also carry a meaning of harshness, that is why I am not using it.

In the vision I was standing among vast, vast numbers of people. We had all passed through the mortal life, so we did not have the physical bodies that were left when we died. We were only spirit as we were before we were born into mortality, but we still looked the same.

Light does not work the same there as here. The light was low, much like the darkness a little after twilight. There were people standing every two to maybe eight feet apart. This massive place was full, stuffed with people. But it was hard for them to see each other until they got pretty close to each other, maybe four to five feet away, especially if you wanted to see their faces and maybe recognize someone you knew. To do that, you had to be about three feet away. The light from Christ was not bright here. They were waiting…

Most all were walking around; many were talking to someone near to them. Somehow there were no language barriers. Much of the discussion was about their past mortal life, when they lived, what family they had, how they died, what they believed, and what they did to deserve to be there in this darkened area. Their concern about their past unrepentant disobediences or ignorance were major concerns as they understood it was their acts or lack thereof that placed them there. No one there questioned the fairness or reasons they were in the dark holding place. It was because they did not follow the eternal rules of life during their brief mortal probation/trials, or they did not hear about Jesus and his Gospel. The rules were what God/Jehovah/Jesus had decreed and shared with us during our probation. The rules or directions were abundantly shared with us during our mortal life by our conscience, promptings from the Holy Ghost or His ministering angels, prophets, good words, or good examples, warnings from parents, neighbors, and friends, the Scriptures, and on and on. All here recognized the true reasons they were here. There was no self-deception here as we use in mortality to try to justify or hide our disobedience. There were no mistakes in our placement here. However, there still is hope here, at least for some that were not the severe offenders.

Those here were from the earliest disobedient and unrepentant descendants of Adam and Eve's children to the recently passed from mortality. It was almost overwhelming in sadness as to how many were here.

For some reason, I could see an incredibly long distance, the vast area was all full of people with their spirit bodies. To my right, about 200 feet away, was an opening or trench, deep in the ground. It was maybe fifty feet across. All knew about it, that it was not to be crossed or even entered. In our mortality, many would investigate and even try to cross such a thing. Not here. The rule was absolute, none questioned, none argued. No one even went close to the gulf or gulch or abyss or whatever name you want to use. It was empty of light. If someone went into it there was no way out, that I know of. It was one of the boundaries to the confinement.

Being here carried a feeling something like being under water.

On the other side of the gulf was an incline in the ground, gently rising as a hill to the elevation of about 300 to 400 feet above our level. On top of the hill was a flat area or plateau of unknown size. I could not see past the edge, but somehow, I knew what was there. It was full of light. In the mortal world that amount of light would have illuminated this lower level also, but not here. Here light had different rules that it followed. The repentant and obedient of God, during mortality, were there. I could not see them as they were not standing near the edge of the hill. The surprising thing was the light. That area was full of light, the light was brilliant almost yellow/white, like fire. This light was the only color I could see in this vision, all the rest was shades of gray, dark gray, and some darker. (All the clothes they wore here were dark grayish.) But the action of the light was the surprise. The light stopped at the downslope of the hill and went up in an elevation to who knows how high. Everyone here could somehow see or knew of the light and knew the type of people that were there.

Everyone here knew why we were here, for some sort of disobedience to God not repented of in mortality. No one was going around complaining about the placement; we knew there was no lack of God's love for us. There was His love and justice in our temporary placement as there will be in our placements for the eternities, the Eternities. How incredibly sad, even tragic, in that we all had the opportunity to follow our conscience and God's teachings to some extent. Those that did not receive much information about God during mortality would receive it here.

Despite all this the love of God was known and felt here. A little more on this later.

Directly in front of me, less than a quarter mile away, was a bridge or causeway type of ramp. It started on top of the hill and crossed the abyss and had some supports holding it as it gently sloped down to our level. It was about 400 yards or so in length. Those at this level were not allowed on the bridge. There was not any trying to cheat or sneak onto the bridge. There were no bridge guards. Rules here were rules and they were obeyed without question. I could see the walkway clearly. There were people on it. It was easy to see them. They were enveloped in light. That light went a short way out from them and stopped. They were like walking candle lights as they crossed the bridge. Each was coming here to teach an assigned person about Jesus and his Gospel. God's love for us was not finished, He has more, so much more for all of us. That was the end of the vision.

Praise to our Glorious God! God is Great. ALL PRAISE TO OUR GLORIOUS GOD! His work and glory and mercy and justice are by no means even close to being finished!

I understood those who were crossing the walkway from the light to the darkness were servants of Jesus. Joseph F. Smith shared much with us of his vision of the area of light. Jesus had the area of light organized for so many reasons and for so many things to do.

These servants were crossing the bridge to meet with us, here in the darkness. They would come here and teach the specific person they were assigned, about Jesus. The Holy Ghost can probably share with you more of the feelings of those here as they journey in the dark area.

Just a little comment, there are different degrees of glory for all of us to be placed into for the **eternities**. The lowest degree is still a degree of glory, a good place, compared to our present mortality. But it pales in comparison to the middle kingdom and that kingdom pales in comparison to the celestial kingdom where the faithful and repentant will spend the **eternities** with God the Father and His Son, Jesus, doing majestic and wonder filled things through the eternities.

Soon hereafter I will discuss a view of one of the cities of the lowest kingdom of glory on a different planet. That huge city full of some of the best known of this life, that were so disobedient to so many things. There will be peace and order there, they will be presided over by the meek and humble followers of Jesus.

Another irony is the ones who preside over them will be among those persecuted by them in mortality. The greatness of the Father and the Son and the Holy Ghost will light the eternities, worlds without end.

Raul (Not his real name) was my closest friend in Vietnam. He died shortly after I returned home. I prayed for over forty years to know why one of the very best of us was allowed to die in that rotten war. As I have said many times, God has answered all my prayers. This answer took so many prayers, and over forty years before I received a full answer. It will be easy for you to know why it took so long. The same concept was involved as with V and sharing the vision with her only after she had the dream.

Here I had to have and understand the vision of the spirit holding area of darkness, which we just reviewed, before I could understand what happened to Paul. Paul was killed in action towards the end of 1970, shortly after I left Vietnam. One of his great traits was, I suspect he looked at most everyone as his spiritual brother or sister from a Heavenly Father. Everybody really liked Raul and he liked them first. It was finally shared with me that Paul was called home early from mortality to go to the good assembly place, the place of the bright light as one of the good, repentant, and obedient.

There were between two and four million Vietnamese killed during the US involvement there, both combatants and civilians, plus all those that died in the previous French war there. Raul was called home, out of this mortal life. He was assigned, as many others were, to go to some of those who died in that war. As they would discuss their mortality, Raul would have a strong association with them from the moment he shared with them the truth he had died in that war also. They would have a common death that would help bond them and they would more readily listen to Raul discuss the glorious and majestic Jesus and His plan for them to be happy with their families through the eternities.

It should be noted that we carry our personalities, experiences, unrepentant weaknesses, sins, and so much more into the next life. Just as God will force no one here in mortality to believe in Him, in the next life the same rule applies. Raul will be one of those lights that cross the gulf to visit those in the darkness. Those with different and strongly held misconceptions here in mortality will carry them there to the darkness. Raul's bond with them will make it easier for them to hear and understand the love and will of Jesus that Raul will share with them. That teaching from Raul will help them move to the next stage of their trek through the eternities of God's will.

Future Cities in Future Kingdoms in the Next Life. I will share just one more short experience. Please remember the account recorded in New Testament in the book of Luke, of the talents or pounds and the cities. My oldest son, David, has shared several of his dreams with me. Part of this explanation comes from one of his dreams. There are many different things that will happen during our movement through the eternities. This is of a specific time not the complete journey.

In the future, a time past that of the dark holding area discussed earlier, there is a large city of many cities in the lowest of the three kingdoms of glory, still a good place as a result of the Grace of God. It is populated with so many individuals. There are so many here, they were some of the unrepentant, rebellious, and disobedient in mortality, that are assigned here. Even so our Great Savior decreed this place to be good place, although less so than the other two more increasingly obedient kingdoms. The pains here are self-inflected. Each individual here, at least in the back of their thoughts, is to some extent distressed they are not in a much more advanced kingdom, as an eternal consequence of their mortal life choices. Each had the opportunity to choose better, but they did not. Each could have followed God or at least followed their conscience. That gnashing of teeth phrase is descriptive to help explain their early arrival condition, until they appreciate the great Grace of God that gave them this good eternal existence.

The large city is full of the unrepentant, through the ages, that had been in great disregard or maybe something a little less than hatred, for Jesus, His teachings, and His will.

This time is in the distant future. Time being more for us in mortality than for use in the eternities. This was mentioned or even possibly explained but probably not completely understood as recorded in the book of Luke (cities). I had been assigned to preside over this city for a time. I was to share my love and understanding of Jesus and His will with the citizens of this city. I will not name some of those that were there, but it is not too hard to reason. **Some had well recognized names across the world, from politics, entertainment, business, and so on. In mortality, they stood in opposition of God's will and ways. Yes, some boldly assisted in and supported the killing of the unborn...sexual perversion...grind the face of the poor and workers...kill...lie...steal...pull others away from Jesus to false gods of this world. They were politically correct so to speak as they tried to tear down the US Constitution and the principles that it stands for, that was God's loving gift to foster freedom in the world and so on and so on... They stayed unrepentant in mortality.**

I see some of them in our time, on TV and on the news spewing their dogma that comes from evil spirits. I wish I could meet with them and beg them to reconsider and repent of what they are trying to teach others with their doctrines of devils. Oh, if they could see themselves in the future and what they are giving up there for their disobedience here. Is abortion, pride, money, power, taking from workers the bread they have earned, forcing government rule over the families, and of course trying to replace Jesus' love for us with a forced woke doctrine of devils.

If this offends you and you hate me, I am sorry for that. However, the eternities are coming, and I will endure your hate for the opportunity to share this saga with you and I pray and hope you will turn from hate and seek Jesus and you will not end up in the lowest kingdom for the eternities. **Especially because Jesus is not there**. Please...please...you have my faith, hope, prayers, and my tears that are now blurring my sight for the unrepentant. Please?

All there that hated Jesus, His will, and ways, to some degree as they followed the influence of evil spirits, and the doctrine of devils...

They were unrepentant...

Is it that hard to see, hear, feel, and know good from evil and repent when we are wrong?

On this future day, my son and others had traveled across a vast distance through space to be there on that distant planet for a special day. It was my turn to be released from this duty of representing Jesus in presiding over this city to go on to other things. My son asks me how some specific former world politicians and other former celebrities were progressing. I mentioned to him that there was not much change in them.

There was a good man who had lived in Idaho during his life that was going to assume my former position. There was a brief gathering to celebrate the change and most importantly to give glory to our Redeemer for His constant love for all of us. My son was talking to the new leader of that large city. He asked the new leader what was he going to do with the ones I had mentioned who were not progressing or doing well. The new leader said he had "some ideas." That is the end of that view of that point in the eternities.

Years later, I live in Idaho and wonder if I knew this new leader, or if he even lived during the same time as me. I suspect he does.

As before, I was going to be finished with this book now, but maybe there should be some more added. My hope is that by adding some more experiences someone, somewhere, will be encouraged in their desire to learn more about our Savior, Jesus the Christ. Although, I do realize there will be serious hate generated in some. I am so sorry for this by-product. For those that hate, please remember I am nothing extraordinary beyond you that read this volume. I am only your brother here in mortality. Yes, I am your brother in Christ.

Dreams. For the past decade and more, family members and some friends have brought their dreams to me to be interpreted. I will share with you how this has been accomplished. There is a process to be followed, at least for me.

First, you must be humble and not think you are anything special, better than anyone else. You may think that this part is hard. Well, this part may be a bit easier than you may think if you recognize that you are ordinary, as I, in most respects.

The dreams come most often in the form of a parable or metaphor that has been given them for their benefit, to help them with something or add to their understanding of some part of this life. So, they tell you the dream. They are counting on you, hoping. You really want to help them with the interpretation.

However, at first you do not know and cannot by yourself know the meaning of the dream. This gives you such a sinking, helpless, and very humble feeling, very humble. Plus, you do not want to appear dumb or as a pretender. Though compared to our Lord, I am so very dumb. That understanding is so very humbling.

The process continues by asking for help. But, asking is not enough, you have some work to do before the request for aid is going to be answered. Clear your mind of the stuff of this life. Then listen and feel closely to the words giving meaning to the dream, remember God deals in the exact meaning of words, as previously discussed. Open your mind for any doctrinal relationships from the words and any parts of the dream to concepts that God teaches. **Ask** in prayer for **permission** to be an aid to the person with the dream to help them, to be a small part of Thy will in this circumstance. Be confident that the way you live is in harmony with God's commandments and live in the faith that the Holy Ghost is anxious to answer if we are living those ways that are pleasing to Him.

Remember that a ministering angel probably gave them the dream and we are aiding them in understand something God seemingly gave to their subconscious. So, we are only trying to aid in bringing the meaning to the conscious awareness.

Sometimes it takes all this, sometimes the understanding comes very soon as I clear my mind, and sometimes the understanding comes as I hear the dream, word by word. On occasion, I must use more faith. After some time of following this process, I must open my mouth and start giving the interpretation even though I may not understand all the meaning yet.

This is the hardest way to do the work. I start speaking not knowing what I will say, I must just start speaking from an open mind and let the Holy Ghost supply the words. If it is the hardest path, as I speak the interpretation comes, both of us learn the meaning at the same time. Sometimes, for complicated dreams, I ask the dreamer to start at the beginning again and I share the meaning a little at a time. I share a little of the understanding at a time, not knowing where the interpretation is going until the last. I need to a remember, it is not my dream. God sent it and He must share the understanding if it is to be of value to the receiver, at least of at a conscious value. Sometimes the dream is so complicated we take a part at a time and after we have all the parts, we piece them together to see the overall picture.

Generally, the dream is of more worth to the receiver, where it can be more fully understood given the persons present mortal awareness. So, the Holy Ghost, or an angel speaking for the Holy Ghost, must be sought and permission must be given to find a reference to the dream. They are the closest ones that have the understanding, and they are anxious to share it with us if we will follow our faith to the source of all wisdom. So, ask permission to receive the interpretation. Ask to be a helper, to the glory of the Father and the Son, Jesus, and the Holy Ghost. Be aware and not be tempted to accept any praise for the help! The help is from God, not from us.

There are dreams sent from above and dreams that are bad. The dreams are easily recognizable as to their source. Dismiss the bad dreams with your prayers for His help and love. Sometimes I have had to struggle awfully hard to dismiss my bad dream in progress. Do not keep thinking about bad dreams and get depressed or deceived.

Publishing this book, or at least trying to, has not been pleasant. For years having no success in publishing this book is only part of the story. Just one example is, while working in downtown Salt Lake City, I took a preliminary copy of this book to a large publishing company for their review in hopes of getting them to publish it. Sometime later, I was notified to come to a meeting at their office. There, I was told they were not interested in this work, and I felt some contempt from them for me even attempting to get their help. As I was leaving, one of the staff boldly declared, "Since your experiences are so much like Joseph Smith's, why don't you go start your own church?"

Yes, from time to time there is hate. Beyond that, and even worse, I must deal with my own disappointment and inadequacy with not being able to better explain and record these many experiences, plus handle the lack of success in disseminating of this work that God has given me. I need help and more patients, but mostly I need a new and better heart.

Early this morning, I realized that more should be shared in this writing.

I try to be brief, sometimes maybe I have been too brief, and not sharing enough details.

K. This is a short glimpse of a future point of a dear friend. But first a little background. K was one of the best I ever met. She had progressed much here, and she really loved. She admitted being a "stinker" when she was young and changing her nature much. I have heard it said that love is the beginning, middle, and end of the road to discipleship. That love from K was shared in abundance with my wife, Beverly, and our middle son, Joshua. A big personality was used to spread her understand of Jesus and her love for all. For a couple years, we lived close to her and her special husband. We would get together often on Friday nights along with others in the neighborhood. Each gathering was always special. We moved far away and would still correspond. But we still miss those Friday evening socials that were held at our house.

She contracted cancer.

Being in Utah on business, I went to see them. She said, according to the doctors, she only had a couple months left in this life. So, they were putting things for that time.

The Spirit whispered to me that the timing was wrong. It was shared with them K would live with the cancer, but she would have several years, not a couple months. Being the special person, she was, she recognized the truth of what was just shared and immediately stated they would finish a room downstairs and she would spend the time she had doing extended family research and temple work. She had several more years of health sufficient to do some of that work before the exceedingly difficult times came. Those exceedingly difficult times came, and her family served her as she had served them. I suspect this was a time their family bond was stretched and strengthened more than before, especially for her children. She kept a cherry and humorous temperament until the last. May God bless K and her family. She was such a bright spot in this life.

That was the last time I saw her alive. Later, I was privileged to attend her funeral. Her loss was stinging even though I knew she was in a much better place. But the sting was still so strong.

Years later, I had a vision of her palace in some point of the eternities. This vision was not looking at her or her home. I was standing near her looking at her backyard. I am thankful for the vision. However, I do not fully understand why this view was given. I suspect, but the full reason was not given. Still, it was given for some reason we may understand with some prayer, thought, and contemplation after we finish this view. I suspect that the vision was at least partly a parable.

The Joy of the Next Life. I will start with the less important details as some of them may be some sort of image to help us understand the more important part of this viewing. The view was of a grassy type of area, so perfect that it was much more beautiful than a fine carpet. There were some trees. They were large but not huge, very fine. There were no limbs until about nine to ten feet up on the trees. This gave a wonderful view of the area. There was water, sort of glassy water, farther out the back, beyond the lawn, less than a hundred yards away. The sort of water could have been a mirror, crystal clear, like in some lake pictures with no ripples. The water came to the grass with no muddy area between. (I am not doing justice to this view with my words)

The most important part was the peace and happiness that was here. It was beyond my understanding. I was not allowed to feel it all, but I was allowed a little understanding. I have felt a few very happy times in my life. Take that and compound it many times and I cannot understand as I have not experienced that in this life. I felt an intensity of the joy that she lived in but not the joy itself. The intensity was like not being able to hear an incredibly loud music but only feeling the vibrations that shake you. The intensity of the joy was overwhelming. Constantly, continually, through the eternities, to live with that incredible intensity, with that great intensity of the happiness and joy of the Lord and all your surroundings! What a supreme reward for obedience and repentance to the will and ways our Lord and Savior. A supremely majestic and eternal blessing…

This view taught and emphasized only one of the many blessings of our Lord. How can we not seek to know our Redeemer? No wonder those disobedient and unrepentant will experience gnashing of teeth along with the other consequential activities that are expressions of their great sorrows for not following Christ in mortality. They could have shared in it all! Yes, in all that Jesus has. He offers it all, for all eternity, but so many of us choose disobedience. And even more we choose to be unrepentant in our disobedience and political correctness. We choose not to search for Jesus, but only give an occasional thought or prayer. We spend our time and thought in the worship of other gods, the gods of this world. This type of life leads us to end up in the dark world looking up to the top of the hill and seeing the Light, while we are in darkness, filled with intense sorrow and long held remorse.

Evil Spirits. I should share a little more on evil spirits. Not a good subject, but maybe I can share something that will help inoculate or help defend.

I was driving to work. It was an hour and a half trip in the early morning. As usual, the CD was playing a *Church of Jesus Christ* conference talk feeding my need to gather more perspectives and wisdom on how to improve and be better. The drive was about an hour complete. It would not be dawn yet for some time. I was sandwiched in the third lane to the right of a four-lane freeway. That early, many big rigs were trying to get into the Bay Area before the morning rush hour. The fast lanes were moving faster than I wanted to go. This was just a regular commute that had been happening for me for almost two decades. Although the sky was still dark, a thick darkness seemed to be surrounding me. I knew what was happening. A powerful evil spirit or several of them somehow decided to surround and do some kind of harm to me. Please remember they are very smart and lust to convince us to do bad things or to hurt us in any way they can conceive.

The darkness soon started to affect my concentration on my driving and my vision started to be troubled. At this point, I would normally pray for help. I was aware God knew of the evil plans long in advance and had made plans to help me. He had, I suspect, many ways to protect me. I strongly suspect God would rather have me use all the resistance to evil that I can before He "bails me out" from another bad circumstance. You know, that "try to grow some here before you call for help," thing. Probably a powerfully bright, light kind of bright as well as intelligent, angel was not too far away, just watching and observing.

So, I decided, with a prayer in my heart, to try to figure out a strong resistance or defense to this darkness. I knew if this went too much further, I would be in an auto wreck at highway speed. My decision was to move the car to the right lane and then off the freeway so I could stop as far off the freeway as I could. I could not see well enough to know where the trucks were that were in the slow lane. If I tried to change lanes, it could be a disaster with a big rig. The darkness was still getting worse, and something had to happen now.

One thing I know for sure is that evil spirits are full of hate. They intensely hate Jesus and, to a lesser extent, all of us who try to follow Him. So, I could make them intensely miserable by singing out loud about Jesus. So, I started to sing the hymn "I Believe in Christ." I sang the first verse. I started the singing and soon the darkness stopped increasing.

With a little more singing, the darkness started to lessen. I only memorized the first verse, so I started singing the first verse of "The Spirit of God Like a Fire is Burning." By the end of the first verse, the darkness was almost gone, and I finished with the first verse of "I Need Thee Every Hour."

Now the words of these songs are full of so many things, only one of which is a pronouncement of our worship of our Lord. They represent our love for our Savior; thus, they are incredibly noxious to evil spirits. I suspect the evil ones could have endured the words if they were really determined; however, I am not anything of too much importance and I suspect they thought one ordinary unimportant mortal is not worth enduring hearing such descriptive and praising words about Jesus our Savior and Redeemer. Added to this, there are good angels everywhere, and there was at least one good angel there and he may have commanded them to depart as I expressed my faith in and love for Jesus. Anyway, for whatever reason, they left and took their darkness with them. All hail to our King of Kings and Lord of Lords. I wish He would return and take all the reins of all kingdoms. What wonders are to happen when He does…

For those who want to laugh at me, you might say it was my poor singing that chased them away. Let us all laugh at me together, or at least laugh with me. Even if it is at my expense, let us laugh; we need to laugh more than we do. Please laugh.

More on Healing the Sick. I would like to share a little more on healing the sick.

Prayer is always available to us to petition Heavenly Father in the name of His Son and our Savior, Jesus, for his aid in helping someone that is sick or injured.

There is so much more to healings. I will speak directly to those that hold the Melchizedek Priesthood, and to those that are servants of the Christ, those who will give a healing blessing to all that ask, those repentant of our failings, and to my brothers and sisters in Christ, in whatever religion they follow. And especially those who have love and compassion for the sick, who will seek a blessing from our Lord for them. To those who choose to be an instrument in the hands of our Lord.

Jesus, again in our time, heals the sick and injured, as He did in ancient times, to His everlasting majesty and glory. But now He allows servants to have a little portion of activity in accomplishing His wondrous will. He allows us to stand close to Him in His wonderful work.

I will skip over the use of consecrated oil and the anointing and sealing of the oil. James, among others, has something to say about this. As well as, the general order of the administration, these things have been regularly taught and generally understood by followers of Jesus.

It takes faith to be healed; at least part of that faith is manifested by a sick or injured asking for a priesthood blessing. Sometimes the sick or injured are such that they cannot ask, so another can add their faith to the mix and ask for the blessing on behalf of the one who cannot ask.

At this point, the faith of the one needing help has been initially exercised by the act of asking and hoping and looking forward with faith. It is to be understood we are seeking God's majesty and all-knowing will, not our limited understandings. Do we have the faith to be healed? Probably, so if you had enough faith to ask for a blessing from our Lord? The next question is, do we have the faith to move on to the next life or possibly suffer further and longer, if that would be the Lord's will, for reasons we do not understand now, but He does. His will is always the best, even if we will not fully understand it until the next life.

Hopefully, whatever God directs, we will come to understand and desire more than our personal wants. If the Lord calls us home, will we joy in this also? This can be a great trial of our faith. New Testament authors have taught us that it should not be a surprise that trials come to us. This leads to another subject, the subject of trials we will not cover here. But please remember the vision of the pre-mortality life where the wonderful young woman, after talking with and being taught by Father, chose a life of an incredible trial, so that she in her infirmity could be the needed blessing to the lives of her family that they so very much needed.

Now that the request has been made by one who is sick or injured let us review the activity of the Melchizedek Priesthood holder that is to voice the blessing. Please review the thirty-second chapter of second Nephi in the Book of Mormon, Another Testament of Jesus Christ. Especially look to verse 9 where we are taught to pray always, "We must not perform anything unto the Lord save in the first place we shall pray unto the Father in the name of Christ, that He will consecrate our performance…" This comes near the end of the teachings of Nephi. I suspect that Nephi had a "I almost forgot to write this down" moment and added this important wisdom near the end of his writings.

So, we must pray again before we perform a priesthood blessing. Pray to Father in the name of Christ for His help here in the blessing to be given the one in need. So far this is not too hard to understand and perform, no matter what religion we follow. He does not tell us what to pray for, but He does mention "consecrate our performance." So, we know things will go better after that prayer. But what are you going to pray for?

There is more to the prayer. To me, there is some specifics that need to be learned and added. In the Doctrine and Covenants, Chapter 35 we are taught in Verse 8 – "For I am God, and mine arm is not shortened; and I will show miracles, signs and wonders, unto all those who believe on my name." So now we know there will be miracles "unto all those who believe on my name," and it is God that will show them…**not us**. Although we can be an instrument in that activity.

How come more blessings are not accompanied by miracles and wonders?

Verse 9 – "And **who so** shall **ask** it **in my name** in **faith**, they shall cast out devils; they shall heal the sick; they shall cause the blind to receive their sight, and the deaf to hear, and the dumb to speak, and the lame to walk." "Ask" is a most important word here.

Please forgive me and allow me to go to first person here. I was asked to give a priesthood blessing not too long ago. I had learned that prayers are to precede the blessing I would perform. The next step in the process I learned I should ask. I know to simply ask is slothful; there is some work for me to do first. (Please remember my failure in the prayer for the hawk. Further, a good man once asked for a blessing to do a great work. He was given the blessing but later failed in the attempt to use it. It was later explained he gave no thought but to ask. I do not want to fail for that reason.) The one who ask me to give a blessing is in terrible pain in his lower back. Doctors said he had problems in his back that required surgery.

I know the person well. The person tries to live the commandments and has faith in our Christ and is a good example to me. And maybe most importantly his family needs him in good health and strength. Now it is up to me to serve my Master and represent His will. I hold the Melchizedek Priesthood, but it is not my priesthood, it is the Lord's priesthood. I am only an unworthy servant. God will heal not me. So, I go in prayer and **ask** what is, Thy Will and Love for this good man, that is in need. I plead/ask for a miracle from Thee for the one in need, an immediate healing for him so that the pain will go away with no need for the medical surgery, so that he can serve his family needs, needs that are great. I remember the acts of our Savior when He met those in need. Where there was some faith on the part of the needy, He healed them, most often, immediately.

I then ask for **His permission** to use His priesthood, (or would it be more accurate to ask to be a conduit for His will to pass through us to do His will and to be an instrument through which He performs His majestic wonders) in His name, and to His glory. But I absolutely know that my Lord knows so much more and loves so much more than me. His ways are so much above and beyond, so much more, and better than mine. So, I have asked for what I know, or at least strongly suspect, will be the very best for this sufferer. Then I ask for even more, something so much better than my will. Something based with eternal understanding and consequences that only God can know and produce. Please, **thy will be done**. What will Thou have me do or say?

The prompting came into my mind that I may pronounce a blessing that immediately heals. I was so thankful for the response that is so filled with His ever-present compassion and love.

Further, I ask if our combined faith is sufficient to accomplish this wonderful outpouring of Thy will. I am further impressed the injured one has many good ancestors that have passed this life. They will be unseen attendees at the blessing. This new information is gratefully received. So, if they are to attend then their faith will be involved and added. It is now clear that there will be an abundance of faith present at the blessing. More than sufficient to bring to pass our Lord's will.

Now I go to visit the one in such pain. I go to represent our Lord, knowing so much more than I would have if I had not pondered, prayed, asked permission, and asked not amiss. With hope, faith, and confidence in our Lord and His will, I have been strengthened to serve my Master. I go knowing what the outcome will be, which of course, further adds to my faith. I now have a sure knowledge of Our Lord's will, or at least part of it.

I share with the sufferer that some of his passed ancestors are in attendance. (I suspect that information leads to increased faith on his part.) Then the blessing is given. Among other things I pronounce – "You are healed right now." The presence of the Holy Spirit is strongly felt at that moment. Within a short period of time the faith of the sufferer catches up with the blessing from the Lord. He stands takes some steps as he drops the crutches to the floor, runs to the bathroom and loses the contents of his stomach. Then, a few seconds later, all the pain is gone, he is healed. All rejoice in the spectacular love of the Lord our Savior.

There is so much more to be shared, possibly another time. But there should be enough experiences shared here for you to put the puzzle together when the need or when the call comes to you. Is there enough for you to know at least one perspective of what to do and how to ask? To ask permission to do God's will, so **Jesus** can heal another? Now you know how I craft the prayer with all the suggested elements, to include enough of that which is necessary, to be allowed to be an instrument of healing from our Lord to His eternal glory? The Lord wants us all to learn and grow. With your faith and activity, just ask for the Holy Ghost to fill in the parts you need help with. The Spirit is so anxious to teach us the ways of our Redeemer.

I anxiously wait for another to ask for a priesthood blessing. The love of our Savior and Redeemer will be poured out upon the needy with the faith to ask and to be healed.

During the above blessing of the sick, another brother was involved in the blessing. A couple years later he needed a knee replacement to continue to walk. I was called to perform a priesthood blessing for him. I have known and loved him and his family for years. So, I went through all the above activity in hopes of being allowed to pronounce an immediate healing of his knee with no need for the medical surgery. I think I forgot to mention there was fasting on my part of the first blessing and fasting on behalf of my friend here. The request to pronounce an immediate healing was not given. I was disappointed. However, I learned there was something more important that was going to be given. There was another ailment or ailments that I was not aware of that were going to be healed or at least lessoned, and that was pronounced in the blessing. His "health in the future was going to be better than" his "health now." Another healing from Jesus, all to the eternal glory to our Lord and Savior. How can we be thankful enough for what He has accomplished for humanity?

I still anxiously wait for another to ask for a priesthood blessing.

This healing is out of order. I was going to pass on sharing it but this early morning I feel it should be added here. About six years previous there started to be a slight or small burning in my abdomen. Soon it was steadily worse. I was home and shortly thereafter I was in bad shape. I called some priesthood holders in search for a blessing. A good friend, Dean, was at work and said there was another brother at his work who would also aid in the blessing. I got in my car and drove about four or five miles to his office. I was very weak and concentrating hard while driving and later while walking. I got to his office, and he met me at the door. We rode the elevator up to his floor and went to a room where they administered a priesthood blessing to me.

Among other things, I was told the doctors and nurses would be blessed to know how to best take care of my illness. Well, that is not what I was hoping for or expected. However, the will of our Lord is supreme and better than what I could imagine so to be thankful was my course. I was very weak and drove home with concentration as to not hurt anyone. When I got home, it was obvious that I was in bad shape and needed the emergency room, fast. Something needed accomplished first. I needed to pray, and then I would go. The praise of our Father for His majestic will and His wonderful Son, our Lord and Savior who teaches Father's will to us, was reviewed with thankfulness. I started giving thanks for so many times the Holy Ghost has taught me about Jesus, His will, and ways. I have so much to be thankful for it took some time. I lost track of the time while in prayer. Then there was so much more to ask for, certainly not all me, my wife and young son, my other children's needs also. Again, there was always so much more to be thankful for.

For some reason, I lost track of time. The severe burning in my abdomen had disappeared. At that point I stopped praying, wondering why I could not feel the pain. The pain was gone, the pain was completely and surprisingly just gone. I gave thanks some more and finished the prayer. As I got up off my knees a glance at the clock. It told me the prayer had lasted over three hours.

Now there was no reason for the emergency room, there was no more severe pain, no pain at all. Things changed. The very weak and shakiness was completely gone also. I was so much different than when the prayer was commenced. What had happened and the more serious question was why this had happened. I still remembered the priesthood blessing and the things that will happen. So, my present was a little confusing. Some medical people will be blessed to know how to best deal with my sickness. I thought that meant now. So, yes, I am confused. Confusion is not so rare with me. The Lord was involved, so if I cannot fully understand at least, I can be thankful and just continue with my life.

Maybe a week or so later, Bev and I were doing our evening walk around the neighborhood for our exercise. The pain came back much faster and more severe than before. We walked slowly to our home where I got into the car and Bev drove me to the hospital. They did a scan and in about an hour and a half I was on an operating table at the hospital.

Before the operation, the nurse told me, a surgeon was going to repair a rupture in my small intestine.

The surgeons did a masterful job. They removed about sixteen inches of my small intestine. There was no bag needed in my side after the operation. The day after the operation I did not need any more pain medication and my company brought me a computer so I could help with the company work. The third day I could weakly get out of bed and walk the halls. The fifth day they finally released me to go home. One of the very skillful surgeons who accomplished the operation told me there were two ruptures in the intestine not too far apart. He said the first rupture, for some reason he did not understand, had healed itself. I knew how and when the first rupture was healed. So, they took out that part of the intestine also.

It should be stated we have so much to be thankful for. God is so mindful of us all, all not just some.

The Spirit shared with me there should be another person who will add to this writing and to discuss and further explain some of the experiences and help our understandings with the addition of another perspective. I do not now know for certain whom that other person will be. I have searched with no success. At this point, this work is being shared just from me. As mentioned previously, two others have made comments that caused me to add to this writing. Maybe that is enough.

I have mentioned some church leaders in a negative light. I certainly do not intend that we need to be above failures. We all fall and hurt others from time to time. Our failures in no way represent failure of our God and His Church. The mention is to inoculate you from an occasional leader that hurts. If after being hurt, I had walked away from God, His Church, and His teachings because of the bad experiences I had with a church leader I would have lost, as you have seen, so many wonderful experiences. Hold on to the iron rod (the word of God) as much as you can. May God bless you in your trek through the eternities.

My Testimony. I wish to share it with you along with my love for you. Who can live and not come to understand the difference between good and bad? In our life we prize the good or we prize the bad. Good originally comes from God, and later a little of the good comes from those that recognize the difference and choose to align themselves with the good and participate in doing good. Should we not seek the source of all good? What wonder filled discoveries there are waiting for all who seek our God, and the God of all nature and worlds without number. Our God is anxious to be found by us and will aid and encourage us in our search for Him.

There is pain, blood, and tears in the difficulties, trials, failures, disappointments, and fear that accompany our search. Do we want to know Jesus the Christ enough to endure and cross over all the obstacles of the search? Should we be surprised that the great and eternal rewards that accompany our trek through this life cannot be found without our paying in pain, blood, and tears for a reward that will change our eternities in such a marvelous way. More so when we realize our Savior has paid with His blood and His life to be able to take away our sins and dry our tears and let us repent of all our sins. Yes, we can give away all our sins in the process of learning to knowing God. This is our great choice, the choice of all choices, the choice that will define our eternity. Do we choose the Father and the Son and the Holy Ghost, or do we choose to be blinded and swallowed up by the bad and the trappings of our world? May our glorious and majestic God bless you in your supreme life choices that are accompanied by the eternal consequences. Jesus awaits with open arms…

One More Dream. I keep saying just one more. Here we go again; there is another viewing to be shared. Here is part of another dream from my oldest son. I will share some preliminary information to help us understand the dream.

As we can easily understand, after this life so many of even the good among us will have serious faults that we did not overcome in our incredibly challenging mortality. Even given the fact that Jesus gave us His teachings and baptism and the sacrament and on and on. We overcome our faults a little at a time and we will run out of time (life) before we can complete our transforming task. Joshua discussed previously, died before the battles were finished.

This is a type of what will be a frequent conversation in the next life. So, in the future life it will be often asked, "Where is Tom or Sue, or…?" Then another will answer, "He or she has something to work on." After they learn more about their problem and make some changes, they did not finish in mortality; we look forward to being with them again. Now, on to the dream.

A family that had struggled through mortality to follow Jesus, was asking, "Where is one of the members of our family?" The answer is he had "something to work on." We hope to see him soon.

This "something" is a weakness or disobedience that should have and could have been overcome and accomplished much quicker during mortality. When he successfully finished his further instruction, he finally met up with his family. He looked at his wife and family. He asks the question, "Are you, my wife? You look a little like her. Are you, my son? You look like him, but I am not sure. You look different."

The answer will be, "We have been with Father! **He is amazing!** Our words cannot describe the majestic way he teaches! We have changed much from being near Him and receiving His love and further teachings. He is the greatest teacher in all the heavens. Yes, we have changed. We have changed inside and out. Even our looks have changed by being in the presence of Father!"

I love dreams that teach us of God.

Following Answers to Prayers. Here is another experience I was not going to share. However, here it is. In the last couple years, I have asked several times in prayer if I could do certain things that are important and good. Each time I was given positive responses to the prayers. So, I did the things. There was an expectation of positive outcomes, or at least what I thought was positive. Oh well, the outcomes were not as was expected. This happened several times in a row. After the string of negative outcomes, I was more than a little discouraged as the requests were for substantial activities, of great value to more than just a few. (One of the requests was to help change political corruption and another was to reduce the particulate matter pollution from diesel trucks, especially the 2.5-micron level of diesel particulate matter that kills many thousands each year in the U.S., not to mention the suffering it causes all over the world.) So, you guessed it, the lack of understanding of these circumstances was the motivation for and object of my next prayer. Why? The answer came in an unanticipated response. I reviewed the merits of what was requested and my considerable (I have been working on the pollution part for about fourteen years, and the political part for significantly longer) activity that was part of the process and then the negative outcomes. Was my activity not sufficient? I received the positive responses to my prayers, but the outcomes were not what I was trying to achieve. Yes, you are right again. As you suspect, I was surprised and further taught by the response to my prayer.

The response and answer to my prayer for more understanding came immediately after the request for "Why" was finished. It was given. Did you not march when you were a soldier? Did you not turn right and left at the commands? By so doing, did you not learn to follow the commands given to you?

That was enough for me to put the rest of the pieces of the puzzle together. The benefit to me for following the commands of God and even the value of the answers to my prayer requests should not have been dependent upon some outcome I wanted. Whatever I may want is important, but not of major importance when compared to God, His majesty, and His will. His teachings are with such love for us. Following His will, like following the commands to turn left or right, are more important than the direction I turn. My responses to the directions from God are the primary and eternal goal while the outcomes may be of only temporary and temporal concerns, as they obviously were here.

We may have our lesser concerns, which may even seem great concerns for the benefit of all humanity we wish to move forward. But our plans and timing, when compared to Heaven's will, are no more than a dim mist compared to the bright sun, like money compared to the value of our potential station in the eternities. Even much more, the majestic will of our Father in Heaven and His Son, our Savior Jesus the Christ and the Holy Ghost is unparalleled to anything I can think of. Even my fondest hopes are pale in comparison to His eternally wonder filled plans for us.

At this point, I think the perspective is made that my will is so very much less than God's will. That being said, I do not want to put our prayers in a dim light. When we pray, as I learned long ago and explained earlier, **when we pray the eternities change.**

An additional thought can be reasoned out. Our timelines are so pitted with our limited understanding of how we think things really are. While Father's timelines are given from an omnipresent intellect that knows how things really are here and in the eternities.

Even more, His teaching to us is for the here and now and even more for the eternities. Our will is mostly for mortality. Our will shall be swallowed up in and surpassed by the eternal perspective and purposes of our Heavenly Father. I am standing and functioning in my mortal reality. I should remember my reality is happening in a specific dispensation of time. This is the dispensation of time that is shortly before and will include the final great and even tragic things that will happen before our Savior returns to subdue and end the excessive evil that is so prevalent today. Jesus will rule and reign in His absolute righteousness and wonderful will for a thousand years (Mortality still has another thousand years after that). What a breathtaking future awaits. Our Savior and Redeemer, please, please speed Thy return…

And lastly, the outcome of my requests was not dismissed, possibly, (and hopefully) only delayed. He wants us to do good of our own volition and He blesses us in so doing. (Another side note, if the Savior returns soon my requests may become of no effect to humanity, no matter how important they look now. The Savior will change all those problems to good. Although, I do understand that I need to try to make things better each and every day. That is part of my mortal trials.) One thing is for certain, I had things out of order and this instruction was to elevate my perspective. My perspective was short sided, yes, I recognize and admit it. I hope and my intent is to change my will to His will. May God aid us all in our individual repentance and change to a better way.

Looking back, this concept, is not so hard for us to understand. An eternal perspective is much easier for us to read about then to live. Lastly for this specific review, the better approach should have been as my first prayer, a thorough review of what I knew about Father's will surrounding the two issues. Then go further and make my request weaving my will with as much of God's will as I could. Then ask if there was anything that He would share with me about my "weaving" of the two wills.

All this time in prayer also clears my mind and is placing myself in the path of revelation or God sharing something more with me. If, as can happen, the Spirit enlightens my thoughts with something higher than I should eagerly follow that path. If there is nothing yet, I am ready to ask, I have explained why and what I am asking for, so I now ask for something much more, I ask to know Thy will so I can do it if it is (almost always is) different from what I know and want…and wait for a response or review it all again in case I forgot something or got something out of order, and then wait for a response. You can reason out the rest.

Thousands of deaths each year, I am still on that trail with new innovations to a proven technology. Hopefully, a little wiser. Still working to stop the thousands of deaths each year from diesel pollution and still learning.

I am going to take a little space to share some of the trail. I have contacted so many in trying to get help with a proven technology to reduce the killing pollution and reducing billions of gallons of diesel from being burned each year, just in the U.S.

I have contacted leading present and former politicians, state and federal agencies that are charged with improving our environment, with associations and clubs that claim to be environmentalists. I found none, not one that has the power to change the present status quo interested in solutions to this one specific major pollution problem, not one. What is the word that is used for these types of "leaders"? One word is hypocrite, other words are liar, deceiver, phony, socialist, communist, dictator, hater, or anarchist. They are okay with people suffering so long as they have a problem to use to help them control the workers or masses. Climate control, global warming, abortion, racial differences, police brutality, social justice, Covid 19, U.S. immigration, BLM, monetary inequity among other causes are tools that are being used deceive, create hate, control voters, and tear down safeguards for peacefully progressing societies.

There is no perfect people or place here on Earth; we are a fallen people. God organized this planet for a place for us to be born into mortality and be tested. Tested, yes tested for us to choose good or bad and then see the consequences of our choices. Then with more experiences continue to make choices for us to decide who we will be, try to be better or disregard good and choose bad. I could say so much more, but you already know some if not most the reasons, why people, why we are doing what they are doing.

All the while thousands each year are dying, and billions of gallons of diesel is being burned for transportation that is not needed…

Are you tired of hearing experiences about healings? Well, here is one more recent occurrence.

I was praying about the recognition received about the young children in the ward we lived in Idaho Falls. The sisters that have managed the primary (the ward organization that coordinates the teachings of the little ones) have consistently, over the last half decade been simply exceptional in their attention to the little ones. They have showed more love for the little than I have ever seen in any other ward.

I was praying about this observance and seeking to better understand the reasons why this is the case here and now. At an early point in the prayer/request, the Holy Ghost decided to take me away from that prayer and give the understanding that there would be an exceptional sister taken from this ward, called home to Father. It would not be too long before the order in Heaven wanted her back in the immortal realms.

This was not a tragedy from the immortal perspective, there was important things for her to do there, and things here would be okay. From our perspective it would be a major tragedy, we would not know the difference, and we would probably not understand the full meanings of the occurrence while here in mortality. There is an irony here. It was also given that the combined faith of the men and women, though substantial, would not be enough to persuade the Heavenly order and timetable to change. It would take more than the combined adult faith and prayers of the ward. It would take the prayers of at least one or some of the primary children before Father would rearrange the eternities.

The great trial for one family came, the trial was, at least partially shared with the ward adults. There was fasting and prayers from some of the adults. More importantly, there were prayers from at least some of primary children. The young, special sister is still with us. Father rearranged His divine will for the eternities, at least a little, just for her.

Prior to the emergency, I told one of the ward leaders we would have a life and death emergency, but not all the potential outcomes. I suspected we needed to start praying and fasting, asking Father if He would change His divine will and allow the sister to stay here and postpone her work on the other side until her life here was finished. The ward leader advised me not to mention my understanding as it would probably scare many in the ward. Plus, I suspect he thought I would be perceived as weird, and as happened before, even feared or hated. I had great respect for my friend and his council seemed sound, so nothing was mentioned until after the little ones used their faith to aid in the recovery of our young sister in distress.

I took Luke, our youngest son, to see the place where the Hawk incident happened. Then later to where the old school used to be, where the other spiritual experienced happened to me as a ten-year-old.

Types of priesthood blessings for the sick and injured, from what I have seen, seems not to be well understood. I will share what I have learned from the writings of a past prophet named Spencer Kimball. The prayer before and the asking and the other things are accomplished prior as we have discussed. The three types of priesthood blessings are –

> Two Melchizedek Priesthood holders; one anoints with oil and the second seals the anointing and pronounces the blessing given by the Spirit, in the name of Jesus and by the authority of the Melchizedek Priesthood. All to the blessing of the one in need, all to the glory of our Savior.
>
> If only one Melchizedek Priesthood holder oil is not used, but the rest is the same.
>
> If no Melchizedek Priesthood holder available, the priesthood holder is the Savior, and we ask in prayer for His Divine intervention on behalf of the one in need. Obviously, this can be accomplished by a woman as well as a man not holding the priesthood.

As previously discussed, let us review Doctrine and Covenants, Chapter 35, Verse 8 – "For I am God, and mine arm is not shortened; and **I will show** miracles, signs and wonders, unto all those who believe on my name." It is not us that is **showing** miracles it is Our Lord. We are being allowed to help and be part of the process so we can serve and learn.

Verse 9 – "And **whoso** shall **ask** it in my name in faith, they shall cast out devils; they shall heal the sick; they shall cause the blind to receive their sight, and the deaf to hear, and the dumb to speak, and the lame to walk." It states, "… whoso shall ask." Does it state that the whoso can only a priesthood holder? What mother has not taken a sick or injured child in her arms when no one else was around and offered a prayer for the child? Does that mother seek a priesthood blessing from Our Lord at that time to heal the child by a **miracle, sign, or wonder**? After reviewing these things, should a mother, or anyone offering the prayer, be shy about asking for what the Lord said can happen? Do we have faith, faith enough to ask for a miracle, and then ask for even more, Thy will be done?

I suspect the precedent activities mentioned previously for blessings should be observed as part of the preparation and to strengthen the faith of those involved, if time allows. All this is a review of the third type of priesthood blessing.

When I shared the incident of the prayer by Joshua when I was sick, Joshua was using this third type of blessing, wasn't he? But we did not recognize it at the time. The Lord will have order in His Kingdom so respect His order as much as you know. I am not trying to share anything different than His order and Love for us. In sharing this I hope that all that do not hold the Melchizedek Priesthood or have immediate access to that help will ask and use the faith necessary to call for a miracle, sign or wonder from the Lord. If you are in need, find someone who hold the Melchizedek Priesthood in your area and call on them to administer a blessing, no matter what religion, if any, you follow. Priesthood holders are servants of Christ and should do as He directs them. You can add their faith to yours towards the healing of someone in need.

As we try to put ourselves in a greater part of His order, will He not respond? There is still much I have not explained here, but the Holy Ghost is anxious to encourage and teach us to draw closer to our Lord and Savior. Ask Him. There will be help as is the Lord's will. One last comment on this subject is, a very good teacher named Boyd Packer, near the end of his life stated something to the effect there are few things as strong as the prayer of a faithful mother. Mothers use that strength; your prayer is an act of faith being added to your request to an anxiously awaiting Savior.

Ask for the Savior to send a strong angel to heal. That angel was probably sent before the need and is there already just waiting to do as he or she was directed in the courts of Heaven.

Chapter 6

Religion and Politics

How sad it is to view the rogue actions of nations as opposed to the amazing will of "Our Father in Heaven." How mysterious to us are His ways if we have not understood at least a little about Him. He has taught and fostered freedom oh so often while there have been so many of those that oppose freedom and want to dominate and control us.

A Congressional hearing was on TV. As I listened to a congresswoman, I could not agree with much she said. She was siding with an obvious lying high-ranking member of the FBI. A thought floated through my mind that I would probably not like her if we ever met. By now I should be able to recognize such a thought and dismissed it. There was more pondering on her actions. Then the Holy Ghost decided to lightly scold me with a wonderful lesson.

My mind was opened to review the premortal life before we came to earth through birth, we were spirit beings in heaven. We were all sons and daughters of our Father in Heaven. (Now comes the great instruction.) It was shown to me that this congresswoman and I were far closer than good friends there. She and I were very close to each other. There, she had a great and pristine love for me, and I had a great and pristine love for her. We were brother and sister in the best sense, something seldom, if ever, accomplished in more than a small way by brother and sister here on Earth. Our love for each other was epic compared to relationships here. Those types of close relationships were not uncommon there. Sadly, through birth we forgot all as we entered this fallen mortality. I was born into a poor white family that had little to do with God's teachings and she was born into a black family, of which I know nothing.

The intensity of our love there has opened another understanding of the previous life. It is a treasure for me to experience and review it here in the land of our difficulties with love. That intensity of brotherhood and sisterhood far transcends my experience as a brother here, to my sadness and of course my failure to be a much better brother. The epic and pristine love was at the edge of my understanding, I do not suspect I could achieve such love here in mortality, without a new and better heart and mind.

There will be a reuniting of sorts after this life. After this life is over, we will look back and know that we are accountable for our actions, both good and bad. We will be greatly pained by those things we did not do where we could have helped and loved others. We will be joyous for those times we helped and loved those in need.

Specific to my newly remembered sister, if we are anything less than wonderful and loving to each other here, we will have great anguish in the eternities for our failures in mortality towards each other.

After this teaching that was given, the thought I would not like her was completely washed away by the teachings of the Holy Ghost. Leaving me humiliated at thinking such a thought about a sister that should be cherished, given our past life and love. But more than that, if I ever meet her in this life, my only response, given our past life, should be so much different than my first thought. My first and most appropriate expression to her should be, I love you and I am thrilled to finally find you in this fallen mortality. Whatever political persuasion she serves or what color of her skin should be far second to my love I had for her in the past life.

After this learning episode was over, I was thrilled that the Holy Ghost had again taken the time to teach and change me…

I am still left with more to learn about this teaching. Should this be specific to this one woman? Probably not. Is this general to all people? It is time to ponder on this concept much more and hope the Holy Ghost will continue His wonderful teachings of God's will.

It seems Jesus universally applied this love to most all of those He dealt with during his mortality. He did not lose sight of His love for us from the previous life like we do. His teachings of love were great in so many ways. Most of them were by His example and some were by His words.

That love we had seems to linger a little in infants as you can understand. Love, oh yes, He taught us to love our neighbor. But he did not tell us all the whys. I suspect he wanted us to follow Him by faith and later all would be made known to us. Further, when we lived with Father before this mortality, Father taught us to love each other, and we learned to love so very powerfully, far beyond petty differences. That love mostly stayed there as we fell into our lives here. Of course, little children carried some of that love until this life beats and strangles it out of us in so many ways.

Clearly, the Holy Ghost has shown me, and I hope you also, that there should be more love here, different love here. God bless my wonderful sister and your sister, the congresswoman. Oh, how we should love her… Oh, how we should love all our brothers and sisters. Jesus' teachings on love have not been well received by us. Father, I ask in Jesus' name, please, please, help us repent and learn love.

When God teaches, He really teaches.

Rock Solid Politics. There is an old saying, if you want to get along with those around you do not discuss religion or politics. In this volume, I am attempting to discuss both, or maybe I am just attempting to become enormously unpopular.

As you know from reading the first pages of this book, the interest in religion started as a five-year-old at the beach in San Francisco.

From the same reading, the interest in politics started as a ten-year-old at an elementary school under a covered walkway by the cafeteria. The interest in politics was re-emphasized at age fifteen as an answer to a prayer.

God orchestrated these experiences, so for me, there was no confusion as to the reason for my future involvements in both areas.

I very briefly discussed some of my involvement in politics. But for the benefit of those that are not interested in both, I was going to separate the two areas. That may happen in the future.

There are some that seem to think there is a war going on between the political parties in the US. The use of the word war is very perceptive. To better understand this war, let us start way back at the beginning, of sorts. A war between God and satan. A war or better stated "The War in Heaven." To disguise the war some, say there is no satan, some even say there is no God. That disguise will not fool many reasonable humans. I suspect most of those who espouse that line of lies really know the difference but do so for some reason, like having been hurt by someone who espoused a belief in God, so they blame God for the hurt caused by one of us. Or for the sad reason that some really hate God and want to deceive.

Early in this book, I shared the experience where satan came and attacked me, tried to take my body, and then lied to me. I know satan exists, contrary to what some say, that he is only a fable; he exists. As for what were called "his angels" we now call them evil spirits. Jesus cast them out of people when He walked with His disciples. As you remember I have mentioned some of the evil spirit's activities I have encountered.

Let us go back, way back, back to before Adam and Eve were on the earth. That should be far enough.

Here we are in the politics section, and we will now tie politics to religion. The two have always been connected and they are connected today.

Before you go any further with this book, you may want to reread or review the first book in the Old Testament (Genesis) and the last book in the New Testament (Revelations). To be more exact you can go to Rev. Chapter 12, Verses 3 to 13. To help remember it a little, the dragon refers to satan (if you have been wondering the lack of capitalization is intentional), and the third part of the stars of heaven refers to the third part of the spirits (as us they were spirit children of Our Father in Heaven) in heaven that followed satan. Satan and the third part of the spirits in heaven were cast out of heaven for rebellion in the war. Chapter 7, "And there was war in heaven: Michael and his angles fought against the dragon; and the dragon fought and his angles" Verse 8, "And prevailed not; neither was their place found any more in heaven." **Verse 9, "And the great dragon was cast out, that old serpent, called the Devil, and Satan, which deceiveth the whole world: he was cast out into the earth, and his angles were cast out with him."**

Jesus was talking to his followers, as recorded in Luke, Chapter 10, where we read His words, "I beheld Satan as lightning fall from heaven." Jesus beheld; He was there on Father's side. We hear firsthand testimony from an unimpeachable witness, Our Lord, Jesus.

Isaiah also had some things to say about satan.

In Chapter 14, we read "How art thou fallen from heaven, O Lucifer, son of the morning! How art thou cut down to the ground," (Isaiah then adds a political perspective as he finishes the statement) "which didst weaken the nations!" In Verse 16, "Is this the man… that did shake Kingdoms."

Isaiah further shares that satan wanted to "…exalt my throne above the stars of God." Satan wanted to "…be like the most High." It is clear he wanted to rule in God's kingdom.

Yes, Isaiah states clearly that satan will have a negative influence on nations and kingdoms. As he wanted to have his evil way and rule in Heaven, now he wants to have his evil way and rule on Earth. Since he was not born into this mortality and has no physical body for us to see, he must act through mortals. He uses mortals to do his bidding and it is recognizable that there are many that are standing in line to work for him. We have scriptures, recorded histories and our own memories of how men and women representing evil have brought great tragedy to nations that follow them.

God offers us love and freedom and happiness, while Satan offers sadness, force, fear, and unhappiness. This is a simple tool to judge which side a politician is on! Does he or she seek for the security, freedom, and happiness of the people or do they discourage religion and promote divisions, governmental controls, force, and the enslavement by taxes, drugs, and debt. Do they seek equality, friendship, and love or do they promulgate fear, hate, lawlessness, lies, discrimination, voter fraud, plus intellectual and physical intimidation, and intolerance, which are the "doctrines of devils." Do they peacefully assemble and protest for better during the day (Gandhi, MLK), or do they wear masks and destroy, steal, and burn other's property at night (KKK, BLM, Antifa)?

What an irony, Our Lord walked around in protest to the wickedness of the world as he taught the doctrine that would lead to more peace and happiness in this life and the ultimate peace and happiness through all the eternities.

There is a simple choice between good or evil. Do you support good or evil? Do you fear standing for good and opposing evil? It is not hard to know the difference. Your choices have eternal consequences. Just as much as the third part of the spirits of Heaven lost their future happiness when they choose wrong in Heaven. I weep for all who knowingly do not choose good here, there are eternal consequences! Bad choices here have eternal consequences. What are the two words? I think it is repent here in mortality and I think it is consequences in the eternities.

Whenever rulers have followed his evil practices, we suffer, or as stated thousands of years ago, "when the wicked rule the people mourn." That suffering can be individual or reach up to the level of great tragedy and for so many, many millions in the past the suffering has reached holocaust levels.

Evil, unchecked and followed to the end, would end all life on Earth. Why is this so? Simply put, satan and his evil spirits were cast down to the earth. They did not get here by the way God had decreed for all the two thirds of the spirits in heaven that followed Him. Those of us that followed God, in the war in heaven, were allowed to be born here and receive physical mortal bodies. Satan and the evil spirits did not get mortal bodies, so they want to end all others from getting and keeping mortal bodies, either by abortion or wars or whatever.

After Adam and Eve, all that come are born and received what the evil spirits did not nor will they ever receive, birth into mortal bodies. Mortal bodies that are needed to live and learn, to love and hate, to know good from evil and to choose between good or evil and act upon those choices. After our death our Savior and Redeemer of the world offers immortal bodies to us through His resurrection.

God's test for us, is for us to experience what we will do away from His presence. For that we needed to be born into mortal bodies with no knowledge of our past life with God. In this new form and in this greatest of all tests, will we seek after God's teachings, will we choose good or evil. Will we love and be kind or will we hate and take from others. This great test, yes, this greatest of all tests will decide our future through the eternities.

The scriptures are complete with teachings to aid and encourage us. The scriptures are complete with the consequences of the choices of those that came before us. The good or evil choices of those of the past are laid out plainly before us.

Now it is our time to choose good or evil.

Now it is our time to choose religious and political good or evil.

We can and should know what our rulers are really up to. We can know what direction our political servants or our political rulers are taking us.

I will attempt to clearly show the difference between our political servants of good and our political rulers for evil.

Satan wants, as so plainly stated by Isaiah to "weaken the nations" and to "shake kingdoms." God has given us laws to guide us and nations, to foster freedom, safety, and happiness. So many before us wanted freedom, often tribes and nations have made laws to protect the individual freedoms. Evil wants to tear down those laws and nations that protect freedoms because all good, which includes freedom, comes from God's influence. From the time that satan was cast down out of heaven, he hates all things from God. That hate is complete and furious and constant. So, all those that follow satan learn to hate as he does and want to weaken all nations and laws that protect freedom, safety, and happiness. They want to build all nations that hate good and freedom.

Well, in the time since Isaiah (even more on Isaiah later), we have histories of the incredibly tragic effects of evil on people and nations. We have lists of bad rulers that sacrificed children, started wars, even denied the existence of God and the difference between good and evil as they broke all the commandments of God and taught their subjects to do the same, as they try to convince us that everything is relative and there is not good or evil.

Tragically, each time these types of rulers appear, the type that will not follow the teachings of God, there also follows tragedy and suffering. Some nations are full of evil rulers and some rulers are part of good and part of evil, as they try to remain neutral.

Do I even need to mention some of the names? Here in the U.S., we have had quite a string of political leaders that have followed at least part of satan's plan to "weakened the nation." Our nation has been so weakened we are nearly bankrupt of both money and principles. Wars and wars and government greed and waste, LIES untold, corruption, immorality, murders... Plus the 40,000,000 soon-to-be-born humans, family members, yes, soon to be born, babies sacrificed at the altar of liberalism. Yes, some of our US "elected" rulers that are actually disciples, either knowingly or not, of the evil one's lies of false doctrines, "doctrines of devils" as mentioned.

1 Timothy 4:1 "Now the Spirit speaketh expressly, that in the latter times some shall depart from the faith, giving heed to seducing spirits, and doctrines of devils..." Who could say it better of our time!

By the way, when the satanic lies of abortion snare women and men and if they act on the lie, their conscience causes great remorse for the wrongdoing. So, they try to justify their act by covering themselves in liberalism and telling themselves they are okay. Just more lies that satan uses to chain them to him. The truth that will set them free is that Jesus lived and died and lived again to be our Savior. Our Redeemer suffered to give us the opportunity to repent of our sins. There is something stronger than our sins. It is the love of the Christ that atoned for our sins. Then it is our opportunity to use the atonement by our act of choosing to acknowledge our mistakes and then repent of them. Then we must act the act of change to a better and accept His loving forgiveness as we resolve to never commit evil again. That is the only way to be free of the terrible and eternal consequences of sin! The blood of Christ is stronger than sin.

Yes, my sisters and brothers of the forty million U.S. deaths, repent and ask God for his absolute love to come to us and repair the torn parts of our souls and the torn parts of our nation. If we seek Him, we can find Him. He is anxious to be found, to heal our pain and lead us to a better way of life here on earth and especially into and through all the eternities. Jesus is the only escape from our great sins. You, choose this day who you will serve, as Joshua did. Keep the blood of abortions and other evil on your hands as did Lady McBeath and suffer through the eternities. Or seek Jesus who has suffered for all our sins and will allow us to repent and is the only one who can and will forgive us, through the eternities, worlds without number...

Satan wanted to rule in God's kingdom but not the way God rules. The serpent wanted his way, an evil way to rule. God would not allow evil to rule in heaven. So, God had satan and those that followed satan cast down and out of heaven. We can cast away our thoughts and actions that follow satan.

Now here on Earth in our mortality the war continues to rage on. Except now in our mortality, we do not remember our life in heaven. Only Jesus had enough memory of the pre-existence to be able to tell us that satan's fall from heaven looked like lightning.

Without a memory of the pre-existence, we must piece things together as best we can. The scriptures can help immensely. They give us the glimpses as we have just reviewed. Plus, we have a conscience. This light from Christ is a gift to each of us for our mortal journey that will help us to know the difference between good and bad. At least it does until we do so many bad things and go unrepentant long enough that we can no longer feel the influence of our conscience.

However, while it functions in us, we can know good and bad. We can distinguish between good acts and bad acts. Hopefully, we will be thankful to our God as we have the good feelings for doing good towards others and be even more thankful to our God as we have the darker remorseful feelings for doing unkind things because God has given us the opportunity to repent and do better.

Politicians, evil politicians that hate Jesus and His free nation have been very successful at "weakening" the U.S. and have institutionalized "doctrines of devils."

What can we do…?

From an old song, "This land is your land; this land is my land… this land was made for you and me."

We should do something. Well, this is what I did.

I am certainly not rich nor bombastic, so the media would not even talk to me about my presidential campaign. Yes, the media decided who should represent each political party in our 2016 President Election as they gave them all the media attention. What irony, national and local media pushed Trump to the head of the Republican ticket with most of the media attention, confident that he would lose by a great margin to any Democrat, and then choked and went into convulsive slobbering fits of hate, when he won.

Well, I did stand for something, and I did try… I attempted to the presidency, as I was directed to do, so many years ago when I was a ten-year-old.

If you have read this book, you know who I am, a servant of Jesus Christ. As a U.S. President, you know I would seek His will, as in blessings of the sick that we have discussed, and then do it. God would be the head of our government and I would ask His help in all things, receive His revelation, and then do His will with the help of the faith and prayers of all Christians and all from the other religions that would unite with us in prayers to God for this nation and the world to be peaceful and happy as we ready ourselves for Jesus' second coming. As anxious as He is to forgive us as we repent, we could collectively pray the prayer of Daniel of repentance, seeking individual and national forgiveness. All this in the hope and faith that the incredible terror and destruction that has been foretold that precedes His return will be removed or lessened in time and severity.

Sadly, only a tiny few of you may have seen this before the 2016 elections. The following was my **2016 Presidential Campaign Preamble:**

Why Is Stan Warner a 2016 Republican Candidate for President of the United States?

As a ten-year-old, a fire was lit inside me to learn all I could about God and his dealings with mankind, both religiously and politically. Almost sixty years ago the study started. In my adult life the study has been continuous, intense, exhaustive, and filled with discovery and at times with majestic wonder.

I will use all the wisdom available to guide this nation. I will stand against all enemies, foreign or domestic, to help our people be free, happy, and prosperous. I am a servant of the Lord. Evidence of such is chronicled in my book, you can understand how God answers my prayers in wonderful ways. I will pray before each national decision asking the Lord for the best decision to serve His children. As a nation we can unitedly seek His will and do it, to our great blessings. With me, the Lord will be the ultimate leader of this nation as He offers to guide us in politics if we will ask and follow His majestic and heavenly wisdom.

Satan has had great influence over some of the leaders of our nations, to weaken our great country. Some doctrines of devils have even become some of the laws of this nation. Together we can follow the Lord's lead to heal our country. Individually and nationally, we can pray as Daniel of old, to nationally repent and ask for His forgiveness, and the blessings of His leadership.

The history of mankind has generally been, the gluttonous few, rule and take from the workers. The few take from the many by means of conquest, slavery, serfdom, lies, drugs, and taxes.

From time-to-time severe oppression drove our ancestors, in humility and faith, to call upon God for His help. Here in the New World, with God's help and the blood of the brave, Freedom was achieved. Many of my family has served in the military through the Revolutionary War and Civil War (my fourth great-grandfather, from New York, had a family before he served and died in the Civil War), World War II (my father and uncle served), Korea (my uncles served), and lastly, I served in Vietnam. As has been said many times, Freedom is not Free.

Our Heavenly Father inspired and aided our Founding Fathers to establish us as the first free people in modern times. They founded our great nation upon a mostly God inspired Constitution. A couple things were still needed. Freedom was to be universal and took another war and a couple amendments to secure. The families of our nation paid an incredibly high price to end slavery. Both my wife and I lost family, on both sides of that war.

Freedom, precious freedom, has never lasted long. The Old Testament and volumes of history have chronicled our brief episodes of freedom. There are always, corrupt leaders that are planning how to take from the many and give to themselves special privileges, yes to steal what they have not earned.

Thomas Jefferson warned us that all that is necessary for **evil to triumph** is for good men (and women) to do nothing.

Even further, have we forgotten the warning from the Old Testament - **When the wicked rule the people mourn.** Federal corruption is so widespread it is hardly even news. Our money is wrongfully taken from us. We work, the government takes, and we mourn. The Washington D. C. corruption is unchecked and growing and GROWING!

Federal politicians betray our country in exchange for foreign money.

Our Constitution, the great safeguard of our freedom, has been and is being trampled upon and changed by both Democrats and Republicans. The reason for the changes is to steal our freedom away from us, our children, and our children's children until nothing is left. They change and violate the Constitution to set up the power to take that which they have not earned. From whom, from us, the workers.

Some say that the Democrats are at fault, others say the Republicans are at fault. Sadly, I must agree with both. This great corruption/evil has been brought to you by many Republicans and Democrats, yes, liars and thieves. Those that do not honor God and the freedom He wants us to have.

These are bold words, calling many of our leaders liars, and thieves. I will take a moment to be specific (as if you do not already know). This example will be specific to one person because of the limitations of both time and space. However, this is generally seen in many leaders of both parties.

The last televised Vice-Presidential debate (2012) is a clear example. When the challenger was given time to speak the incumbent, Vice President, would speak over or interrupt him, time and again. He would ruin his feeble chance to explain his views. In an aggressive and forceful manner, the Vice President took the time of the challenger. He took what did not belong to him. Did he steal from another, in front of all the viewers? In a small way did he proved to us that he was a thief?

Even further, the Vice President looked directly at the camera, to us viewers, promising that he would protect Social Security. He had been in power in the government for decades. In those decades Social Security has been greatly mismanaged even looted, to say the least. Even further, while he was Vice President the government has squandered trillions and trillions of dollars. Please, somebody tell me the Democrats and Republicans while squandering many trillions of dollars put at least one of those trillion dollars into Social Security to make it secure for so many that were forced to pay in so much and need it now and in the future. Well, at least $100 billion out of trillions? The answer is no, they did not secure Social Security. Democrats, yes, our Democrat leaders, pretended defenders of the old, or should I say liars to the old, stealers from the old. How secure is our Social Security? I told the voters twenty-five years ago, when as a Democrat I ran for Congress, this was happening and would increase in severity. But most of those voters voted for the national Democrat's agenda. The Vice President's statement did not represent his past or present. Did he lie? He showed no remorse for doing both acts, to the contrary he seemed very pleased with himself.

Please, help the federal representatives. Too long in the sewer of power and they can no longer smell the stink. Who do they represent? Not us. Please do not vote for them more than twice. Please help them, they are addicted to power, send them home to relearn how to live with an oppressive federal government that takes from us, the workers and gives it to those that did not earn it, a reverse Robin Hood syndrome.

Jefferson told us – "what more is necessary to make us a happy and prosperous people, one more thing fellow citizens, a wise and frugal government that will keep us from injuring each other and leave us otherwise alone… and will not take the bread from the laborer."

I stated twenty-five years, ago our federal government is neither wise nor frugal. Now our federal government has contempt for us and is socialistic. It is just a matter of time until a future President, with federal force, will cancel the next federal election and declare him/herself President for life… How do you spell "voter fraud?"

In full honesty, not all federal politicians are liars and thieves. There are a few that are statesmen and not lying politicians, plus a bunch of the newly elected. The power center will start by getting them to agree to small compromises here and there. Eventually their pride convinces them they are better than us, the workers they represent. Then they will join the other liars and thieves.

Our freedoms and our very government are in mortal danger. Not yet from foreign nations force but from internal corruption and overspending/squandering/stealing and from foreign money buying federal influence. Yes, from national Republican and Democrat liars and thieves. They are deciding what part of our God inspired Constitution they can trample upon and not alert the sleeping voters. I am here to say wake up and vote them out, while we still have a free vote, or we will lose our entire God given freedom.

I know the national wrongs and evils that have been accomplished. I know how to change our nation's course back to good, prosperity and freedom. I have known that for a long time. To this end, in the late eighties and early nineties, as a Democrat, I ran for Congress twice, once in California and once in Washington State. I outlined the problems and future consequences if we did nothing to stop the assault on our Constitution, our economy and on our freedom. During those campaigns, I further learned how ingrained these evils are in our national Republican and Democrat leaders.

During those two Congressional campaigns I explained how the sixteenth (income tax) and seventeenth (direct election of US Senators) Amendments plus the Federal Reserve System have broken significant safeguards given us in the Constitution and to our political and financial freedom. Further, I outlined how the federal government spending was spiraling out of control and how the Social Security was being mismanaged/looted, big time. These five issues, if left uncorrected, would allow power seeking federal politicians and bureaucrats to become tyrants far greater than King George and bring this great nation to total ruin.

Now, twenty-five years later, history has sadly proven my warnings true. Oh, so sadly, our Republican and Democrat presidents, Congress, and federal courts trample on the Constitution as they wink and smile at each other. They think that the hard-working voter is too busy working and paying taxes and not smart enough to see through political lies. Well, I declare we are smart enough to recognize lies and deceit of the politicians, but do we have the courage to stop them.

Kennedy and Reagan are the only recent presidents that can be called good. We needed them to represent us through difficult times, and they succeeded. And yes, they did make some mistakes. By the way, they both called for big tax breaks to unleash the investors to move our economy and create jobs. I agree with both, but they did not go far enough, our present taxing/stealing activity must end.

In the **second paragraph of the Declaration of Independence** we read wonderful words like **"all men are created equal** and **endowed by their Creator with certain unalienable Rights."**

Thomas Jefferson further explained in that same writing - **"all experience hath shewn, that mankind is more disposed to suffer, while evils are sufferable, than to right themselves by abolishing the forms to which they are accustomed."**

That is so true today. In the same paragraph Jefferson further wrote – **"But when a long train of abuses and usurpations, pursuing invariably the same Object evinces a design to reduce them under absolute Despotism, it is their right, it is their duty, to throw off such Government, and to provide new Guards for their future security."**

Stealing our freedom and money is not a **light and transient cause.** We should have stopped the corruption long before now, but **we have been more disposed to suffer, while evils are sufferable, than to right themselves.**

No more suffering the evils, vote out the career politicians.

We do not want to have to go through another Revolutionary War, we need to right ourselves now.

We must **wake up**; choose different leaders that are unalterably committed to defending and repairing the Constitution. If not, we again may be spilling our blood to try to regain our freedom.

Sadly, I see no presidential candidate, either Republican or Democrat, which knows how to and most do not even want to reestablish our God-given freedom for all.

If you reread the second paragraph, better yet reread the whole Declaration of Independence, and then think and ponder, are we being represented or ruled, you will recognize there is an evil in our government. This was the future evil recognized by Thomas Jefferson as he wrote in the second paragraph of the Declaration of Independence "…a long train of abuses and usurpations, pursuing invariably the same object evidences a design to reduce them under absolute despotism…"

Our review of the last one hundred years (since 1913) of history evidence that conspiring politicians have been successfully tearing down our Constitution. **Our Constitution is mortally wounded and will fall if not healed by repair.**

We need the Lord's help or we will fail as a nation.

Our freedoms are safeguarded by the Constitution and those that still love freedom. There are many that are actively following a "shred the Constitution and destroy freedom" agenda. Spend the country into bankruptcy is only one plan to kill our country and freedoms. Is this not plainly visible.

Scriptures warn that there are those that will **weaken and destroy our nation.** Can we not see so many of our politicians/rulers have become followers of satan and embraced "**doctrines of devils**" as they lead us and this nation to ruin. How are they doing this -

The godless killing of the soon-to-be born children. In the future the names of politicians, justices, and celebrities like…you know who, will be remembered for their championing of this great evil, remembered for thousands of years in mortality and in the life beyond. How long will God stay His hand from exacting justice upon us for the killing over 40,000,000 soon-to-be-born children… Our nation is still unrepentant of the American holocaust called abortion.

Direct election of US Senators – the seventeenth Amendment (mortal wound #2). Now senators do not represent the states any longer but represent big money, big business, and big government/socialism.

A national income tax – the sixteenth Amendment (mortal wound #3). To take the fruits of our labor and send it to D.C. to finance the doctrines of devils and buy rulers their reelections and bankrupt this nation. The Founding Fathers made an income tax illegal.

Activist Courts - Courts that abandons the Constitution, no longer know good and bad and forces the mention of God away from us. Can you hear satan's laughter? What more?

A Federal Reserve System.

Uncontrolled federal spending.

Encourage and even celebrate perversion.

Let drugs cartels and drug manufacturers into our country to make slaves of our brothers, sisters, mothers, fathers, husbands, wives, and our sons and daughters.

Federal politicians and bureaucrats above the law and control/twist the law to protect the influential.

Squander Social Security, even lie to us about the status of Social Security.

Federal political influence for sale, how many betray our country for foreign money.

Immigrants into the US that hate God and this nation.

Send our military into harm's way for the profit of some.

Force our military to kill and die in offensive immoral wars in foreign and distant lands.

Tax the worker to poverty.

Make us work to support the rich and the idler.

We do not aid the homeless.

Allow usuary interest rates past 10% to make the rich richer and further enslave the worker and the poor.

Send our jobs and manufacturing to other countries.

Tax breaks and special privileges for the rich.

Pollute our population to death.

Allow and even encourage voter fraud.

Persecute political opposition.

FBI and federal justice system as a punishing arm of a political party.

Deny voter privileges to citizens, allow non-citizens to vote.

Protect big business by allowing them to buy or destroy their competition.

Federal usurpation of State power.

Federal control of education.

Federal government waste.

Federal government corporate welfare.

Federal government medical insurance that is designed to fail, and on and on and on…

Today the Constitution is mortally wounded, and our freedoms are of a limited duration.

This must be stated very plainly. If a doctor treats a patient's symptoms and does not treat the cause of the symptoms the patent may die.

President Wilson and other rulers/politicians broke major parts of our US Constitution with the passing of the sixteenth and seventeen Amendments. Even the likes of President Kennedy and Reagan did not make positive long-term repairs to our nation. They were treating the symptoms only. We must fix the cause of the problem, the repeal of the sixteenth and seventeenth Amendments, if we want any real chance to save this nation. No other ruler/politician, even those that "claim" to follow the Constitution even bother to look in that direction. Sadly, I seem to be the only one even discussing this supremely important issues.

This national life and death issue coupled with our national (ruler/politician) rejection of God shall seal our national fate. Yes, unless we change our individual and national course, our God-given nation with our God-given freedoms will evaporate as steam does when it is released into the air. It will just be gone, with the accompanying catastrophic consequences...

That is why Stan Warner is a candidate for President of the United States of America.

That was the end of my Preamble.

Well, well, history has recorded what happened from 2016 to 2020. So sadly, just as I said, it continues... My heart is so heavy.

That was a lot of sadness to read and worse to live.

Please, let us all take a deep breath then spend a little time saying a prayer for our nation that is under such a siege, with so few defending it.

Warning. This is for nations and for us individually. As we look at the past, we see warnings were given. Noah spoke to the people of his time. Repent, was his cry! Repent of the wicked deed you do. The cry went unheeded. Where did the warning originate? Not from Noah, the warning came to Noah from God. Time and opportunity were given to those that were choosing to do bad things to change. The people had a warning to change or suffer the consequences of sin. All but eight people died, all but eight died from the flood. All but eight...

How many times has God sent warnings before He cleaned a nation of wickedness? How many times have the inhabitance of Jerusalem been warned? Has a nation ever been destroyed without first being warned? They had been warned by prophets of the Lord that they either repent or be destroyed.

Before Babylon destroyed Israel, they were warned. But the nation generally hardened their hearts and did not heed the warning. Many were killed, many of those remaining were carried captive into Babylon as slaves, with trails of blood and tears.

I have read and even studies the writings of ancient prophets as they discussed the conditions associated with living in the Americas. It has been profoundly taught that, "in as much as we are righteous, we will prosper in this land," the Americas. But, in as much as we are wicked, we will eventually suffer greatly. There have been at least two other great civilizations that inhabited the Americas. One was completely wiped out and the other was more than half wiped out and the rest were nearly wiped out because of the European incursion into the Americas. Those that survived were brutally treated. What was the total of all that suffering, can it be even understood, much less be quantified?

Why have I shared this dark review, obviously to bring our heads and hearts to think and feel as I say the following. This is our time, our mortal probation. Are we different from all the others, from those that have lived in the history of the family of Adam and Eve? Do we think our wickedness is hidden or unrecognized? The basic teachings of God stand as rock solid as ever. But do we see ourselves as "enlightened" above the need for God. I do not need to state the obvious. Do we need a prophet to state what we as a people have been taught by Our Lord, repeatedly? We desperately need to repent individually and collectively if we want to avoid the coming consequences of our disobedience and unrepentance. Individually, we are only one heartbeat away from the eternities and our destiny that is occasioned by our life choices. The destiny of our nation is just an accumulation of the sum of the life choices of the citizens.

Our national destiny could be peaceful and filled with happy communities, families, and individuals. Or it could be as at former times where nations were greatly depopulated with the balance becoming subject to brutality and terrible sadness with trails of blood and tears.

Our life choices as a nation and as an individual are happening every day, every hour, and every minute. The great sadness now is that this nation's choices are such that there is a recognizable trend. Simply stated, the trend is unmistakably to disobedience to the teachings of Our Lord. Simply stated we are in great trouble nationally. Our great wealth, our great oceans, our great military, our great history cannot save us from our great disobedience to God's Laws. Our great cleaning awaits us. As past prophets have pronounced, we will see terrible consequences for our disobedience. Then they would insert a "however" and state our God's arm is still outstretched. Meaning God has His arm still outstretched to accept our repentance and has His forgiveness still available, and His arm is still outstretched to accept our prayers. However, it seems that His arms are largely empty of us. This is so simple a simple man like me can state the obvious without being the prophet.

One side note before I finish the above. Do you see the question that has arisen? It is as old as Adam and Eve. Why is God so willing to forgive us? Thinking about this will lead to a review of Our Heavenly Father. Our Father in Heaven, great be your name… Yes, He is the Father of our spirits. I will cross our science now. (This is my thought here, certainly not revelation as you can see.) I suspect that Father did not create all of us, as our earthly mother and father did not create all of us here. Their union produced a body into which our spirit was sent to reside during our mortal testing time. The visions I shared showed spirits in Heaven and after this life in the holding area.

A second deviation or side note. Has our Father in Heaven mistakenly sent male spirits into female bodies and vice versa? Of course not. Are there serious problems from time to time, of course, more often than we want? Do we understand all the "why's," not in this life? But like the vision of Heaven where Father was teaching the young women, one of the great ones plus us at the same time, we cannot understand much without heavenly help.

But the evil ones with their doctrines of devils and with modern "medical science" have been most successful at letting us choose what we will be. This incident was told to us by Elder Packer and happened; I think in a southwestern US school. A very young student brought a kitty to school. The question arose whether it was a boy kitty or a girl kitty. One little one said, "I know how we can tell; we can vote on it." Voting does not change nature and nature's God. However, voting or choosing will cause our future. Second side issue not finished.

Back to our first side note, trying to reason out all we can, our work before asking in prayer, about why God is so forgiving. I suspect that Our Father in Heaven did not create our spirits but added to what we were and perfected whatever we were to give us the opportunity or possibility to become like Him. Is that not what generally what happens here in mortality. If we review what Jesus said, Our Father in Heaven, not just Jesus' Father in Heaven. That leads to much more and different lines of review that we can briefly cover here.

At this point in my quest, I suspected I did enough review and study to ask the question. The first part of the prayer/request was since Jesus seems to have saved us from the fall by His suffering and dying for us so we can be forgiven and resurrected, has He taken over the place of Our Father in Heaven and Our Father become something like taking a step up the ladder as our Grand Father? Those acts of His could not have been completed without Him loving us more than we can understand. Obviously, He learned and remembered how Father loved us the same as He remembered the fall of satan as lightning, among so many other things. As you can see this request was getting a little long winded.

The answer came. "I Am your Father in Heaven; I will always be your Father in Heaven. Nothing will ever change that." That answer was given along with a strong feeling of His love. That, for me answered the question why God is so anxious to forgive. As mortal mothers and fathers we are a little the same. Maybe that is the biggest key to help us understand why God is so forgiving.

I received a little information about a near future world tragic event. I was given that something tragic was going to happen in the world and in the U.S. very soon. Receiving this was something like the five-year-old experience at the beach at San Francisco. Also like the knife incident and the two towers incident and other incidents.

I was given that there were going to be two incredibly terrible actions, one before the other, by a rogue nation that would eventually lead to World War III. One was nuclear and the other was a man-made plague. I was not given which action would happen first, other than one of the acts was going to occur very, very soon. More important than the terrible acts, a remedy was given to the future consequences, even before the events happened. We could stop the terrible attacks and the WWIII that will happen!

In haste, I wrote the following letter, outlining the near future problems and the coming war with the Heavenly inspired solution and sent it to the embassies of all the major nations of the world, plus to a couple US Senators.

The only reply I received to the information was the FBI or some other US security agency intercepted one letter, sent it back to me, and stated I had no right to send the letter to Russia. I am inserting the entire letter here, a little late to stop the coronavirus, but still enough time to stop the next more serious plague, nuclear detonations, and the eventual WWIII.

China WWIII Alternative

September 23, 2019

by Stan Warner, US citizen,

Former Candidate for US President

> China, the CCP rulers not the people, will start WWIII with surprise nuclear attacks as soon as they convince themselves they can succeed, per their "Art of War." The CCP has been at a Stealth War with the Free Nations of the world for decades.
>
> The Free Nations can wait for the near future WWIII and the resulting carnage, or they can unite to stop the China CCP rulers now.
>
> **Soon, surprise CCP nuclear detonations will happen to Free Nation's military and civilian locations.** Remember this Stan Warner warning of September 2019. If nothing is done... By the way, has anyone asked the CCP how

their designing a man-made plague is progressing? If not stopped the CCP, in their quest for global domination, will cause many more deaths than WWII.

A United World must stop the China CCP rulers, before the carnage, by using the following mandate – CCP

Immediately stop military, political, cyber and trade aggression.

Immediately free Tibet and Hong Kong to India and the UK.

Immediately free **Xinjiang Uygur** – To be part of **Russia, Pakistan, Tajikistan, Kyrgyzstan, Kazakhstan, India.**

Immediately free **Yunnan** – To be part of **Vietnam, Myanmar, Laos**.

Immediately free **Nei Mongol** – To be part of **Mongolia, Russia**.

Immediately turn over all nuclear weapons to India.

Immediately turn over all arms of war to Germany and Austria to be distributed to the free Provinces of China.

Since CCP rulers evidence a lack of care for the Chinese people or any other people, they will probably refuse the United World demand.

Consequently, the United World will initiate a total blockade of all air, land, and sea routes to and from China.

China rulers will either attempt a war with the United World, where they will be quickly and soundly defeated or dissolve the present corrupt and war-obsessed leadership and attempt to negotiate non-war-like relationships and terms.

If a war, all countries that actively stand against the CCP war machine will take Chinese provinces. China will no longer be able to confront the world safety.

If a regime transformation with no war, the provinces will be held by foreign nations for twenty years. During that time the foreign nations will help set up self-governing provinces and help to improve the living conditions of the Chinese people. At the end of that time most provinces will become independent nations and choose their form of government or they stay aligned with the host foreign nation, whichever they choose by independent and free elections. All senior CCP officers and senior military officers take immediate retirement, with no prosecutions for acts prior to September 2019, never again to be active in government or military.

Foreign predatory debts to China are erased.

Foreign Nations responsibilities after CCP regime change. The following is conditioned upon National activity to stop CCP aggression.

China - Provinces, Regions, Municipalities

Beijing – Held by **Germany, Austria.** Germany, Austria takes over control of the national government of China as they transition control to the individual provinces.
Tianjin – Held by **Germany, Austria**.
Shanghai – Held by **Brazil, Argentina**.
Chongqing – Held by **India, Algeria.**
Hong Kong – Helped by **UK** to be transitioned to self-rule.
Macau – Held by **Switzerland.**
Anhui – Held by **Saudi Arabia, Nigeria.**
Fujian – To be part of the nations of **Taiwan, Singapore.**
Gansu – Held by **Sweden, Norway, Finland.**
Guangdong – Held by **UK, Australia, New Zealand**.
Guangxi Zhuang – Held by **Indonesia, Vietnam**.
Guizhou – Held by **Thailand, Malaysia**.
Hainan – To be part of **Philippines.**
Hebei – Held by **Netherlands, Hungary**.
Henan – Held by **Canada, Egypt**.
Heilongjiang – To be part of **Russia**.
Hubei – Held by - **Italy, Greece.**
Hunan - Held by – **Poland, Denmark, Czech Republic**.

Jiangsu – Held by **France, Spain, Portugal**.
Jiangxi – Held by **Mexico, Chile**.
Jilin – Held by **Turkey, Bangladesh**.
Liaoning – Held by **Republic of Korea**. Japan and Republic of Korea establish and regulate secure shipping lanes in the seas near China.
Nei Mongol – To be part of **Russia, Mongolia.**
Ningxia Hui – Held by **South Africa, Algeria.**
Qinghai – Held by **Columbia, Peru.**
Shaanxi – Held by **Belgium, Romania.**
Shandong – Held by **Japan.** Japan and Republic of Korea establish and regulate secure shipping lanes in the seas near China.
Shanxi – Held by **United Arab Emirate, Qatar**.
Sichuan – To be part of **India**.
Xinjiang Uygur – To be part of **Russia, Pakistan, Tajikistan, Kyrgyzstan, Kazakhstan, India**.
Xizang (Tibet) – Helped by **India** to be transitioned to self-rule.
Yunnan – To be part of **Vietnam Myanmar, Laos**.
Zhejiang – Held by **US, Israel, Ireland**.

That was the end of the letter. As we all know, COVID-19, the coronavirus, arrived a month or so after the warning was sent in the letters.

So, I guess we just wait for the next more serious plague since China was so successful with the present plague. I expect that before the next more serious plague is released, China will have a tested and mostly successful inoculation. They may achieve their ends with only plagues, but so very sadly I expect the other tragedy will follow when they see fit.

Just a brief addition here. In the past God allowed Babylon to be conquered Israel after the inhabitants of Israel were disobedient and unrepentant. There are many other similar occasions, just to mention one more is the Noah episode where the disobedient and unrepentant were washed away. Are we generally a disobedient and unrepentant people? Could it be too much to see the war obsessed CCP as just another Babylon…

I suspect we all missed some of the wisdom that was inserted into the China warning, I know I did until I gave it more thought. Maybe I have been too brief in explaining things, especially with the China warning. I will add a little and we can see a little more wisdom almost hidden in the warning.

These warnings started when I was four or five years old at the beach in San Francisco. In this book, it was one of the first incidents recorded. Since then, as you can remember there has been a long string of them through my life, not all of them were mentioned in this book.

When this warning came it was given in pieces. The two offensive attacks were given, but not the order, just one was close to happening. The date of the letter I sent was September 23, 2019, it took about a week or two to research and write. As I knew one of the two attacks would happen soon, I worked fast to put the pieces together as soon as I could so the warning would go out, with time to stop the attack. Still not knowing which one of the two would come first.

I was given the solution in parts. The first part was that the world would need to be united to stop the threat. The second part of the solution was to have a united world blockage of everyone from China. After that came the breakup of China by provinces. That part I had to figure out by myself. So, I tried to roughly align geographies, GNPs, and populations of provinces with the foreign country groups plus taking into consideration special associations and the like.

Here is the wisdom I did not recognize at first. If the nations would have united and fully blockaded China, the CCP virus would have stayed in China and not have spread all over the world as quick as it did, with the world opportunity to act instead of only reacting. The world could have seen China trying to deal with the virus from afar and isolated. We had a timely warning, but no nation that received the warning letters took them seriously, at least to my knowledge, not even to investigate a little. However, it seems that we cannot escape living the consequences. The rest you can reason out as your personal discovery from the circumstances as now recorded in recent history.

Maybe we need a breather after that letter. Let us all ask Father to intervene. But maybe He already has.

There are certainly so many weaknesses in me, as you can tell. If there are errors in this work they are, of course, to be charged to me and me alone. I write these things, as best I can, as a most unworthy follower and servant of Jesus Christ, the Savior and Redeemer of this world as well as worlds without number.

I just finished organizing some information on the second coming of Jesus.

Chapter 7

The Wonderous Second Coming of Our Lord, So Close

To keep this brief review brief, the Life and Teachings of Jesus the Christ, the Savior and Redeemer of all humanity will be left to your own study.

He ascended into the Heavens, after his resurrection, about 2,000 years ago and His followers have been anxiously awaiting His majestic, healing, and cleansing Second Coming ever since then. When will that glorious event happen? A few religious leaders have pronounced dates for that event, that have come and gone without the Second Coming.

Let us see what we can find by restudying the scriptures.

Mark Chapter 13 is a review of the troubles and signs preceding the Second Coming. That seems a good place to start.

Mark 13:32, "But of that day and that hour knoweth no man, no, not the angles which are in heaven, neither the Son, but the Father."

So, if we think we can find the **day,** or the **hour** of the Second Coming let us quit now and not waste our time. However, that statement does suggest things that are not mentioned.

Mark 13:33 – "Take ye heed, watch and pray: for ye know not when the time is."

Mark 13:36 – 37, "Lest coming suddenly he find you sleeping. And what I say unto you I say unto all, Watch."

Clearly, He is commanding us to wake up "watch and pray." That presupposes that we learn what has been offered us about the last days. So, we learn what we can by means of studying the scriptures and prayer.

Mark 13:28 – 29, "Now learn a parable of the fig tree; When her branch is yet tender, and putteth forth leaves, ye know that summer is near: So ye in like manner, when you shall see these things come to pass, know that it is nigh, even at the doors."

Okay, we will not be given the **day** or the **hour**, however, we are told we can know the season.

Next let's review some words of Daniel. Daniel, oh Daniel, God bless you for your service to Him and to your people and even to us in our day. His prayer in Chapter 9 stands as instruction and encouragement to us and was sufficient for God to change the future for so many then and for us today. In Dan. 9, Daniel found from Jeremiah that there would be seventy years of desolation of Jerusalem. History has recorded that occurrence. It seems to me those words were a type of something to come.

Then Daniel gave the spectacular prayer as he represented all Israel in a complete confession of their many sins and a masterfully heart felt plea for mercy and forgiveness, both individually and nationally. If only we could learn to pray like Daniel, and even more importantly if we had a prophet/leader that could offer that prayer for us. We can offer that prayer for us, our families, and friends.

During the prayer, Gabriel (the same Gabriel that later instructed Mary) came and talked to Daniel. Gabriel stated seventy weeks are "upon" the city. At the end of the seventy weeks "to make an end of sins," "to bring in everlasting righteousness," "and to anoint the most Holy." That is definitely the Second Coming, where there is the end of the great sins as Christ takes the lead of His precious Kingdom. To bring everlasting righteousness, what a wonderful thought, much more when it is a reality! Further to anoint the most Holy, that reference to the most Holy is obviously Jesus. The "anoint" is clearly the Anointed One or Christ. Yes, that is the time Jesus the Christ is here again. These words point to a time when God the "most Holy" would stop, at least the great sins and bring everlasting righteousness. Everyone from Daniel's time knew there was plenty of sin, even gross sins. That was what Daniel was praying about in the first place. Now there is even more sin, so are we praying like Daniel?

This is not new information from Daniel. It has been there since Daniel wrote about the occurrence and since there has been an Old Testament. Then add all the wonderous and tragic and wonderous time of Jesus. Ending with His ascension into Heaven and everyone looking for Him to come again. All this gives new relevance and excitement to Daniel's vision.

The seventy weeks is a hint for us to investigate. That is a declaration of where the bridge starts. That hint directs us to a greater study of those scriptures than we would accomplish without it.

The seventy weeks were divided into a sixty-two-week period, a seven-week period and a one-week period. And at the end of the one-week period will be the end, the end of wickedness and **the return of our Lord!** But how can we understand this timeline?

The easiest part is one week equals seven days.

A day is the most basic and easiest recognized period. In the scriptures, it has several meanings. First, it represents one revolution of the earth from morning to the next morning and so on. In Genesis, it is used as a tool to separate periods of time. As used in the Creation periods, the day seems to represent an exceptionally long periods of time in which separate activities took place. It seems each activity is represented by a time, a time of a different value. The first day, or period, represents the time it took for, "God created the heaven and the earth, divided the light from the darkness." The second day, or period represents the time it took when, "And God said, 'Let there be a firmament in the midst of the waters…'" and so on to the seventh day. Using that application of day to a period does not seem to help me directly other than a day can have several meanings of time.

The meaning that appears to give us some understanding of Daniel's vision comes from Ezekiel chapter 4, where Ezekiel gives the number of days that will represent the siege and famine that shall happen to Jerusalem and gives one day to represent one year. A similar accounting is given in Numbers, Chapter 14. So, let us try that application.

We have three periods of time that total 490 years.

(Seventy weeks x seven days per week = 490 days, each day = one year = 490 years.)

The end of the 490 years is the season of the Second Coming. Maybe we can identity some events that fit Daniel's timeline that will give us a reference to the starting point and to our present day.

There are three periods mentioned:

Sixty-two-week period 62 x 7 (days per week) = 434 days (one day = one year) = <u>434 years</u>

Seven-week period 7 x 7 = forty-nine days = <u>forty-nine years</u>

One-week seven days = <u>seven years</u>

There are not too many pronouncements in the verses that offer hints, so let us look at the words about the starting point with "the commandment to restore and to build Jerusalem."

During the Crusades, Jerusalem changed hands several times. We even know when the dome of the Dome of the Rock collapsed and was rebuilt. One time the towers and some of the walls were rebuilt and then the walls were shortly after torn down again, in the eventuality that the Christians retake Jerusalem, to prevent Christians from having a fort type of defense. But that was around 1000 years ago. If that were the key the Second Coming would have been 490 years later. The Second Coming obviously did not happen then, so that is not the key.

A key that has been suggested is the activities of Sultan Suleiman the First. Also known as Suleiman the Magnificent who was the Sultan over the Ottoman Empire at a zenith of its greatness. In 1535, the incredibly powerful Sultan ordered the repair of the Dome of the Rock and the rebuilding of the walls of Jerusalem. Most of the walls we see today are those constructed because of his orders. (Thank you to Sultan Suleiman and the Ottoman Empire; great job.) The construction started in 1537 and was completed in 1541.

Reviewing Daniel's words again, they say in Chapter 25, "...that from the going forth of the **commandment** to restore and to build Jerusalem." There are three dates: the date of the order is 1535, the other dates are start and finish dates. I suspect we should use the date of the order as Daniel used the word "commandment," not something like started for completed.

Starting with the year 1535 + 490 years = the year 2025. So possibly that is the wonder filled year of the season of the future great event. Since there are other hints given by Daniel, we need to further investigate them. Then there is still even more work to do that we will discuss later.

How did we get the sixty-two weeks period that we used above? Some of you read Daniel and know the answer. We are now reading from Chapter 25, "and threescore and two weeks: the street shall be built again and the wall, even in troublous times." A score is twenty, three score is sixty weeks, and two weeks is a total of sixty-two weeks. Sixty-two weeks x seven days per week = 434 days. Remember one day equals one year, so the 434 days represents 434 years for us.

We started the timeline in year 1535 and we add 434 years to take us to year 1969. Now if this 1969 date is the true date Daniel was telling about, there must have been "the street shall be built again and the wall, even in troublous times." I am officially an old person, so I can remember the 1967 war in Israel. Those were certainly "troublous times" with great destruction. For me, it is reasonable there would be rebuilding of streets and walls in Jerusalem for some time. For me, the timeline fits very well, at least, so far.

The next piece of the puzzle is the seven weeks or forty-nine days that represents forty-nine years. From 1969 plus forty-nine years, will take the timeline to 2018. Later, we will discuss this date from another source.

At this point, we are at the end of the forty-nine years, in 2018. To me, the words from Daniel are not clear enough to me to make any specific assessment. Chapter 26, "And after threescore and two weeks shall Messiah be cut off, but not for himself." When in doubt study harder. So, let us use the forty-nine years as a place holder and now add the last part which is the one week or seven days that represents seven years.

The seven years take us to 2025 and the end of the 490 years. This could be the end of all wickedness and the time when Christ reigns for a thousand years in peace. But there are lots of other spiritual hints we need to investigate and see if they fit with this timeline; if not we may be missing the mark. Further, given some dates may be in early winter while other dates are late fall, thus causing us to possibly be a year off one way or the other. Daniel's words are clearer in Chapter 27, "And he shall confirm the covenant with many for one week: and in the midst of the week, he shall cause the sacrifice and the oblation to cease, and for the overspreading of abominations he shall make it desolate, even until the determined shall be poured upon the desolate."

For the seven years, the first parts are regular with what he calls oblations and sacrifice happening. That sounds like normal life. Then "in the midst of the" seven years the fairly regular "sacrifice and the oblation to cease." The second part of the seven years is the abominations mentioned so often, that will be horrific, at best. Dan 12:1, "and there shall be a time of trouble, such as never was since there was a nation." This is massive destruction and loss of life, worse than the Babylonian or the Roman conquests. The slaughter will happen to many or maybe most of the people. But the first part of Chapter 27, above, he states "he shall confirm the covenant with many for one week." This is an obvious reference to a covenant between God and "many."

What does God want from us? To follow His word and will, those that do are His people. He shall confirm the covenant with who other than His people. They have a great place in the Eternities and a help here in mortality. This is even mentioned again in Chapter 12:1, "and at that time thy people shall be delivered, every one that shall be found written in the book." That book is a recording of our decision to and actions in following God. It is a record of our actions and choices in mortality. Do we love or do we hate? Have we been good, kind, obedient, honest, truthful, repentant (sacrifices), and all the things God has told us to do? It is clear, those and only those good people "shall be delivered" during that tragic time. There is much, much more to share describing the abomination and desolation, but you can easily find that information.

We need to spend a little time talking about the timing from the "midst" used in the seven years. There is more in Chapter 12:7, "and it shall be for a time, times, and a half...all these things shall be finished." Remember the time-line we are using is one day represents one year. Then when it is mentioned "time" will be one year, "times" will be two years, and a half will be half a year. So, the "midst" was speaking of the middle of the seven years, that is three and a half years. Then, after the second three and a half is until "all these things shall be finished". In the second three and a half years is the abominations and desolations spoken of several places in the scriptures. More things that will happen in the second half, the three and a half years is given in Chapter 12:2, "And many of them that sleep in the dust of the earth shall awake, some to everlasting life, and some to shame and everlasting contempt."

Catch the word everlasting, the rewards for being good or bad are EVER-LASTING! Another bit of information is given that "many of them that sleep in the dust of the earth," so the earth will give up many to resurrection at that time, not just resurrection but also, at least some type of judgement, and an everlasting placement of some kind. Remember this is before the end in the last three and a half years by the end of 2025, and remember, maybe a year one way or the other. The resurrections could start any time between, using the timeline we so far have discovered, between the middle of 2021 and the end of 2025.

It may be that the good ones of the past are to be alive again before the triumphant return of our Lord so they can accompany Him, can bow, sing, weep, and pray, for Him on His return.

Now it is time to go to the Book of Revelations, lots more information there. Rev. 11:2, "But the court, which is without the temple leave out, and measure it not; for it is given unto the Gentiles: and the holy city shall they tread under foot forty and two months."

Here we are at the three-and-a-half-year period we have been discussing. The second half of the seven years will be unbelievably bad. I suspect it will start in an ascending manner in severity. At some point in the last three and a half years, part of Jerusalem will not be in full control by the nation of Israel. Here it is stated the court, which is without the temple leave out, the Gentiles will have control of part of the city. What urban warfare that will be. Will the Jewish people just give it up or will they fight for it? We are told here that the Gentiles who want to take over Israel will be there in the second half of the seven-year period.

To continue Rev, 11:3, "And I will give power unto my two witnesses, and they shall prophesy a thousand two hundred and threescore days (another reference to three and a half years), clothed in sackcloth." I suspect that, given the description, part of the last three-and-a-half-year period will be too much for the Israel Defense Force to handle alone.

So back to the Covenant, for the sake of the good of that area, "he shall confirm the covenant for many for one week." For the sake of protecting the good ones, God is going to send two witnesses. So, God is blessing Israel for the first three and a half years, and then He is going to send two witnesses to do similar things Moses did so long ago for at least part of the second half of the seven years.

Some nations and people want to take Jerusalem by force from the Jews. Those nations will send many millions of troops to fight in the last battle. There was only one Moses that held the priesthood of God through the Exodus and look what happened. This time God is sending two priesthood holders with the same power. The description of their activities is, "fire prodceedeth out of their mouth, and devoureth their enemies: and if any man will hurt them, he must in this manner be killed." The priesthood operates by words not by the physical strength of the priesthood holder. So, the things that happen will be a result of words from their mouths. Words of power, represented by the word fire.

It is my sincere hope that Egypt does not join in this fight against Israel. This hope for Egypt is partly borne of the lineage of all those, like me, of the Israelite tribes of Manasseh and Ephraim as they are the children of Joseph and his wife, Asenath, the daughter of Potipherah priest of On or Or, I cannot remember. Ephraim and Manasseh were half Egyptian. Does Egypt remember their history and dealings with Moses? Will they fight against some of their distant blood relatives and against two Moses type servants sent to Jerusalem by God? Will Egypt remember the old saying, they have once "been there and done that, most certainly don't want to do that again,"?

An interesting aside will be that to hold the Melchizedek Priesthood the holder will be a follower and servant of Jesus. They will "witness" about Jesus and His will, to who, to the hoards attacking Jerusalem, or to the defenders of Jerusalem, or both. Both might not want to hear about Jesus. We will see how that turns out. It has been and is my hope and prayer that both sides will soften their hearts to receive the witness's words about Jesus, words of love and life eternal and will not need to receive the witness's word of war that will destroy. The carnage decreed does not have to happen, just as it did not happen in the time of Jonah. If we pray, as we were taught by Daniel, God can change the decreed future tribulations as He accepts our cries of repentance. I hope those prayers erupt from both sides.

Please, let us all open our hearts, minds, and arms to the love of Jesus. God is always anxious to forgive us if we recognize our faults and want to change to a better. If all concerned listen to the witnesses the whole conflict could change to a better. A wonderful thought but how many in our time repent and seek God. The ancient Prophet Mormon had the same concerns and look how that turned out.

We now have two sources telling us about the last half of the last seven-year period.

Even though we see the last three and a half years will be terrible, the stage is set for that experience. It would be nice if we had at least one or two more confirmations of our timeline. So, we will go to book of Revelations and talk about seals.

To start, we need to begin with a teaching of Peter. In 2 Pet. 3:8 we are given a relationship between the Lord's time and our time, "But, beloved, be not ignorant of this one thing, that one day is with the Lord as a thousand years, and a thousand years as one day." So, for us, we are given another relation about time. How interesting, each thousand years of our humanity is equal to one day of the Lord. From the fall of Adan and Eve, we have had a little over six days of the Lord or a little over 6,000 years for us.

This is further discussed in Revelation Chapter 5 verse 1, "And I saw the right hand of him that sat on the throne a book written within and on the backside sealed with 7 seals." Each seal represented a thousand years of our mortal history. In Rev. 8:1 talks about opening the seventh seal that represents the time from 2000 to 3000 A.D, "And when he had opened the seventh seal, there was silence in heaven about the space of half an hour."

Taking the, about the space of half an hour, to be in the Lord's time that would equal 20.8 years. The "about" could be shorter or longer so for the sake of simplicity let us use twenty-one years. We previously discussed why we could be off by a year, then adding the about we are still not too far off, if looking at this in our years.

If we use the year 2000 as the opening of the seventh seal, then twenty-one years forward would be the year 2021 for the end of the silence in heaven. That would put us very close to the middle of the last seven years 2018 to 2025. The mid-point of that period, the year 2021 half is when the extreme difficulties start. Remember we could easily be off a year or so, as previously discussed.

Now it is time to look at the meaning of the "silence in heaven." In Rev. 8 we find that there are angels with trumpets prepared to sound, waiting, or "silence."

Seven angels have trumpets and **prepared** themselves to sound (silence). When the first angel sounded his trumpet (the end of silence), there followed hail and fire mingled with blood and the third part of the trees was burnt and the green grass was burnt. In 2021, do we see trees burning or forest fires? Of course, we do. And with each of the remaining angels sounding their trumpet (no silence in heaven when the trumpets are sounding) there was further destruction. The balance you can read in Rev. 8-9.

Then, after the silence, the great tribulations are in full swing to the incredible sadness of all that are courageous enough to read now or we will soon experience. The silence in heaven is the time before the sounding of the trumpets. That time after the seventh seal is opened (2000 A.D.) and the angels are silently waiting for about half an hour in God's time or about twenty-one years in our time. That puts the end of the silence in the middle of the last seven years or "about" 2021 plus the year or so as discussed. At that point, we have seen forests burning more than regularly.

That time fits, and the forest fires fit, the piece of the puzzle fit. All the others that predicted when the end would come, but were wrong, could have reviewed these same things and came to the same conclusion, but they did not. When that time comes, there will be no doubt that the great desolation is upon the earth, piece by trumpet sounding piece. The end of the silence in heaven begins the terrible times when the trumpets are sounded and the destruction of the wicked is so great that no life will be left except those days will be shortened. So, we have multiple confirmations from the scriptures telling those good people to be wise and prepare and do not be counted as the five foolish virgins.

More confirmations of our timeline come from two total eclipses of the sun. Matt. 24:29, "Immediately **after** the tribulations of those days shall the sun be darkened."

As we have discussed the tribulations, by our review the Christ should be here about 2025. I googled the full eclipse of the sun; there is one in April 2024. Further, Isaiah told us that before the Lord starts destroying the wicked "the sun shall be darkened in his going forth." Isaiah 13:10. There was a total eclipse on August 21, 2017, also which occurred about the start of the seven-year period.

That is the end of a white paper on the Second Coming of Jesus, I compiled and inserted into this book. This is not given as a vision or understanding placed into my mind. It is a reasoned review of the scriptures that we have had in our possession for so long, nothing more.

There is much more about the Second Coming, but not for this brief review.

This review of the Second Coming coupled with the experiences of this lifetime saga should be more than enough for us to use as an aid and encouragement to our hope and faith, to persuade us to make a full review of our present status in relationship to God. What is our status with what God has given us to do and more importantly what our Christ has given us to be? The eternities in the next life, for all of us, come at some unknown time when we die. Mercifully, we have many warnings of generally when the Christ may return and all the stuff that happens shortly before His return. If that is immediately in front of us, will we choose to repent and mend our ways and redouble our efforts to be good or will we continue as we are now, as those in the time of Noah and the like. After our prayers and contemplation, will we share a **warning** with those we love, with those that are near and dear to us? Do we have enough love for others to move us to that action? May God bless you in your choices in such a pivotal time so close to the end of our mortal life choices and the eternal consequences of those choices.

My love for you is such a very, very small part of this saga compared to the eternal love that Jesus offers us. However very, very small that love is, I give it to you embedded in and woven through this writing, with a great hope that you will end up living through all eternities in the highest Kingdom of Glory along with God the Father, His Son Jesus, the Holy Spirit, your family and the most obedient and repentant of all mankind, being surrounded and enveloped with the most intense love, happiness and joy that can ever be achieved, going on through the eternities doing incredibly wonderful things with incredibly wonderful, loved ones. May God bless you forever with no need for eternal remorse.

The City of Enoch. I will be very brief as I have with all this writing. As I have said so often, I thought this writing was complete. I was not going to share this experience; however, it seems now I should share.

One of the important events associated with the "Second Coming" of our Lord is the return of the City of Enoch. In faith and hope to better understand this event, about ten years ago I was pondering on the subject. The process is important so I will share the order of what happened.

It has been made plain to me that much of what the Lord shares and does for and with us comes through the Holy Ghost and often then through ministering angels. (Sometimes He even uses us to accomplish His will, giving us a wonderful experience in being part of His will.) Remember the incident of the man in Utah that had the car wreck with the deer.

Well, here this was, a request for further spiritual information. So, there will be work for me to do before the question will be favorably answered. I use the word favorably as I strongly suspect if I just asked without me doing my part the answer would be a "no response." Leaving me wondering if I ask God for something I should not ask for or a dozen other thoughts. Remember the prayer for the hawk when I was a ten-year-old.

Here it is obvious I should start by reviewing what the scriptures say about the subject. The cost was great to get the scriptures to us so it would be foolish of me to not use them.

So, we know the City of Enoch was taken off the earth because the inhabitants were good, exceedingly repentant and obedient, leaving mostly the wicked, disobedient, and unrepentant on the earth. That seems to be the lead up to the Noah and the flood experience that occurred only after the warning given from the Lord delivered by Noah to the remainder left here on earth. I want to say the Lord loves us lots and would never send a flood to cleanse the earth without a clear warning first. On this point I have thought several times what would happen to San Francisco if the Lord warned all the obedient to leave San Francisco for a weekend.

At this point, the City of Enoch is gone. Let us meditate on this and review what we can reason. Enoch had well over 300 years with his people. If the number he started with was, let us say one hundred, and assuming each couple had about ten children or more, with the long-lifespans, then, no wars and probably no major diseases, the population could be extremely large. Especially if the Lord blessed them with great crops and water and who knows what extra blessings they were given. Safe to say, it was an exceptionally large city of a farming and ranching lifestyle, maybe more. However, who knows what technology they may have achieved since then? Maybe they stayed agrarian or maybe they explore space with a much more advanced technology than we have. The righteousness of that civilization with the help of God could do anything that God allows. You can reason where I am going with this thought…

The population may have reached much, much higher than the population of the U.S. today.

We have seen what happens to cities as they grow. Most often, if geography allows, they grow in a mostly circular arrangement. Further, that city should be many, many times the size of anything we have seen in history or in the present. I suspect that it would extremely dwarf the entire L.A. basin by many, many, times over.

Next for me, I took as a starting point that the Garden of Eden was in a land in the present North America. Further that in the taking of the city, was of the city (land with farms and buildings) with the people not just the people. So, is there a huge circular piece of land that is missing around there? At this point there will be those that say this is not in harmony with science. I agree it is not in harmony with the science that is in academic favor today. But if we assume our present academic view of science is perfect and complete, we can certainly disagree. The science I know, is, as are we are, on a trek through the mortal present, heading into the eternities, where it will be perfected.

At this time, my thoughts were turned to the Gulf of Mexico. After some thought and review the Gulf of Mexico seemed to fit. A little later there was some communication from the Holy Ghost. "I received what I had prayed for," like the prayer for the hawk. As time passed, I kept this all to myself.

About five years later, there was a book written about the unique experiences of man from Utah that suggested the City of Enoch would return, at least in part, to the Gulf of Mexico. Well, at that point, the "cat was out of the bag" so to speak. It seems that he knew, many years before the information was shared with me. So, I am sharing this experience with those of you that have not read the other book.

By the way, what happens to the water that will be displaced by the returning city. I did not make that part of my request and the answer did not include anything about that. Recently, I thought about trying to calculate the amount of displaced water and how that would affect the land around the Gulf and the oceans of the Earth…and then taking that in prayer. But it seems I will just leave that question for time to answer. Although, I would probably not have that approach if I lived near the Gulf.

In the book by the special man from Utah, calling himself Spencer, he talks about the displaced water. More information on that subject is in the book from Spencer. Plus, there is more information on parts of this subject from the teachings of the Prophet Joseph Smith.

In giving this subject a little more thought, who knows how many others, through the years, have been given different parts of information surrounding the return of the City of Enoch or on sundry other subjects. I suspect there have been voluminous amounts of information given to others, but that they have decided to keep the information to themselves. If we had all the other's information, we may have a vibrant picture of many concepts and future events. As you can tell I am willing to share with you most things in hopes that they may become valuable to you.

History is Family History. For this section, I wish we were walking in the sand and shallow serf at a deserted ocean beach as we talked to each other.

I have much to share and I must be very brief. Oh well, I will do my best.

As a young husband and father, long ago a patriarch laid his hands on my head and stated my linage is of Joseph through Ephraim. Curiously reading the accounts of Joseph and Ephraim and their descendants started me on a lifelong study of my family and extended family history. The first thirty-five years was very difficult. But then I was back far enough with most lines of ancestors to start tying into the research of accomplished genealogists. Sometimes finding one more distant grandfather or grandmother would tie me into a string of ten or thirty or many more generation of ancestors. Going far back, those who were recorded were mostly notable for some reason, often royalty of some kind.

One line goes back through about fifteen high priests to Arron, the brother of Moses, and then back through Abraham to Adam and Eve. Another line goes back to King David and back to Adam and Eve. Among my favorite ancestors is Joseph of Arimathea and his daughter Anna. Of course, I would study each of the notable ancestors and I was almost always thrilled with what I learned. According to genealogists, Joseph was the half-brother to Heli the father of Mary, the mother of Jesus. Anna was cousin to Mary. Anna, her father Joseph, Mary, and several others fled Judea to the tin mining region of southern England where Joseph had long standing business dealings. There Anna married a Druid king of a small kingdom. Her posterity is mingled through Scotland, Ireland, and England and later across the channel.

More than just simple history is available. Now the Old and New Testament are family history lessons. Some wonder filled lessons are learned after an in-depth review that would probably not have happened without the family tie encouragement.

Just one example, King Hezekiah, is a distant grandfather. The king's father had been a bad leader. He let the people worship satan and even sacrifice children in that worship. Immediately after Hezekiah became king, he stopped that practice and tore down the places of satanic worship. With some questions as to the source of the strength of the new king and those that may have been helping him, led me to more scripture searching. Of course, his wife was the first question and then advisors as well as what is recorded about his nature and beliefs.

I do not remember the name of his wife, however, I discovered she was the daughter of Isiah. The daughter of Isiah, which explains much. She had to be an immense influence and aid and encouragement to the new king in courageously and aggressively serving God, as well as having such an inspiring and wisdom filled father-in-law, the Prophet Isiah. What an enlightening and wonderful family history discovery, for several reasons. Isiah a distant grandfather, lots to restudy from him.

There is a Y in the trail of this thought process, or two lines to follow this one I have been on.

One is how does this information and perspective fit us today. Well, the priests that taught the people to sacrifice children to satan, do we have them today. Of course, we do. We have satanic priests teaching the practice of abortion. These priests and priestesses are spewing their dogma, disguised as women's reproductive rights. They are using the media plus their legislative, executive, judicial leadership status to spread their "doctrine of devils." Some of them even seem to be high priests and high priestesses of these "doctrines" as they use their great influence to persuade for evil. Mingled with my broken heart my only further comment on this is we desperately need to repent and seek forgiveness from our Lord. Please, please let us not go unrepentant into the next life.

Those last words were so heavy and sad. However, the contrast is this other path. I suspect that finding all the new family history research ties, like my first cousin Mary and, of course, her son, our Lord Jesus, is a second cousin many times removed. Plus, all the others from Abraham, Isiah, King David, Arron and on and on, will inspire me to be better for the rest of my life. Even more to this trail is it seems evident that many and probably a vast number of Europeans and North Americans and well as so many across the entire earth have much if not most of the same family history. You just have to do some family history research to find out and then be inspired for the rest of your life. Will you spend a little time to see that you are a close relative of Jesus, Mary, Moses, and so on plus a direct ancestor of so many others like Abraham, Joseph, Isiah, David, Joseph of Arimathea, and on and on. Yes, the story of Joseph and Rachel, and especially that part about the cattle, and sheep will have more meaning now.

"**My Chains Are Gone**" is part of a wonderful song. My chains are gone because the Lord allows me to have His love, gospel, repentance, baptism, sacrament, prayer, direction, and forgiveness for my sins, sins that chain me away from Jesus. Then as I fail and fall, I get up and try again and eventually become a little better. I will never be good enough, on my own, to enter the Celestial Kingdom with God. My hope and faith are that after I do all I can do; the grace of Jesus will make up the difference and save yet another.

Further it is my hope that by studying these experiences the Holy Ghost gives you conformations of the truth of them and they become your experiences, for you to use, the same as I do. Just as a tradesman needs tools to do their job, these experiences can aid us in understanding the trials of life and more. Also, you have so many personal experiences of your own to help you with your trek through mortal life.

Forests and Trees. How many times have I thought that I was finished? Well, here is some more.

It is Sunday morning, and I woke up a little after four a.m. and spent about an hour in prayer and meditation. I was given a larger perspective of things in this book. It seems I missed something, like the old saying goes, "You can't see the forest for the trees." So, I will add that new understanding or maybe just a different perspective here.

This is a condensation of a theme of experiences, a little like the Old Testament experience where I ask for permission to do a shortened review or rewrite of it. There are a couple of themes that Heaven orchestrated in my life that I mostly shared in this narrative, but I never consciously put them together in my understanding. You may or probably did recognize them, but I did not so I will share the first one here.

At the start of the spiritual experiences, I shared the San Francisco beach experience. Where some Heavenly being told me how to avoid my brother and me from drowning just before the rogue wave crashed over us.

That is the start of the secondary theme. This theme is a listing of the times the Holy Ghost or ministering angels have guided me to avoid a closely approaching potential death or serious injury, represent God to give healing or misunderstand the timing of approaching death. I will list them; some were not reported in this writing –

1. The San Francisco beach and the rogue wave.
2. At kindergarten in Oakland, being put in danger by older students.
3. Request to let me die and return to where I came from before this life, when the Heavenly man appeared.
4. Being attacked by the evil, unseen man.
5. Swimming across the Sacramento River in the path of a river barge rounding the bend.
6. In Vietnam, several occurrences.
7. In Vietnam, my stopping a planned fragging of my company commander, a second lieutenant at Phu Bai.
8. In Vietnam, my stopping the planned fragging of my company commander, a captain at the MACV compound Hue.

9. In Vietnam, walking through a village with Paul seeing the NVA soldier.
10. Not salting my food and later a high-voltage contact.
11. Several high-voltage near misses at the electric Municipal Utility.
12. Writing a safety program that remarkably reduced the serious accidents at the Municipal Utility after there were a few deaths.
13. In Sacramento, after witnessing a serious auto accident, being stopped from stepping in front of a car as I went to help.
14. The first healing of the sick where I did not follow the direction of the Spirit.
15. In Sacramento, at the hospital, not telling the woman when she would "pass on."
16. In Seattle, the incident with the knife and the rope.
17. In Seattle, the incident of the two towers.
18. Telling K she had years longer to live than the doctors told her.
19. The vision of the throne of God and the ministering angle that stopped the man from dying in the auto accident.
20. Praying about the pain in my abdomen.
21. The dark spirit/spirits trying to disrupt my drive to work one early morning.
22. Learning much more about the priesthood healing and immediately healing process.
23. Knowing about a female that would be "called home," only children praying for her would change the natural order.
24. The China CCP plans to kill using nukes and a man-made plague.

Again, this is a secondary theme. It was reconsidered to give us a perspective of the overall review of this area.

Now we can review the first theme, hopefully putting the primary theme together as we just did with the secondary theme. Except the second theme only dealt with life and death and healings. The first theme is immeasurably more important. It deals with our relation to God and the eternal joy and happiness of each of us. Our eternal joy and happiness through endless time, with those we love! What are we willing to do to achieve that eternal position? What forbidden things are we doing now that will eventually deny us that breathtakingly magnificent eternal existence. Further, how do we overcome our resistance to change because of our failures to do and be better? An irony is the second theme is fully incorporated into the first theme.

May I, may we, recognize our faults, find remorse for our transgressions, repent of them, and follow Jesus' example and teachings before it is too late. That has been and still is a theme coupled with the teachings that will come directly to us from God. He is anxious for us to have heavenly communication now as it has been throughout the history of mankind. May God bless us in our choices and through our eternities.

My prayer is that we may feel and come to recognize, the love God has for us. God is so Great.

All Praise and Thanks to Our Great Lord!

THE END

Printed in the USA
CPSIA information can be obtained
at www.ICGtesting.com
LVHW021700240924
792026LV00012B/258

9 798885 272674